Viewing Violence

Viewing Violence

How Media Violence
Affects Your Child's
and Adolescent's
Development

Madeline Levine, Ph.D.

DOUBLEDAY
New York London Toronto Sydney Auckland

PUBLISHED BY DOUBLEDAY
a division of Bantam Doubleday Dell Publishing Group, Inc.
1540 Broadway, New York, New York 10036

DOUBLEDAY and the portrayal of an anchor with a dolphin are trademarks
of Doubleday, a division of Bantam Doubleday Dell Publishing Group, Inc.

Library of Congress Cataloging-in-Publication Data

Levine, Madeline.
Viewing violence: how media violence affects your child's and adolescent's development /
Madeline Levine. — 1st ed.
    p.   cm.
Includes bibliographical references.
1. Mass media and children.   2. Mass media and teenagers.
3. Violence in mass media.   I. Title.
HQ784.M3L48   1996
302.23′083—dc20   95-48266
CIP

ISBN 0-385-47686-8

10   9   8   7   6   5   4   3   2   1

This book is lovingly dedicated
to the memory of my father, Louis Levine,
who taught me to follow both the rules and my heart.

Contents

Acknowledgments

Looking back over the past two years, I am astounded by the kindness and generosity of the many people who took an interest in this project.

While we agreed, disagreed, and occasionally locked horns, I am very grateful to Dick Wolf, Charles Rosin, and Greg Weisman for helping me understand the complex and often conflicting demands placed on those who create some of our best and most popular television.

The staffs of Senator Paul Simon and Representative Edward Markey were tireless in tracking down obscure government documents and keeping me current on legislation that changed with mind-numbing speed.

My greatest debt is owed to those researchers whose work on media violence and children has helped illuminate this important and troubling aspect of our culture. For the many hours it took to make sure that I understood their research thoroughly, I would like to thank Leonard Eron, L. Rowell Huesmann, Leonard Berkowitz, Jerome Singer, Joanne Cantor, Albert Bandura, Edward Donnerstein, Ronald Drabman, Aimee Dorr, Sarah Stein, and Don Roberts. Special thanks to Calvin Settlage, whose early comments on values were particularly important to me.

Two people deserve special mention for their interest in this book and their largesse of time and spirit. They were kindling wood for this project, sparking me to look beyond the "facts" of media violence and children and into the heart of what is troubling our country. George Gerbner, who has spent a lifetime helping to clarify the ways in which the media affect us and our children was exceedingly generous with both his time and his knowledge. Most important, however, over the arduous task of writing a book was his contagious enthusiasm that people can have a significant effect on righting wrongs. I am profoundly grateful to him. To Richard Heffner, whom I cannot quite place in any category, because his intelligence and breadth of knowledge are so great that he defies categorization, my deepest thanks. Our many discussions had me think and then rethink my assumptions about rights and responsibilities.

To Eric Simonoff, my agent and sometimes friend, therapist, babysitter, and sounding board—thank you for the vote of confidence long before I deserved it. There is no greater gift than to take seriously someone's need to be heard. To Eadie Klemm, his assistant, thanks for always knowing when all I really needed was a sympathetic ear.

To Lori Lipsky, my editor at Doubleday, who works magic in ways I can't even begin to understand, thank you for using your dazzling intelligence to massage this book into its present form. To her assistant Frances Jones, for walking me through the sometimes baffling process of publication, and to the copyeditors and proofreaders who worked to make this book as readable as possible, thank you.

To my friends and to the many people in my community who provided me with hundreds of clippings that they thought might be of use to me—everything from the *Harvard Law Review* to the Marin Day School newsletter—thank you for your interest and support. To my dear friend DeeDee Epp, thanks for your love and for keeping me connected to the outside world. To our dear "Maga," who loved and cared for my children so thoroughly that I had the peace of mind to devote myself to this project, I am very grateful. And to my Uncle Obbie, who would regularly call at two in the morning just to make sure I knew "what the jerk said about television." Thanks for the late-night humor and for watching out for me.

To Suzanne Lippsett, who worked on the original proposal for this book and who taught me to divest myself of academic language—to realize that a single idea clearly communicated was worth a dozen that were poorly communicated—thank you for your crash course in straightforward writing. To Rachel Tak, who ran our local video store, and was a model of responsible business, always checking with parents before allowing those eleven-year-old rapscallions out with *Blue Velvet*, thank you for ignoring all those overdue video charges.

Thanks to Nancy Boyden, who helped with mountains of photocopying and difficult librarians. And a very special thank you to researcher Karen Capadona, who took every one of my phone calls starting with "You'll never be able to find this out" and somehow managed to find it all out.

To my mother, Edith Levine, for her unflagging support and belief in me. Thank you for listening to hours of frustrated, euphoric, jagged phone calls. To my husband, Lee Schwartz, who barely let a day go by without taping some clipping or commentary to our bathroom mirror. Thank you for your love and support and for allowing me the space to complete a project that took me away from the family more than any of us liked.

And most especially to my three sons, Loren, Michael, and Jeremy. Thanks for enduring late carpool pickups, missed basketball and soccer games, and endless nights of frozen pizza and take-out food. I have learned more from you three than from all the psychology courses I ever took. Thanks for letting me use all those embarrassing anecdotes about you—you won't get teased for long; kids' memories are short. You three guys are the greatest blessings I will ever know.

Introduction

On February 10, 1992, my oldest son, then two days shy of his twelfth birthday, asked me if he could see the movie *Silence of the Lambs*. Having recently seen it, I said no without hesitation. Cannibalism, murder, and mutilation seemed to be the stuff of nightmares, and I saw no reason to expose him to such ferocious brutality. Our ensuing discussion was predictable. I said that *Silence of the Lambs* (or *Terminator*, or *Die Hard*, or *Nightmare on Elm Street*) was not "appropriate" for his age. He said, "It's just a movie, Mom. It can't hurt my development." Being the son of a clinical psychologist, he has learned, in self-defense, to speak his mother's language.

I was struck by his insistence that he was the only one of all his friends who had not seen the movie. As a psychotherapist and the mother of three boys, I am not easily fooled into believing the anthem of adolescence "I'm the only one." He assured me that he was telling the truth, and I was certain that he was exaggerating. "Go ahead and call," he suggested. So I did, believing that other parents would share my point of view. After all, we live in a middle-class, well-educated community with parents who are genuinely and regularly involved in their children's activities. I was certain that other parents would agree that a movie like *Silence of the Lambs* was an experience to shield children from.

One by one I called his friend's mothers, all women I had known for years, whom I respected and who were without exception "good moms." Yes, in fact, their sons had seen the movie, some with parental permission, some without. Some of the parents and all of the kids felt "it was just entertainment." A few of the more outspoken children even questioned why I found it difficult to "distinguish reality from fantasy." While all of the kids felt that the movie was "very scary," none said that they had any nightmares related to it.

So, here I was, a forty-five-year-old Ph.D., mother of three, significantly disturbed and shocked by a movie that a group of eleven- and twelve-year-olds had taken in stride. My training and experience as a psychologist told me that these children should have been traumatized by the psychotic, graphic sadism of Dr. Hannibal Lecter. Developmentally, young adolescents are concerned with issues of physical growth and awakening sexuality, the replacement of parental values with peer values, and an emerging sense of identity. At its best, *Silence of the Lambs* simply does not deal with the emotional issues relevant to young adolescents. At its worst, it presents a sadistic, perverted central character in an intriguing and even playful way. In addition, I would expect it to raise anxiety about sexuality and physical vulnerability. Yet these children were remarkably unmoved. Why weren't they upset by this movie? Why weren't they horrified?

Almost every week, I am approached by a concerned parent who asks me, "How much TV is safe for my child? When does it become harmful?" I frequently am asked my opinion about the suitability of some movie or another. Parents appear to be simultaneously concerned with and indifferent to the amount of media violence viewed by their children. On the one hand, we read articles, attend lectures, and consult with experts on how media violence affects our children; on the other hand, these same children are exposed to levels of media violence inconsistent with everything that is known about healthy child development.

I have written this book both as a psychologist and as a mother. A great deal is known about the harmful effects of media violence on children, but much of it is technical and inaccessible to the average parent. Without this information, parents are likely to continue to minimize its harm. As a psychologist, I hope to sharpen parents' awareness of the unique ways in which children at different ages experience the media. I will present what social scientists have long known about media violence: that it encourages aggression, desensitization, and pessimism in our children. But since all passion inevitably flows from personal commitment, I have written this book because I do not want my three sons growing up in a society that routinely glorifies violence, and denies social responsibility.

This book is divided into four parts. The first part looks at the role of the media, and particularly media violence, in the lives of our children. Both television programs and movies are used to provide examples. The vast majority of research has been conducted on television, although it seems likely that many of the findings are equally applicable to movies, which regularly feature far more brutal and graphic depictions of violence than either cable or broadcast television. This first part traces the development of television in this country and examines more than forty years of research on the subject of media violence and children. I try to untangle the thicket of research, focusing on those findings that parents will find most useful in understanding how their children are being affected by media violence.

The second part defines what is meant by a "developmental approach." It clarifies the major variables that affect how children experience the world at different stages of development—the nature of their attachments, how they handle aggression, how they think, and the process by which they develop a conscience.

The third part of the book examines how children at specific stages of development think, act, and feel. Parents will be helped to "see" the world through the eyes of their child. The effects of media will be considered in detail for children at different ages. Suggestions and illustrations will help parents make decisions about which films and programs are appropriate and which are inappropriate.

Finally, the fourth part of the book focuses on how parents as well as government, schools, and the media themselves can best approach the problems created by a system at odds with itself. Is it possible to both "serve the public interest, convenience, and necessity" and "recognize the special needs of children" while still turning a profit? How can we, in our varying capacities as parent, educator, politician, entertainer, and, most of all, citizen, preserve a healthy cultural environment for our children? A list of resources at the end of the book provides parents with phone numbers and addresses of the major networks and suggests how to contact government agencies involved with media regulation. This directory also helps parents and other concerned citizens locate organizations that are active in media reform and media literacy.

Part One

Warning: Viewing Violence Is Dangerous to Your Child's Health

1

What We Know

The debate is over.

Violence on television and in the movies is damaging to children. Forty years of research conclude that repeated exposure to high levels of media violence teaches some children and adolescents to settle interpersonal differences with violence, while teaching many more to be indifferent to this solution. Under the media's tutelage, children at younger and younger ages are using violence as a first, not a last, resort to conflict.

Locked away in professional journals are thousands of articles documenting the negative effects of media, particularly media violence, on our nation's youth. Children who are heavy viewers of television are more aggressive, more pessimistic, weigh more, are less imaginative, less empathic, and less capable students than their lighter-viewing counterparts. With an increasing sense of urgency, parents are confronting the fact that the "real story" about media violence and its effects on children has been withheld.

Speaking before the U.S. Senate Committee on Governmental Affairs, Leonard Eron, one of the country's foremost authorities on media and children, said:

> There can no longer be any doubt that heavy exposure to televised violence is one of the causes of aggressive behavior, crime and violence in society. The evidence comes from both the laboratory and real-life studies. Television violence affects youngsters of all ages, of both gen-

ders, at all socio-economic levels and all levels of intelligence. The effect is not limited to children who are already disposed to being aggressive and is not restricted to this country.[1]

Every major group concerned with children has studied and issued position papers on the effects of media violence on children. The Surgeon General's Scientific Advisory Committee on Television and Social Behavior, the National Institute of Mental Health, the U.S. attorney general's Task Force on Family Violence, the American Psychological Association, the American Academy of Pediatrics, and the National Parent Teachers Association have all called for curbing television and movie violence. Their findings represent the inescapable conclusions of decades of social science research. Doctors, therapists, teachers, and youth workers all find themselves struggling to help youngsters who, influenced by repeated images of quick, celebratory violence, find it increasingly difficult to negotiate the inevitable frustrations of daily life.

America has become the most violent nation in the industrialized world. Homicide is the leading cause of death for large segments of our country's youth, and we have more young men in prison than any other country in the world. The roots of violence in our society are complex. We are well informed about the contributions of poverty, child abuse, alcoholism, and drug abuse, but we must also consider the role played by the images that our children see on the screen during their three and a half hours of daily viewing.

A major gap exists between research findings and what the public knows about the harmful effects of media violence on children. This is not surprising. Public education often lags behind research, especially when economic stakes are high. Tobacco executives, for instance, are still insisting that "the scientific proof isn't in yet to link smoking and cancer."[2] The entertainment industry stands to lose a great deal of money if violence, a particularly cheap and reliable form of entertainment, becomes less popular.

Ordinarily when science discovers a matter of pressing public concern, it relies on the cooperation of the media to ensure that this information reaches a wide audience. Much of the success of the antismoking campaign was due to the media's active efforts at educating the public. Similarly, the media have played a significant role in educating Americans about the advantages of wearing seat belts, the need for child car seats, and the inadvisability of drinking and driving. As a result, we have seen a significant reduction in children and teenagers dying in motor vehicle accidents. Yet violence among youngsters and teenagers has skyrocketed. Researchers speak with one voice in telling us that this is partly due to the incessant glamorization of violence in the media. However, the entertainment industry's self-protective stance has resulted in these findings being ignored, denied, attacked, or misrepresented.

In May 1995, presidential hopeful Bob Dole delivered a blistering attack on the entertainment industry. "A line has been crossed—not just of taste but of human dignity and decency," admonished the senator. He called for an end to the "mainstreaming of deviancy." While freely admitting that he had not personally seen much of what he attacked, and while seeming to ignore the paradox between calling for an end to violent images while simultaneously supporting a repeal of the ban on assault weapons, Dole struck a chord of national discontent. Headlines across the country announced, "DOLE SCOLDS ENTERTAINMENT INDUSTRY."

In typical punch and parry fashion, the entertainment industry responded within hours. "HOLLYWOOD SCOFFS AT DOLE'S REBUKE OF SHOW BUSINESS," proclaimed feature articles the next day. Using characteristic hyperbole, director Oliver Stone called Senator Dole "a modern-day McCarthy."[3] But of the dozens of articles crossing my desk in this frenzy of accusations and counteraccusations, not one dealt with substantive issues. The entertainment industry can ill afford to "scoff" at the legitimate concerns of parents who feel that their children are awash in images of violence and cruelty. Nor can concerned citizens simply "rebuke" the entertainment industry without being knowledgeable about the problems. Informed dialogue precedes change. The importance of the effects of media violence on child development is far too great to be abandoned to the arena of parental grumbling and political opportunity.

It seems that we are regularly presented with evidence connecting horrible crimes with exposure to the media:

Serial killer Nathaniel White described how he killed his first female victim while imitating a scene from the movie *Robocop II:* "I seen him cut somebody's throat then take the knife and slit down the chest to the stomach and leave the body in a certain position. With the first person I killed I did exactly what I saw in the movie."[4]

In New York City, a grammar school child sprayed a Bronx office building with gunfire and explained to an astonished police sergeant that he learned how to load his Uzi-like gun because "I watch a lot of television."[5]

Nine-year-old Olivia Niemi was sexually assaulted with a discarded beer bottle on a deserted beach in San Francisco. The four girls who took part in the attack said they were imitating a scene from *Born Innocent*, an NBC television movie they watched three days before committing the crime.[6] The movie, which takes place in a girl's reform school, shows a new inmate cornered by four girls and graphically raped with the handle of a plumber's helper.

It is time to move past the debate of whether or not the entertainment industry is "responsible" for these crimes. The question is not whether the media are the cause of crimes like these (they aren't), but whether the media are an important ingredient in the multiple causation of crime (they are). Violence is most frequently the endpoint of a confluence of personal, social, and environmental factors. Television has become a powerful environmental source of behaviors, attitudes, and values. In many homes it threatens the traditional triumvirate of socialization—family, school, and church. *Excessive and gratuitous media violence is an easily reversible contributor to crime.* Quite simply, we need to tell our children stories that will contribute to their healthy development and enhance positive behaviors, rather than allowing the media to encourage negative ones.

By the time they graduate high school, children will have spent 50 percent more time in front of a television set than in front of a teacher. The average American household has television turned on more than seven hours a day, and the average American child watches three to four hours a day.[7] The vast majority of this time is spent watching programs not targeted to a children's audience—game shows, soap operas, and MTV. Television makes no distinctions among viewers. If you are four years old and able to turn on the television, then you are privy to the same information as a fourteen-year-old or a forty-year-old. Television has changed the nature of childhood; it has eradicated many of the traditional barriers that protected children from the harsh facts of adult life. No wonder youngsters who are heavy viewers of television are more pessimistic than light viewers! They have been exposed to a world of violence, sex, commercialism, and betrayal far beyond their emotional capacities. Hours spent watching the O. J. Simpson trial make the world of adults look grim indeed.

George Gerbner, dean emeritus of the Annenberg School of Communication, believes that television "tells most of the stories to most of the people, most of the time." Television "cultivates" the viewer's perceptions of society, encouraging the belief that the real world is more or less like the fictionalized world of television. Television has become the melting pot of the twentieth century. It provides us with a shared set of beliefs and assumptions about how the world works. Television is such a fundamental part of life that one in four Americans say they wouldn't surrender their sets for a million dollars.[8]

Network executives are quick to exploit our sense that television is a kind of cultural glue binding us together as a nation. In a *TV Guide* interview, Judy Price, vice president for children's programming at CBS, said, "A kid can't be the only one on the playground not to watch *Power Rangers.*"[9] This statement highlights one of the prime objectives of media promotion. In addition to making things familiar and desirable, the media must create an appearance of social necessity. "A kid can't be the only one on the playground not to watch *Power Rangers*" implies that the child who is prevented from partaking in this quintessential American experience will be denied full participation in the social life of his or her peer group. While shared media experiences are certainly part of group conversation at playgrounds, workplaces, and homes around the country, parents should not be made to feel guilty when they act to protect their children from excessively violent programming.

These manipulations by people in the entertainment industry are distressing but revealing. Media executives are loudly demanding that parents take more "responsibility" for their children's viewing. "When are you going to stop blaming the media and start looking at the home environment and the fact that parents are supposed to monitor what their children are watching?" admonishes a well-known Hollywood producer.[10] However, parents and politicians who support the "V-chip" (which would allow parents to screen out violent programming) are told by industry leaders, who oppose the chip, that violence must be evaluated on a "case-by-case" basis. It is no accident that parents feel so helpless about controlling access to media they disapprove of. While giving lip service to the need for adult supervision, television executives act to circumvent parental authority.

Television itself should not be demonized. It can serve as an effective instrument for human development and enrichment. Wonderful programs, including many on the Public Broadcasting Service (PBS), have proven that television can teach children new skills, enlarge their worldview, and promote prosocial attitudes and behaviors. But commercial television has a different agenda from personal and cultural development. Its agenda is to round up the largest and most affluent audience it can and deliver that audience to an advertiser.

Advertisers like programs with good track records and proven formulas for gaining an audience. That is why so much of what television offers appears repetitive and predictable. We may have access to hundreds of stations, but in fact the kinds of stories we see are surprisingly limited. As a result, television cultivates a common perspective. All too frequently that perspective includes a reliance on violence as a habitual, acceptable, and even admirable way of resolving conflict. This trivializes the enormous human toll that violence always exacts.

The media, as major disseminators of attitudes, assumptions, and values, can ill afford to ignore their responsibilities while asserting their rights. While the National Rifle Association insists that "guns don't kill people; people kill people," the fact is that people do it with guns. Similarly, television doesn't kill people, but it provides the ideas, the social sanction, and often even the instruction that encourages antisocial behavior. Those who profit from the enormous opportunities for financial gain and status that the entertainment industry provides must act as citizens as well as business people. And it is the responsibility of all citizens, not just parents, to provide America's children with a culturally healthy environment.

The effects of the media are not trivial. For example, it is well known that suicide rates increase after the suicide of a celebrity *if* there is extensive media coverage. The highly publicized suicide of Kurt Cobain, lead singer for the rock group Nirvana, resulted in many copycat suicides of mostly male adolescents. "When Kurt Cobain died, I died with him" was the note left by an eighteen-year-old who, along with two other friends, executed a suicide pact following Cobain's death.[11] This is not to suggest that the news should not have been reported. But science has provided us with

n research to be able to predict that the kind of sensational
:peated coverage that Cobain's suicide received was bound to
t in an increase in adolescent suicides. Parents need to be
:e that sensational coverage of crime and suicide by young ce-
ities can be emotionally devastating for vulnerable teens. Pa-
:tal awareness, supervision, and discussion are critical variables in
ading off additional tragedies.

While examples of copycat crimes are particularly distressing,
ney underscore the power of the media that reach into virtually
:very household in America. Setting social norms can never be
considered a "trivial" task. If you are elderly, it is not trivial that the
media insist on reducing you to a dotty simpleton. If you are an
African American, it is not trivial that the media vacillate between
worshiping you as a sports hero, laughing at you as a buffoon, and
reviling you as a thug. If you are a woman, it is not trivial that every
female newscaster must be ten or twenty years younger than her
male counterpart. If you are a parent who tries to convey the values
of hard work and good education to your children, it is not trivial
that Beavis and Butt-head have become the supermodels of teenage
sloth and indifference.

Images have consequences, often distressing and even tragic
ones. My eleven-year-old son and I turned on the news one evening
to hear a quick disclaimer about "disturbing images" followed by
scenes of dead and critically injured children. In a neighboring
community, a van had slammed into a school playground killing
one child and critically injuring several others. In the two seconds it
took for me to reach over and change channels, those blood-soaked
images were burned into our minds. That night my son had great
difficulty sleeping and many nightmares. Were those scenes necessary? As news, did that footage teach us anything we need to know
about the world or how to conduct our lives? I don't believe it did.
Rather, I believe the television station was following the time-
honored bromide "If it bleeds, it leads." Media executives who
invoke First Amendment rights to justify such irresponsible programming are cowards. Grant Tinker, before becoming president
of NBC, called poor television programming "a national crime"[12]
and suggested that network executives who did not live up to their
responsibilities be jailed.

The basis of all societies is a reasonably shared set of values.
We may define ourselves individually as Democrats or Republicans,

liberals or conservatives, antigovernment or progovernment. Surveys show, however, that most Americans agree that there is a basic set of values that define our society.[13] These include loyalty, responsibility, family, integrity, and courage. It is respect for individual rights, accompanied by a tolerance for diversity, that has characterized America since its founding.

The word *rights* came up repeatedly in my discussions with various media executives: individual rights, creative rights, and, most predictably, First Amendment rights. I am not a political scientist and this incessant referral to First Amendment rights as a way of deflecting criticism sent me scurrying to my son's high school social studies text to refamiliarize myself with the Constitution and the Bill of Rights. I had almost forgotten that there is a Preamble to the Constitution which puts forth the overarching principles of our democracy. In the Preamble there is no mention of rights. Rather, the tone and language recognize that America was founded on the notion of communal responsibility rather than individual rights. The Preamble talks of "*common* defense" and "*general* welfare."

The Bill of Rights, the first ten amendments to the Constitution, is familiar to the public. Whether it's the gun lobby invoking a self-serving version of the Second Amendment (which never said that some desperate, unemployed eighteen-year-old is entitled to an arsenal of semiautomatic weaponry, but rather that a "well-regulated militia" is entitled to bear arms) or First Amendment absolutists like director Oliver Stone, who echoes the sentiments of many in the entertainment industry when he equates criticism with censorship, America has turned her attention from responsibilities to rights. Rights are not entitlements, they are immunities. None of us, whether we are parents, politicians, media executives, or special-interest groups, can afford to forget that along with the extraordinary range of rights that we enjoy in this country is an equally extraordinary range of responsibilities.

When executives in the entertainment industry insist that profits come before responsibility, they do not live up to their commitment to serve the public. When we as parents allow our children to sit and watch hours of thoughtless violence, we do not live up to our commitment to protect and nurture our children. America's children are being hurt. They are hurt when they are the victims or perpetrators of mindless violence, illustrated and glorified by the media. They are hurt when they see the world as a corrupt and frightening place in which only consumer goods bring satisfaction and peace of mind. They are hurt when they have become so dependent on rapid-fire, prefabricated visual effects that they can no longer conjure up their own images or dream their own dreams. It is time to stop hurting our most vulnerable population. It is time to start protecting our children.

2
Television in America

Television was introduced to the American public by the Radio Corporation of America at the New York World's Fair in 1939. Not incidentally, the first image to be publicly broadcast on a television screen was the dollar sign.[1] At that time television was viewed largely as an object of curiosity, although the well-known journalist and children's author E. B. White wrote with uncanny clairvoyance:

> I believe television is going to be the test of the modern world, and in this new opportunity to see beyond the range of our vision, we shall discover either a new and unbearable disturbance of the general peace or a saving radiance in the sky. We shall stand or fall by television—of that I am quite sure.[2]

Not even E. B. White's prescience could have prepared him for the kinds of experiences that television would soon be bringing into virtually every American household. We would see some of our most beloved political leaders, John F. Kennedy, Robert Kennedy, and Martin Luther King Jr., murdered before our collective eyes. We would watch televised courtroom trials of serial killers like Jeffrey Dahmer and Ted Bundy describe crimes of unspeakable inhumanity. We would see seven popular astronauts reduced to a plume of smoke in the *Challenger* disaster. Ninety-five million people would sit in rapt absorption as O. J. Simpson, a sports superstar, sped down a Los Angeles freeway to avoid arrest for the double murder of his ex-wife Nicole Brown Simpson and her friend Ron Goldman.

We have been delighted by, indifferent to, or offended by characters like Archie Bunker, Murphy Brown, and Roseanne. Almost every child in America knows Big Bird, Bert and Ernie, and the Cookie Monster. Barney, a purple dinosaur created by a mother in Texas who was unhappy with the programming available to her young son, has proved wildly successful. While critics attacked the "banality and simple production values" of the program, youngsters fell in love with Barney's kind and reassuring manner and message. Seventeen kindergartners sang his "I love you, you love me" anthem as they cringed in terror in a disabled elevator during the New York World Trade Center bombing. For nearly thirty years Mister Rogers has played friend, educator, and psychotherapist to children, reassuring them that "you're special" and "I like you just the way you are." Karate has become the social interaction of choice as youngsters pay homage to the Teenage Mutant Ninja Turtles and Mighty Morphin Power Rangers in playgrounds across the country.

Television and the movies have become such a common reference point that Vice President Dan Quayle made Murphy Brown's pregnancy a political issue in his 1992 bid for reelection. President Bush appropriated a line from Clint Eastwood's *Dirty Harry* movie and invited the Iraqis to "Make my day" during the Persian Gulf War. Following the release of Spike Lee's popular film *Do the Right Thing*, members of Congress saw fit to use that phrase sixty-seven times in a four-month period.[3] Sixteen of those references were invoked during arguments for a congressional pay hike. Presidential hopeful Bill Clinton appeared on MTV to bring his agenda to the program's 15 million potential voters.[4]

Americans, regardless of race, religion, gender, age or socioeconomic group, have been bound together by the shared cultural experience of television. We have watched with attention, interest, and sometimes disbelief as television has poured the world into our living rooms and bedrooms. Television, which was in only 9 percent of American households in 1950, is now in 98 percent of them.[5] Most homes have two or more television sets as well as cable and a VCR, all of which allow access to an ever expanding range of media offerings. Children are watching, on average, close to twenty-eight hours of television every week.

George Gerbner has observed, "The longer we live with television, the more invisible it becomes."[6] Television and the media in general have so successfully saturated our culture that we barely recognize their influence. America's corporations spend $45 billion a year on advertising designed to cultivate desire and change our behavior.[7] Our attitudes and actions are shaped in ways that are subtle, persuasive, and often outside our consciousness. Most people in this country cannot remember a time before television.

While Americans have embraced television, the concerns about its role and influence are long-standing. In 1961, the recently appointed chairman of the Federal Communications Commission, Newton Minow, delivered his famous "vast wasteland" speech. In his inaugural address to the National Association of Broadcasters, he said:

> When television is good, nothing—not the theater, not the magazines or newspapers—is better. But when television is bad, nothing is worse. I invite you to sit down in front of your television set when your station goes on the air and stay there without a book, magazine, newspaper, profit-and-loss sheet, or rating book to distract you—and keep your eyes glued to that set until the station signs off. I can assure you that you will observe a vast wasteland. You will see a procession of game shows, violence, audience participation shows, formula comedies about unbelievable families, blood and thunder, mayhem, violence, sadism, murder, western bad men, western good men, private eyes, gangsters, more violence, and cartoons. And, endlessly, commercials—many screaming, cajoling, and offending.[8]

Thirty years later, on the anniversary of this speech, Minow observed, "In 1961 I worried that my children would not benefit much from television, but in 1991, I worry that my grandchildren will actually be harmed by it."[9]

Minow's worries are shared by all those interested in the effects of media on child development. Historically, there has always been concern about the ways in which children can be manipulated by "outside ideas." In Plato's *Republic* Socrates asks, "Then, shall we simply allow our children to listen to any stories that anyone happens to make up, and so receive into their minds ideas often the very opposite of those we shall think they ought to have when they grow up?"[10] All forms of media have been the subject of widespread concern at one time or another. Radio, silent movies, and comic books have all had their share of critics. Mass media bring into the home ideas and sensibilities that are beyond the control of, and often in conflict with, parental values.

As the American family changes, and often fragments, the concern about the effects of media on children has accelerated. In 1971 there were about 550 studies on children and television. In 1980, this number jumped to almost 3,000. Parents today feel less able to control their children. Isolated from extended family, and often economically stressed, American parents spend less time with their children than parents in any other nation in the world.[11] Many would argue that television has replaced all other institutions as the single most powerful transmitter of cultural values.

Both common sense and my experience as a psychologist tell me that parents are still the most active agents in a child's socialization. However, there is no question that television teaches children many things about our culture. Television reflects, creates, and perpetuates our social order. It teaches who's in charge and who submits. It illustrates who gets away with things and who is likely to be punished. Television takes us "behind the scenes" of our society. Here, men dominate the airways, women are a subservient minority, real minorities barely exist, and when they do it is usually only in stereotyped fashion. Television communicates the hierarchy of power relations in our society. Too frequently it teaches boys how to be perpetrators and girls how to be victims.

Research on the effects of media has focused on several areas, its effects on children being the most prominent. Is violence on television harmful? In what ways? Who is most likely to be harmed?

Unusual circumstances have allowed social scientists to look at what happens to communities when television is introduced. In 1973, Tannis McBeth Williams and colleagues were presented with the unique opportunity to study an ordinary Canadian town about to receive television for the first time.[12] The town, which the researchers named Notel, was not an unusual or particularly isolated town, but because of its location in a deep valley it had never received television. The researchers had a year in which to accumulate data on many variables, including children's aggression, before television transmitters were installed. For comparison, data were also collected on two nearby towns, one called Unitel, with limited television service, and one called Multitel, with ordinary television service. The results of the study were unequivocal. Two years after the introduction of television, children in Notel displayed an increased level of aggression. This increase took place regardless of gender or initial level of aggression. The study also showed that the introduction of television increased sex role stereotyping among children and decreased their reading scores, creativity, and involvement in community activities.

While this research took place in Canada, the bulk of research on the effects of media violence has been conducted in the United States. When researchers have studied media effects in other countries, results have been generally comparable. It is unfortunate, but perhaps not surprising, that in spite of a vast body of scientific knowledge, the media themselves have been superficial in covering this issue. We are often led to believe that this is an area of debate within the academic community. Minimal differences in research findings are sometimes used as "proof" that conclusions are unwarranted. But the vast majority of research has consistently shown the damaging effects of excessive and gratuitous violence.

The truth is that violence is not generic and neither are children. Different kinds of children at different ages are affected by violence in different ways. The reasons for the social problems of this country are long-standing and complex. Many other factors besides media violence—lack of job opportunities, availability of guns, drugs, and poverty—must be considered when making a thoughtful assessment of this country's high murder rate and high rate of incarceration. It is foolish to suggest that television, or any single factor, is responsible for these problems. But television's role needs to be clearly defined in order to clarify the ways in which we can protect children from its negative effects. The next chapter looks at some of the major studies that have been conducted on the effects of media violence on children. Research has identified and focused on three major areas of concern:

1. Does media violence encourage children to act more aggressively?

2. Does media violence cultivate attitudes that are excessively distorted, frightening, and pessimistic?

3. Does media violence desensitize children to violence?

The research answers each of these questions with a disturbing "yes." A familiarity with these studies and their implications provides the backbone for later chapters designed to help parents make informed decisions about their children's viewing.

3

Research and Theory

Does Media Violence Encourage Children to Act More Aggressively?

Children are great imitators. Even in the earliest months of life, infants can mimic the facial expressions of their caretakers. Children learn how to eat, dress, use the toilet, and interact with those around them because their parents and others are constantly providing examples of how to do things. Children are not particularly selective in what they imitate; countless parents have been reminded to pay attention to their language when their three-year-old utters "Oh shit" in frustration. Sometimes it seems as if there is nothing that escapes the attention of the young child. Although imitation is not the only way that children learn, it is the earliest and sets the stage for future learning.

Given that children are relentless in their imitation of people around them, it is logical that they would also imitate people they see on television and in the movies. From Davy Crockett coonskin caps to Teenage Mutant Ninja Turtle bandannas, costumes based on television characters have always been extremely popular. This type of imitation of screen characters is not limited to young children. A generation of adolescents rolled up their T-shirt sleeves and cultivated the sneer and swagger of James Dean and Marlon Brando. Many of today's teenagers seem to have shopped at a single store, so alike are they in their choice of flannel shirts and baseball caps, a style of dress begun and perfected by the grunge bands of MTV. Throughout the life cycle we imitate others in order to learn new things and to reinforce our identity with a particular group.

Stories of children imitating characters from the media with tragic results are reported with some regularity:

> A five year old boy set his home on fire, killing his two-year-old sister, following a *Beavis and Butt-head* episode. The boy's mother described him as "addicted to *Beavis and Butt-head*," two moronic preadolescent MTV cartoon characters who enjoy fire setting and other antisocial acts.[1]

> An adolescent boy was killed by a car and several of his friends seriously injured while imitating a scene from the movie *The Program*. The scene shows young men attempting to prove their courage by lying down along the center divider of a busy road between lanes of cars.[2]

> A thirteen-year-old boy and his friend were acting out the Russian roulette scene from the movie *The Deer Hunter*. The young boy died instantly after shooting himself in the head.[3]

These stories are all tragic, but thankfully they are also rare. Clearly most children do not simply imitate what they see on the screen. Instead, out of the multitude of behaviors, images, attitudes, and values that children are exposed to, they choose only certain ones to make their own. When frustrated, one child cries in a corner, while another kicks and punches, and yet a third seems to take the frustration in stride. While imitation may be the earliest form of learning, no child becomes a carbon copy of the people around him or her. As for the effects of media violence on children, if imitation was the only or even the primary form of learning, we could predict tomorrow's headlines from today's *TV Guide*. We cannot, of course, and that is because what children learn from the media is usually far more complex than simple imitation.

Some of the earliest research on the effects of media violence on children was conducted by Albert Bandura at Stanford University in the 1960s. For more than three decades, Bandura has looked at the ways in which children construct their selves out of the range of possibilities available to them. His early work focused on the circumstances under which children became more aggressive by observing aggression. His Bobo doll studies are considered classic experiments in psychology and have done much to clarify the ways in which children are likely to learn from media violence.

Bandura's Bobo doll is a large inflatable clown that is weighted to pop back up when hit. In a typical experiment, Bandura divided nursery school–age children into three groups—one control group (a group that does not take part in the actual experiment) and two experimental groups. All children were initially put into a room filled with attractive toys. The control group was then excluded. One experimental group watched a filmed sequence on a simulated television set. This is what the children saw:

> The film began with a scene in which (an adult male) model walked up to an adult-size plastic Bobo doll and ordered him to clear the way. After glaring for a moment at the noncompliant antagonist the model exhibited four novel aggressive responses each accompanied by a distinctive verbalization. First, the model laid the Bobo doll on its side, sat on it, and punched it in the nose while remarking "Pow, right in the nose, boom, boom." The model then raised the doll and pummeled it on the head with a mallet. Each response was accompanied by the verbalization "Sockeroo . . . stay down." Following the mallet aggression, the model kicked the doll about the room, and these responses were interspersed with the comment "Fly away." Finally, the model threw rubber balls at the Bobo doll, each strike punctuated with "Bang." This sequence of physically and verbally aggressive behavior was repeated twice.[4]

The children in the second experimental group saw the same sequence performed live by an adult male. After this, all three groups of children were brought into a room containing many toys, among them balls, a pegboard and mallet, guns, and dolls. Children who were in the control group displayed few or none of the aggressive behaviors. However, children who had viewed the attacks on the Bobo doll, either on television or live, displayed a considerable number of aggressive behaviors similar to those they had observed. What was perhaps most interesting about Bandura's findings were the novel ways children found to express their aggression. One little girl took a doll and twirled it around by one leg, slamming it into the Bobo doll. Another young boy grabbed a pistol and began shooting the doll. Not only did the children imitate adult displays of aggression, they also added their own particular spin. This is why we say that children frequently "model" their behavior rather than simply imitating what they see.

There were a number of criticisms of Bandura's research. Detractors said that of course children learn behavior from adults, but that doesn't mean that they would copy television, particularly cartoon violence. Others said that the fact that a child acts aggressively toward a toy doesn't mean that the child would be aggressive toward a person. Further research laid these objections to rest. Children who were aggressive with the Bobo doll were also more aggressive toward peers. Other studies found that children could learn aggressive behavior from a cartoonlike figure just as readily as from a live adult.[5]

The fact that a child does not act aggressively after observing violence does not mean that he or she has not learned an aggressive solution. Performing and learning are not necessarily the same. Of the children who observed the adult acting aggressively toward the Bobo doll, most became more aggressive, some did not, but they all *learned* about behaving aggressively. Many of us have had the experience of reacting angrily in some trivial situation, like being cut off on the freeway, and responding with obscenities and an itchy middle finger. A few minutes later we may wonder "Where did that come from?" It comes, of course, from the large repertoire of aggressive responses that we have learned and stored but generally have enough control to bypass. The fact that a child does not go out and shoot someone after watching *Demolition Man* does not mean that he or she has not learned that shooting is a plausible solution.

It is simplistic to look for a one-to-one relationship between violent programming and children's behavior. As children grow past the preschool years, their aggressive behavior becomes less imitative and more a reflection of their developing interpersonal style. While a three-year-old may imitate a Teenage Mutant Ninja Turtle kick more or less exactly, the older child, with a larger repertoire of behaviors, just seems to get pushier. Watch a theater full of young adolescents after a showing of *Die Hard*. They leave the theater pushing and shoving and generally more physically active than if they had seen a comedy. While they are not exhibiting a new behavior, it has become easier to express an old aggressive behavior such as pushing or shoving. Provocation or frustration increases the likelihood that learned aggression will find expression. Several cities have experienced melees and even homicides following the showing of particularly provocative movies. The ordinary jostle that one might experience leaving a crowded theater becomes a trigger for barely contained rage.

While true imitation of a fictional crime is rare, it does happen. In 1987 a disturbed young man named Michael Ryan committed Britain's worst mass murder. Dressed in full Rambo gear, he slaughtered sixteen people, including his mother, before turning his gun on himself.[6] The largest and most appalling example of movie imitation is that of the twenty-six people who shot themselves through the head playing out the Russian roulette scene from the 1978 Vietnam war epic *The Deer Hunter*.

To ask the right questions, we need to switch the focus from "Do television and movies teach children to be more aggressive?" (they do) and instead ask "How effectively is aggression taught?" Under what circumstances are children most likely to express the violent solutions they have learned? An extensive body of research suggests that several important variables determine how effective a media message will be in teaching aggression to children:

- Do we identify with the character?
- Is the violence reinforced? Does crime pay?
- Is the violence seen as real or make-believe?

It is important for parents to have some understanding of each of these factors because they all play an important part in answering our basic concern, "Is this likely to teach my child to behave aggressively in response to conflict and frustration?"

DO WE IDENTIFY WITH THE CHARACTER?

Common sense tells us that we are more likely to imitate people who are attractive, respected, and powerful. Jacqueline Kennedy's pillbox hats and simple suits were as popular among aspiring young women in the '60s as Eddie Vedder's flannel shirts and ripped shorts are for adolescent suburbanites in the '90s. Within their respective groups, these two stylish individuals were seen as models worthy of imitation: contemporary, talented, and powerful. Imitating people who are prestigious and powerful allows us the illusion of borrowing some of their authority and privilege.

Research studies have shown that the more we identify and empathize with a character, the more likely we are to imitate that character.[7] It is for this reason that many psychologists are particularly concerned about "good guy" violence. Contrary to popular opinion, it is the "good guys," not the "bad guys," who are responsible for the majority of killings on television—by a margin of almost two to one. Of course, these murders are presented as necessary and justified. As a result, the audience is likely to be sympathetic toward the police officer whose partner was murdered, or husband whose wife has been raped, or parent whose child has been abducted. It is not uncommon in a movie theater to hear applause and shouts of approval when the bad guy is finally blown to pieces by the heroic avenger.

Clint Eastwood, Charles Bronson, Sylvester Stallone, and Arnold Schwarzenegger have all been wildly successful in their roles as vigilante-heroes. The police and judicial system are dismissed as trivial and incompetent. At the end of *Dirty Harry* we see Clint Eastwood toss his badge into the water, a dramatic gesture suggesting that the institutions designed to serve justice in this country are disposable. Many of our most popular movies carry messages suggesting that violence, not due process, is the "manly" and appropriate solution to crime.

We see the awful consequences of this point of view in our newspapers daily. Young men are murdered for "dissing," or disrespecting, another young man. Children are killed for their jackets or their sneakers. These are the tragic endpoints of a culture that glorifies violence, neglects the complexities of social problems, and elevates characters who are vengeful and ruthless to icon status. If we truly want less aggressive and more compassionate children, then we will have to come up with different role models for our children to admire and emulate.

There are bright spots to be considered. Knowing that children are most likely to model their behavior after characters they like and identify with helps us choose programs that feature healthy role models. Just as children become aggressive following exposure to antisocial programming, they can also become more cooperative after exposure to prosocial programming.

Sesame Street, the most watched children's television program of all time, has been the subject of intense scrutiny. Volumes of research have been turned out on both the academic and social effects of the program. Because it is multicultural and avoids gender stereotypes, children find many characters to identify with. Not surprisingly, those children who are regular viewers show enhanced social skills and attitudes. Minority children show increased cultural pride, confidence, and interpersonal cooperation.[8] Caucasian children show more positive attitudes toward children of other races.[9] Positive effects of *Sesame Street*, in terms of acquiring academic as well as social skills, are stronger if the child watches with a parent.[10] This point will be stressed repeatedly throughout this book: *Parental involvement greatly enhances the prosocial effects, while reducing the antisocial effects, of media on children.*

IS THE VIOLENCE REINFORCED? DOES CRIME PAY?

Young children see things in black and white. They reach moral conclusions by observing which behaviors get punished and which don't. Numerous studies have shown that children are most likely to imitate violence that has been rewarded. In one variation of Bandura's Bobo doll studies, one group of children watched an adult beat up the Bobo doll and then be rewarded with stickers and juice.[11] The adult was told that he was a "strong champion." Another group of children saw the adult punished by being spanked with a rolled-up magazine and told "If I catch you doing that again, you big bully, I'll give you a hard spanking. You quit acting that way." Both groups of children were then left in a room with many toys including the Bobo doll and were told to play while the experimenter left for a few minutes. Needless to say, those children who had seen the adult being rewarded for his aggressive behavior were far more likely to act aggressively than those children who had seen the adult being punished.

It is comforting to know that research confirms what most parents know intuitively. Few of us would consider resolving our conflicts at home by smacking or shooting each other. We are constantly trying to shape our children's behavior by rewarding their cooperative efforts and punishing their aggressive and inappropriate behavior. The media's sanctioning of violence as a respectable solution is either overblown or extremely subtle. This book is filled with examples of the kind of in-your-face, out-of-control violence found in movies such as *Die Hard* and *Robocop*. However, in the popular movie *Kindergarten Cop*, a kinder, gentler Arnold Schwarzenegger assaults a child molester. He is then called into the principal's office, expecting to be chewed out for fighting in front of the children he teaches. Instead, after a dramatic pause, the principal asks, "How did it feel to punch out that son of a bitch?" Schwarzenegger is congratulated for his aggression. The audience, along with the principal, considers Schwarzenegger's aggression appropriate, even valiant. Of course, taken as a single example, this seems trivial. Where's my sense of humor? It was a funny scene. But this book is about the *cumulative effects* of media violence. It is about the fact that we hardly even notice anymore that conflict is routinely solved by aggression. In real life, aggressive solutions are rarely rewarded or seen as funny. The truth is that aggressive children and adolescents tends to be ostracized, not lionized, by their peer groups.

Like violence that is rewarded, violence that seems justified is far more likely to be imitated than violence that seems to be unjustified. Psychologist Leonard Berkowitz and his colleagues at the University of Wisconsin have carefully researched the topic of justified aggression. In a typical study, Berkowitz had male subjects angered by being insulted.[12] The subjects were then divided into two groups. One group saw a violent movie in which a "bad guy" was beaten up. The other group saw the same violent movie, but this time a "good guy" was beaten up. After the movie, the subjects were allowed to punish the person who had insulted them earlier. Those who had seen the "bad guy" beaten up were much harsher in their punishment than those who had seen the "good guy" beaten up. Berkowitz interprets these differences by saying that the movie violence against the "bad guy" was seen as morally okay, whereas the violence against the "good guy" was morally unwarranted. The subjects in the experiment tended to see their own behavior in the same light. Justified aggression on the screen made these young men feel that their own aggression was similarly justified.

Ethical considerations prohibit studies in which people are actually allowed to injure others. However, some particularly creative studies have strongly suggested that people who feel they are justified in acting aggressively would do so if given a chance in the real world. Stanley Milgram, at Yale University, conducted a well-known series of experiments on obedience to authority.[13] He studied the willingness of people to administer electric shocks to another person. Although the person being shocked was actually a partner or confederate of the experimenter, the subjects did not know this. Instead they were instructed to continue "shocking" the person in spite of screams and pleas for mercy. When subjects hesitated to proceed, the experimenter emphasized the necessity of conducting the experiment. More than 63 percent of the subjects completed the experiment, despite the fact that it appeared they were torturing another human being. Later questioning revealed that those administering the shocks felt they were justified because they were "following instructions."

Media for children should emphasize responsibility for individual action rather than encourage blind obedience to authority. *Teenage Mutant Ninja Turtles,* for example, is structured so that the turtles take much of their instruction from the old rat Splinter. While Splinter is constructed to be a "wise" character, his orders are arbitrary and often condone violence. Most important, the turtles never question his orders or think about the implications of behaving aggressively. As parents, we spend years encouraging children to take responsibility for their own actions: "If everyone else jumped off the bridge, would you?" Programs for children should encourage reflection and consideration of consequences.

One of the most significant and frightening findings in the area of justified violence concerns attitudes toward rape and the abuse of women in general. Edward Donnerstein, one of the country's leading researchers on aggression and pornography, has repeatedly demonstrated that when subjects are given information that endorses aggression and then are shown violent pornography, their own aggression toward women increases.[14] Exposure to films that are both violent and pornographic and portray sexual aggression as either justified or not harmful ("she liked it," "she was just asking for it"), are capable of encouraging attitudes of callousness toward women.

Many media portrayals of sexual abuse suggest that women like to be treated roughly by men. Pornography invariably portrays women as lusting after a sexual encounter regardless of their initial protestations. However, this portrayal of women is hardly limited to pornography. Mainstream movies such as *The Getaway* portray women as readily debasing themselves in order to experience the kind of sexual excitement that only some psychopathic killer can provide. *Looking for Mister Goodbar, Fatal Attraction,* and *9½ Weeks* all show women humiliated and even murdered as a result of their sexual "addictions."

Almost all of the peripheral women in MTV videos are portrayed as either sexual accessories or nymphomaniacs. Even teachers and rocket scientists are ready to rip their clothes off at the merest suggestive invitation of some irresistible aging male rocker. Research tells us that media promoting the ideas that women enjoy sexual aggression and that men are justified in their use of force against them contribute to attitudes that are tolerant of rape and other forms of sexual abuse.

IS THE VIOLENCE SEEN AS REAL OR MAKE-BELIEVE?

Violence that is realistic is more likely to have an effect on people than violence that is unrealistic. Realistic violence is seen as "telling it like it is"—a truer reflection of the world than violence that is obviously fictionalized. For older adolescents and young adults, television's realism is the most important consideration in the relationship between viewing violence and behaving aggressively.[15] Many cities experienced a rash of violence after the showing of particularly realistic movies such as *Colors* and *Menace II Society*. While the body count may be higher in movies like *Mortal Kombat* or *Robocop*, the fact that they are overblown and unrealistic makes real violence less likely.

Seymour Feshbach, professor of psychology at UCLA, looked at the role that realism plays in cultivating aggression in children. In one experiment children were shown a movie of a riot.[16] Half the children were told that they were watching a fictitious Hollywood movie. The other half were told that they were watching a newsreel of an actual riot. After viewing the film, the children were given the opportunity to push a peer. Feshbach found that the children who believed they were witnessing real violence were more aggressive than those who thought they were watching fiction.

Children at different ages consider very different things to be real. This point will be fully developed later in this book, but it is important to note that Big Bird is "real" for the three-year-old, the Incredible Hulk is "real" for the five-year-old, and Roseanne is "real" for the seven-year-old. It is not until a child is almost nine years old that "real" means about the same thing that it does for adolescents and adults. For younger children, "real" tends to be anything that could possibly happen. For adolescents and adults, "real" is something that is probable, not just possible. From this difference in the concept of "real" it is easy to see how much more vulnerable young children are to being frightened by the media. It is possible for a "big, bad wolf" to come knocking on your door, and the young child is accordingly afraid that this could "really" happen. The older child knows that this is most unlikely and doesn't waste a lot of time worrying about such a doubtful possibility.

Studies show that parents consistently underrate how frightened their children are by things that parents don't consider "real."[17] Joanne Cantor and Sandra Reilly, at the University of Wisconsin, found that parents' estimates of their children's exposure to scary media were far lower than the children's reports.[18] This probably represents a lack of awareness on the part of parents about what their children are watching as well as a lack of understanding about how easily and frequently children are frightened by what they see. Although much of what the media present is clearly unreal to adults, it is perceived as real by children, particularly younger children. Many parents took very young children to see *Jurassic Park*, assuming that their children would understand that dinosaurs posed no threat. While this was a perfectly entertaining and even thought-provoking movie for older children, it was a nightmare for the many young children who were carried out of the theater screaming. Not all dinosaurs are created equal, and *Jurassic Park* is a far cry from *Barney*.

Children understand at a very early age that cartoons are different from other media offerings, that they are less "real." After about age three, children use both animation and humor as cues that what they are watching is not to be taken as seriously as other forms of media. According to some researchers, television violence should have the least effect when children watch cartoons in which aggression is punished, negative consequences are shown, and the perpetrator is a "totally bad person." But before we plunk our children down for hours of Saturday morning cartoons, it is important to remember that even though young children may understand that cartoons are not real, repeated exposure to cartoon violence still increases aggression.[19] Perhaps it's better for a youngster to watch *Biker Mice from Mars* than *NYPD Blue*, but this is not the only choice a parent has to make. If we take the time to carefully review the media's offerings, we can find wholesome, thoughtful, and appealing programming for our children.

Does Media Violence Cultivate Attitudes That Are Excessively Distorted, Frightening, and Pessimistic?

According to FBI figures, considerably fewer than 1 percent of Americans are victims of violent crime in a given year.[20] Why do most Americans believe that crime rates are going up when actually they have been stable over the last two decades? Why do so many of us greatly overestimate the likelihood of being a victim of violence?

George Gerbner has studied this question for more than thirty years. His research suggests that because television reaches so many people and delivers such a consistently violent message, it is able to create a worldview that is accepted by most people, even though it is false. Gerbner and his colleagues have found that heavy viewers of television differ systematically from light viewers on many issues, assumptions, and beliefs.[21] Heavy viewers are more likely to overestimate their chances of involvement in a violent crime, to believe that their neighborhoods are unsafe, and to assume that crime rates are rising. Heavy viewers of television see the real world through the lens of a camera which focuses disproportionately on violence and victimization. Prime-time television, on average, offers us five acts of violence per hour, and cartoons typically subject children to twenty-three acts of violence per hour. Over half of all major characters on television are involved in some kind of violence every week. On Saturday morning children's shows alone, more than 90 percent of the programs and more than 80 percent of the characters are involved in violence.[22] No wonder people who watch a lot of television have exaggerated perceptions about the amount of violence taking place in the real world.

Gerbner defines heavy viewers of television as people who watch more than three hours a day and light viewers as people who watch less than two hours a day. This puts most Americans in the heavy viewing category. Even when controlling for a large range of factors such as age, gender, socioeconomic status, and race, Gerbner found that "violence-laden television tends to make an independent contribution to the feeling of living in a mean and gloomy world."[23] Gerbner labels this the "mean world syndrome."

This is not to suggest that danger does not exist in our world.

As earlier figures made clear, the level of violence in this country is intolerable. While the overall crime rate may be stable, crime has become more random, and there are certain groups, particularly young men, who are at greater risk of victimization than ever before. Whatever real dangers do exist, however, heavy viewing of television intensifies the fears and insecurities of both adults and children. This leads to behaviors such as purchasing weapons "for protection" that are likely to cause additional violence. It is a well-established fact that homes in which there are guns are far more likely to be involved in violence than homes without guns. A large-scale epidemiological study found that for every gun used in a homicide for self-protection, forty-three are used for suicide or criminal homicide or are involved in accidental death.[24] People buy guns to safeguard themselves and their families only to find that they are far more likely to be the victims of their weapons than protected by them.

Regardless of any particular television program or movie, mass media collectively draw us into a symbolic world with a particular set of values. While this book will discuss many particular movies and television programs, it is important to keep in mind that *it is the aggregate of television and other media that is at issue, not any individual piece of programming.*

Certainly *Mighty Morphin Power Rangers* is a poor viewing choice for preschoolers, and Freddy Krueger is an equally poor choice for adolescents. This book provides specific information to help parents with the kinds of decisions they face every day when their child asks, "Can I watch this?" But I hope it also illuminates the idea that mass media, *on the whole*, present us and our children with a consistently inaccurate, pessimistic, and violent view of the world. It is foolish to argue that such a worldview, presented hour after hour, day after day, year after year, would not affect our children. We are all affected by what we see, children more than adults because they have fewer alternative sources of information.

DOES MEDIA VIOLENCE DESENSITIZE CHILDREN TO VIOLENCE?

Perhaps more than anything else about the media, parents worry that their children are being desensitized to violence. Given the large amounts of violence witnessed under the guise of entertainment, it seems reasonable to ask whether children's feelings as well as their behaviors are affected by the thousands of acts of violence they have seen. Parents, educators, and therapists are appalled by the fact that so many children seem to take even the most horrifyingly graphic depictions of violence in stride. As we have seen earlier in this chapter, there is no question that media violence encourages real-life violence among some children. The question of desensitization to violence is equally compelling and more complex, and it probably implicates larger numbers of children.

A mother consulted me after taking her two sons, ages eleven and thirteen, to see the popular action movie *Demolition Man*. She accompanied her sons because she wanted to see "what all the fuss is about." In a particularly gruesome scene, Simon Phoenix, played by Wesley Snipes, holds up a bloody eye that he has just gouged out of another man's head. The mother reflexively let out a scream and covered her eyes with her hands. Both sons turned to her in disgust and embarrassment and told her, "Be quiet! It's just a movie." Neither son seemed the least bit upset by what he had just seen. The mother wanted to know whether this is a "normal" reaction or whether her sons have become "desensitized" to media violence. She worried that their lack of concern about violence on the screen will translate into a general lack of concern about people and a reluctance to be helpful to others.

This mother, along with the many stricken parents who find that their children seem strangely unaffected by even the most sickeningly graphic scenes, has good reason to be concerned. Two decades of research on the question of whether or not media violence can desensitize people have consistently shown that repeated exposure to violence blunts emotional reactions and makes people less likely to intervene or seek help for victims.

University researchers are finding that their experiments are being delayed because their student assistants are unable to identify aggressive acts. The graduate students, hired to help code aggression on television, do not always record pushing, shoving, hitting, and in some instances using a gun as acts of aggression. Research assistants need to be educated about the fact that physical assault of one person by another is by definition an act of aggression. Depictions of violence in the media have become so routine that perfectly "normal" people no longer recognize it.

What exactly is desensitization? It is a type of learning that makes us increasingly less reactive to something. When we are first exposed to a new situation, whether to a violent movie, an upsetting argument, or an attractive member of the opposite sex, our body responds automatically. Scientists who study arousal and its opposite, desensitization, use both physiological measures such as heart rate and psychological measures such as attitude checklists to determine level of arousal.

It is easy to see the relationship between desensitization and learning. If we are sitting at home working on a project and it begins to rain heavily, we may be startled at first, but we quickly become accustomed to the sound and are able to go on with our work. If the rain continued to demand our attention, raised our heart rate, and made us anxious, we would accomplish very little. By itself, desensitization is neither good nor bad, but simply a type of learning.

Young children are aroused by aggressive scenes on television. Research studies have shown that preschoolers show higher levels of emotion when watching aggressive television programs than when watching more neutral programs.[25] Much like the preadolescent who finds himself hacking and choking after his first cigarette drag, young children are initially distressed by threatening and violent images. This arousal diminishes with repeated exposure as the child becomes desensitized to the violence.

This explains why children seem increasingly capable of tolerating more and more explicit scenes of violence in the media. Over and over, in gruelingly graphic movies such as *Natural Born Killers*, *Pulp Fiction*, and *Interview with the Vampire*, it is inevitably adults who walk out in distress or disgust. The large numbers of teenagers in the audience stay put. This is partly because one of the rites of passage of adolescence is to remain unfazed by horror movies. However, it also reflects a lessening of the impact of violence on those who have been exposed to a steady diet of visual abuse from the time they could talk. The more we watch violence, and the less distressed we are by it, the more we risk becoming tolerant of real-life violence.

IF CHILDREN ARE DESENSITIZED TO VIOLENCE, ARE THEY MORE
LIKELY TO BEHAVE VIOLENTLY THEMSELVES?

The phenomenon of desensitization has been studied for many years. Public outrage over several well-publicized events in the 1960s and 1970s accelerated scientific study in this area. In 1964, Kitty Genovese was murdered outside her New York apartment building in spite of the fact that nearly forty people were aware of her distress. No one came to her aid. The My Lai trials in 1971 revealed that, during the Vietnam War, American soldiers witnessed and participated in the killing of unarmed civilians and children with a shocking level of unconcern. Researchers became increasingly interested in the question of whether people who have been exposed to a great deal of prior violence, either directly or vicariously through the media, might eventually exhibit a kind of psychological and physiological "tuning out" of the normal emotional responses to violent events.

In an early study of desensitization, a team of researchers exposed their subjects to films of a tribal ritual involving painful and bloody genital mutilation.[26] While initially very distressed, the subjects became increasingly less emotionally responsive with repeated viewing of the film. Repeatedly exposing a person to a frightening stimulus in order to lessen anxiety is called "systematic desensitization," and it is frequently used to treat individuals with phobias. It is a process all parents are familiar with as they try to coax a frightened child into approaching a feared situation or object. Many a mother, with a quivering child attached to her leg, has slowly approached a frightening dog while reassuring her child, "You don't have to touch the doggy, just watch Mommy touch her. See, that wasn't so bad." Over time, the parent's patience and reassurance, as well as the child's repeated exposure to the animal, helps the child to be less fearful. Desensitization, then, can help children engage in activities that were previously anxiety-provoking.

Unlike the beneficial effects of desensitization just described, desensitization to violence works against healthy development.[27] One particular study can serve as a model for the many done on this subject. This study was designed to determine whether children who watched a lot of television were less likely to be aroused by violence than children who watched little television. Researchers divided the children into two groups: heavy viewers and light viewers.[28] The children watched several neutral films and a brutal boxing scene from the Kirk Douglas movie *The Champion*. The choice of a boxing scene is important because scenes of violence alternated with nonviolent scenes as each round came to an end and the boxers returned to their corners.

Both heavy and light viewers showed no differences in arousal to the neutral films. However, when both groups were exposed to the filmed violence, the low-viewing group became more emotionally aroused than the high-viewing group. Interestingly, even during the nonviolent segments of the boxing movie, children who watched little television tended to be somewhat more aroused than their frequent-viewing counterparts. It seems that it was harder for them to recover from having witnessed violence. The scientific literature as well as common sense tells us that it's easier to engage in an activity that doesn't make us anxious than one that does.[29] It may be exactly this decreased anxiety about aggression that encourages aggressive behavior after watching violent media. Kids who no longer feel anxious about violence are more likely to participate in it.

DOES DESENSITIZATION DIMINISH A CHILD'S CAPACITY TO SHOW CARE AND CONCERN FOR OTHERS?

Studies by psychologists Ronald Drabman and Margaret Thomas show that children who have been exposed to more aggressive programming are less likely to help younger children who are in trouble.[30] In a study with third and fourth graders, children were randomly divided into two groups: One group watched a violent television program and the other did not. The children were then led to believe that they were responsible for monitoring the behavior of a group of younger children whom they could observe on a videotape monitor. The children on the videotape played quietly at first and then became progressively more angry and destructive with each other. While 58 percent of the children who had not seen a violent program sought out adult help before the angry children began physically assaulting each other, only 17 percent of the children who had seen an aggressive film sought adult help before actual physical fighting broke out. The researchers concluded that children who are exposed to media violence may be more likely to consider fighting a normal way to resolve conflict or may be more desensitized and less aroused by violence.

Arousal is highly correlated with swift intervention in an emergency situation.[31] An experiment that examined how bystanders respond to emergencies found that an increased heart rate and the speed of intervention in a staged emergency situation were substantially correlated. More aroused people came to the aid of others in trouble more quickly than those who were less aroused. As we have seen, repeated viewing of media violence lowers arousal level.[32]

In a world in which genocide still comes to us on our nightly news, where random violence becomes this country's most common form of murder, and where handguns are the leading cause of death of large segments of our population, desensitization is perhaps the greatest threat of all. We are losing our awareness of what it means to be human as we become less responsive to human suffering. Although we may never engage in violent acts or endorse violence ourselves, we may not dislike it nearly as much as we should.

Part Two

Developmental Approach

Introduction

On November 20, 1983, ABC aired a highly anticipated and controversial made-for-television movie entitled *The Day After*. The movie detailed the likely effects of a nuclear holocaust on this planet. It chronicled the end of civilization primarily through dialogue, with some particularly disturbing images of people being vaporized midway through the program.

Because of the anticipated fearful response of young children to this movie, elaborate plans were made to safeguard youngsters from being traumatized. Educators for Social Responsibility and many school systems urged parents not to allow children under twelve to watch it. Special counselors were made available in the elementary schools for children who were expected to need help in dealing with their feelings after viewing the movie. Magazine and newspaper articles suggested how parents might help their youngsters cope with symptoms such as nightmares and heightened anxiety. It was one of the few times the nation has mobilized in an effort to protect children from the potentially frightening effects of media.

November 20 came and went. There was no outpouring of anguish from this country's youngsters. The special counselors in the elementary schools found no lines of distraught students outside their doors. No parents, pediatricians, or therapists reported any particular upswing in nightmares, anxiety, or other anticipated symptoms of stress in grade-school children. What researchers did find, however, was that while younger children were unaffected by this movie, older children and particularly adolescents were distressed. The group most distressed by *The Day After* was adults.[1]

All those who were concerned with the potentially disturbing effects of *The Day After* on young children had their hearts in the right place. Unfortunately, they missed the "developmental boat." They assumed that a program that adults found upsetting would be even more upsetting for young children. While this may sometimes be the case, it often is not. This same mistaken assumption drives our current movie rating system, which is based on what parents find frightening and objectionable. Seeing media through the eyes of a child means that we must enter into the world of the child and appreciate that this world is not simply a smaller or less sophisticated version of our own. Children look at, think about, and understand the world in ways that are both qualitatively and quantitatively different from those of adults.

Reactions to *The Day After* illustrate some of the fundamental differences between younger children, older children, teenagers, and adults. There are several reasons why young children did not find *The Day After* particularly upsetting. First and foremost, concepts such as "nuclear annihilation" are far beyond the grasp of young children. As the following chapters show, the ability to think about something conceptually or symbolically evolves slowly over the course of childhood. Young children (ages three to eight) are influenced by what they see in front of them, the "in-your-face" quality of things. Scientists call this "perceptual salience." Young children are most frightened by ghosts, monsters, and things that transform from the mundane to the grotesque. Older children (ages nine to twelve) are more frightened by objectively dangerous events such as kidnappings, accidents, and natural disasters. It is not until adolescence that abstract ideas such as war become frightening. Teenagers, but not young children, understand and are frightened by the threat of psychological as well as physical harm. Teenagers do not have to see something to be frightened; young children do.

The Day After conveyed a sense of horror mainly through dialogue and the emotional responses of the characters. The movie included few graphic depictions of death and injury. Most younger children were so bored that they had wandered away from the television long before the graphically frightening scenes.

While we can never predict children's reactions with complete accuracy, knowing something about the stages of children's development helps us to make informed decisions about what they watch. Psychologists use the term "developmental approach" to describe a way of understanding children that recognizes certain patterns in childhood. This book looks at children's reactions to media from a developmental point of view. This perspective has three major components:

1. It recognizes that children differ fundamentally from one developmental stage to the next. Not only are older children bigger and stronger than younger children, but their thinking and the very ways in which they experience the world are profoundly different.

2. It recognizes that children build on the accomplishments of the previous stage of development. What the older child knows grows out of what the younger child knows.

3. Development includes both change and continuity. While environment certainly plays a large role in determining a child's future, there also appear to be threads of character that remain stable over the course of a lifetime.

This book looks at the world of the child during sequential stages of development. While inexact, age is used to identify developmental stages. This part of the book discusses the following four variables in turn.

- Attachment
- Aggression
- Cognitive development (thinking)
- Moral development (conscience)

Part 3 considers how each variable plays out at successive developmental stages. These variables were selected partly because they cover the customary areas of interest in child development, but more important because they are especially relevant to the issue of children and the media. We will be looking at whether violence in the media translates into real-life violence. Therefore, we need to understand the ways in which children at different ages experience aggression and the strategies they have for managing aggressive feelings. Attachment, for instance, is one way that we keep aggression under control—we may be very angry at a spouse but we don't haul off and hit him or her because we are also attached. There is a reciprocal relationship between attachment and aggression.

Along with aggression, we worry about whether children are becoming desensitized to violence, whether the moral development of children is suffering as a result of repeated exposure to media violence. To understand moral development, we must have a good grasp of the ways in which children at different ages think—how they understand and organize reality. Psychologists call this "cognitive development." Moral reasoning is one type of thinking. As we shall see, it is not necessarily the same as moral behavior. Moral development, the development of conscience, includes both thought and behavior.

A very important caveat needs to be mentioned here. Every child is unique. While scientists can certainly say things about children *as a group*, no one can predict what will be true for any particular child. As parents read this book they must keep in mind that while development proceeds at a reasonably predictable rate—children generally crawl before they walk, and they make sounds before making words—development is also fluid and uneven. One day your child shares his cookies and offers to clean up his room. The next day the same child spits at his younger sister and refuses to put his toys away.

As you read this book, keep in mind that it is intended as a guide, not a catechism. Developmental categories are designated by scientists and researchers who need a kind of shorthand to describe broad groups of children with similar characteristics. Your particular child will fit perfectly in some categories, partially in some, and not at all in others. Mention will be made of conditions that signal real concern and that should be brought to the attention of a pediatrician or therapist. It may be more useful to think of development as a map rather than a straight line. One of the wonders of childhood is how development proceeds in fits and starts. Remember that childhood accomplishments take many years before they are firmly in place.

4

Attachment

Love and physical contact are essential for human development. Anna Freud and her colleague Dorothy Burlingham studied children placed in British orphanages during World War II.[1] Despite attention to these children's biological needs, many of them became apathetic, and some died. Human infants require physical and social stimulation. Recent long-term studies show that children separated from parents before age four and reared in institutions often find it particularly hard to make friends and become effective parents themselves.[2] It seems that loving connections—what psychologists call "attachment"—is a necessary prerequisite for emotional health.

Parents, of course, don't need social scientists to tell them that their babies need to be loved and held and spoken to. Fortunately, most parents know this intuitively and have such strong feelings toward their young that they strive to provide as much love and attention as possible. Social scientists clarify the process by which attachment takes place and can alert us to possible disturbances in this process.

Having a theory of child development helps us make sense out of behavior. Theorists look for general characteristics that can be used to explain a wide variety of situations. Different theories can lead to different explanations. Depending on one's theoretical perspective, a child who becomes aggressive after watching television violence may have an especially strong aggressive drive (according to psychoanalytic theory), may have a defect in his or her ego's ability to manage aggression (according to ego theory), or may suffer from an insecure attachment to his or her mother (according to attachment theory). For the purpose of understanding attachment and aggression, we need to look at theories that emphasize the importance of the relationship between parent and child and that consider individual differences among children. Both attachment theory and theories of temperament are particularly useful in this respect.

Throughout this book I refer to the mother as the infant's most significant caretaker. I do this for the sake of economy, since for most children their natural mother is their primary caretaker. However, under certain circumstances a child's mother is not available and another adult—father, grandparent, or adoptive parents, for example—becomes a "permanent mother substitute" for the child. In this case the process of attachment is the same.

ATTACHMENT THEORY

John Bowlby, an English psychiatrist revolutionized the field of child psychiatry in the 1950s when he delivered a series of papers that emphasized the normal nature of the child's attachment to its mother. Bowlby put forth the notion that psychoanalysis, the popular theory of the day, had put far too much emphasis on the child's fantasy world and far too little on actual events in the child's life. These papers formed the nexus of what would eventually become known as "attachment theory."

Bowlby conceived of attachment as a particular type of relationship based primarily on the mother's ability to protect her child. This protection comes in many different forms; it includes feeding and changing, of course, but it also involves types of psychological protection. These include a soothing voice when the child is upset and the patient and gradual introduction of new and potentially frightening experiences. Most of all, it means the consistent availability of mother as "home base"—the person who is available to her child in times of need. Bowlby believed that in this respect mother was unique and irreplaceable. It is from this base of security and comfort with mother that the child begins to forge the courage that will eventually enable him or her to confront the difficulties, disappointments, and challenges of life. Bowlby believed that the child's earliest relationship with his or her mother serves as a template for the kinds of relationships the child will expect and enjoy in the world.

Bowlby saw attachment as distinct from dependency. Unlike the psychoanalysts of his day, who saw the youngster's dramatic response to separation from mother as indicating an impaired mother-child relationship, Bowlby saw this response as normal. He believed that the child who has been well loved by his or her parents would naturally protest separation vigorously but would eventually develop greater self-reliance.

Bowlby prefigured the work of contemporary psychologists like Carol Gilligan who have questioned many of the assumptions on which psychological theory is based. Rather than seeing "independence" as the ultimate goal of psychological maturity (a particularly and peculiarly male notion), Gilligan and others suggest that it is affiliation and interdependence that characterize healthy adult relationships.[3] Bowlby was one of the first to appreciate that attachment was a healthy and natural state of affairs for people across the life span.

Research studies have shown that the nature of a child's attachment to his or her parents tells us a great deal about how he or she is likely to handle aggression. Children with histories of secure attachment in infancy tend to show little aggression as preschoolers. Instead, these children show high self-esteem, are popular with peers, and, while they can be quite assertive, tend not to be aggressive.[4] Preschoolers who have had unpredictable mothering tend to exhibit what is called "anxious attachment." These children have fewer friends and lower self-esteem and are more dependent.[5] Finally, preschoolers with histories of troubled attachment, whose parents were frequently unavailable or abusive, are often hostile and aggressive toward other children.[6] Children who have troubled attachments or who were deprived of early attachments grow up to represent a disproportionate number of this country's violent criminals.[7]

TEMPERAMENT

While Bowlby and other attachment theorists stressed the importance of the relationship between mother and child, they paid little attention to the inborn differences between children. Tell three different twelve-year-olds they can't see *Friday the Thirteenth* and you will probably get three different reactions. One child will protest mildly. Another will argue at great length, pointing out how absolutely prehistoric your views are, but will finally accept the fact that he can't go to the movie. And the third child may argue, slam the door, and go off to the movie anyway. While different theories of child development will each have its own explanation for why these children responded differently, they all give short shrift to a fact that every parent knows: Children are born different.

Temperament is best thought of as a preferred style of responding. Stella Chess and Alexander Thomas studied children over thirty years and concluded that there are three basic types of temperament: easy, slow-to-warm-up, and difficult.[8] They found that a child's temperament is reasonably predictable and consistent across time and situations. The preschooler who is easygoing and sociable is likely to grow up to be well liked and even-tempered. The young child who zips maniacally around the house is likely to be the kind of adult who runs marathons and can't talk on the phone without pacing.

Temperament is thought to be composed of nine different traits. While my explanations will be brief, it helps to keep these traits in mind as they exert a strong influence on the different ways in which children are affected by media violence.

Activity level. How active or restless is your child? This is an important variable since studies show that aggressive television fare makes children restless.[9] High-activity kids do not "relax" with *Power Rangers;* they just become more aggressive and restless.

Distractibility. Can your child pay attention? Is he or she easily distracted? The child who has difficulty focusing may be helped by the slow-paced style of *Mister Rogers* rather than the rapid-fire style of *Sesame Street.*

Intensity. How strong are your child's emotional reactions? The child who screams in terror at every bug or spider that wanders into the house is likely to be far more upset by the pit of snakes faced by Harrison Ford in *Indiana Jones* than the more placid child who takes things in stride.

Regularity. How predictable is your child in his or her habits: eating, sleeping, using the bathroom?

Negative persistence. This type of child never takes no for an answer. This child has an argument to counter every reason you can come up with about why he or she can't see the *Texas Chainsaw Massacre*. Parents can be driven to their wits' end trying to get the child to change focus.

Sensory threshold. Is your child easily bothered by sensory stimulation: noise, bright lights, smells, textures, and colors? Children with a low sensory threshold are unable to filter out annoying stimulation. They may throw a tantrum because the seam in their sock is unbearably uncomfortable. These children often have difficulty managing highly stimulating media fare. They jump out of their seats at the movies and can be bothered by what they see for extended periods of time afterwards.

Approach/withdrawal. What is your child's first reaction to new experiences—new people, places, food, and clothes? Some children can't wait to see the latest movie, try out the latest video game, or install the latest program on their computer. Other children are tentative in new situations and tend to hang back until they are certain that all is well.

Adaptability. How well does your child cope with surprises, with changes in his or her routine?

Mood. What is your child's basic disposition? It can range from happy to serious to cranky and is another important variable in terms of media viewing. One of the strongest research findings is that children who are heavy viewers of television have a more pessimistic and anxious view of the world than children who are light viewers. If your child's basic mood is on the depressive or anxious side, a lot of television viewing only adds to his or her unhappy feelings.

Taking into account your child's temperament when making decisions about media viewing fare is important. I have seen preschoolers with a low tolerance for new situations and low sensory thresholds go into an absolute panic the first time they are taken to a movie theater with its harsh lobby lights, strange smells, and dark interior. I have seen young adolescents with intense and somewhat depressed natures become preoccupied and ruminative after watching Jason or Freddy Krueger's latest slasher offering. Some of these children have suffered months of nightmares and other symptoms typical of what psychologists call "post-traumatic stress syndrome." While we can say many things about the effects of media violence on children *in general*, every child is different and much depends on his or her individual temperament.

ATTACHMENT AND THE MEDIA

The capacity for attachment is the foundation of our most significant relationships. Attachment affects every aspect of a child's life. It follows that a child's attachment to his or her parents would affect the ways in which that child experiences the media. Many studies have looked at the ways in which family structure and dynamics influence both children's understanding of the media and their vulnerability to what they see.

One of the major tasks of parenthood is to protect children from stimuli that are overwhelming and to allow new information to be introduced gradually. This helps children integrate new information and new experiences into their existing view of the world without being unnecessarily bewildered or frightened.

Even as adults, we know it is much easier to learn when we are not overwhelmed. Learning a new task, such as how to read a computer manual, is easier when there are no competing demands, than it is when the children are screaming, the television is blaring, and we can't figure out what to have for dinner. Over the course of a lifetime, we learn how to "dose" our environment so that we function effectively and efficiently. The young child does not possess this ability and would, given half a chance, prefer to take every last action figure from the local toy store, stay up all night watching adult television, and live on Pop-Tarts and soda. Young children do not have the life experience to understand the consequences of overindulgence.

Parents stand between their children and the world. They protect the young from experiences that are potentially disturbing and help children learn to regulate their desire. These twin functions of protection and discipline are called "mediation." Parents mediate when they set up rules about television viewing—how much can be watched, how late the child can stay up, and what content is appropriate and acceptable. Explanation and clarification are ways of protecting children from being overwhelmed by information or images they are psychologically unprepared to handle. Studies have found that parenting styles influence the extent to which children are affected by what they watch. Children whose parents discipline primarily with reasoning and explanation are least affected by antisocial content on television. Children whose parents rely on power (either physical or verbal) to discipline are most affected by antisocial programming.[10]

Unfortunately, in spite of mountains of evidence to the contrary, most parents do not consider television to be very influential in the lives of their children. Ninety-two percent of parents with young children do not provide any guidance for television viewing on Saturday mornings. This time is packed with violent cartoons designed to hold children spellbound long enough for advertisers to sell them cheap toys and high-sugar junk foods. Seventy-five percent of parents set no limits whatsoever on the amount of television that their youngsters may view, and 95 percent of what children watch on television is not specifically produced for them.[11] Every night between 11:00 and 11:30 P.M., three million children are up watching late-night adult programming.

As a result of their research on parental involvement and young children's understanding of television, Jerome and Dorothy Singer recommend that preschool-age children watch no more than one hour of television per day, increasing to two hours in elementary school. The Singers, who are the founders and codirectors of the Family Television Research and Consultation Center at Yale University, were so impressed with the consistency of their findings that they wrote, "Our results regarding viewing amount are so clear that there is virtually no qualification of the recommendation."[12]

In the Singers' studies, children of similar intelligence who watch a lot of television without restriction from their parents show poorer comprehension, greater confusion between reality and fantasy, more restlessness and aggression, and less acquisition of general information than children who come from homes where parents set limits on television viewing. Apparently, practice does not make perfect when it comes to television viewing. For young children of five and six, parental control of viewing is the single most important factor in aiding a child's understanding of television programs.

Around the age of seven, control of viewing is replaced by the parents' discussion and explanation as the variable that most influences the child's understanding. As we will see in Chapter 6, this coincides with a dramatic change in thinking that occurs at about the same age. Around age seven children are developing some rudimentary skills that encourage more logical thinking. A parenting style that filters and interprets the outside world supports the child's developing ability to understand and sympathize with the world around him or her. Among children of equal intelligence, those whose parents are involved in explaining and discussing television programs with them learn far more than those children who watch alone. It is not enough for a parent to simply be in the same room: Discussion and explanation are the key factors.

Parents need to both express their own point of view and support their children's curiosity about what they see. Children who live in families that foster this kind of communication tend to be less aggressive, less fearful, and more patient. Young boys in particular are helped by parental explanation and involvement, probably because they tend to lag behind girls in verbal skills and concepts. The parents' explanation seems to "fill in the gaps" in understanding that are more commonly found in young boys than in young girls.

It is obvious that children with concerned and involved parents are less likely to suffer negative effects from television viewing. Love, attention, and communication are powerful factors in children's lives and help to protect them against many negative influences. Whether one believes that children are innately aggressive or that their level of aggression is largely a product of their environment, or some combination of the two, there is little question that attachment influences at least the behavioral aspects of aggression. What child hasn't thought (and often said), "I hate you. I wish you were dead." And what mother hasn't in turn thought, "I'd like to strangle that kid." But few parents are murdered by their children, and few children are murdered by their parents. Our attachments to each other soften the anger and even rage that are inevitable over the lifetime of a relationship.

5

Aggression

Many people believe that the United States is the most violent nation in the world. This is simply not true. There are less-developed countries, ravaged by war and lawlessness, that have higher rates of violence. But among the more developed Western societies, the United States has the highest rate of interpersonal violence—three to ten times greater than similarly developed countries. Every year, 10 out of every 100,000 Americans are murdered. In some of our inner cities, war-torn countries of their own, the rate is ten times higher than for the rest of the country: 100 murders per 100,000 inhabitants per year. In contrast, Japan's murder rate is only 1 out of every 100,000 inhabitants. Canada, England, Wales, and Australia all lose 3 people per 100,000 inhabitants.[1]

Much, but not all, of this difference can be attributed to the easy availability of handguns. There are approximately 225 million guns in private hands in the United States.[2] In 1993, more than 24,000 Americans were murdered, 16,189 with guns.[3] A child is murdered in America every three and a half hours.[4] The majority of these children are shot to death. If we include suicides and accidental deaths, again mostly attributable to guns, American children are lost to preventable causes at a rate of one child every two hours.[5]

Outside of San Francisco, two young boys' desire to handle a gun was so strong that one child climbed through a bathroom window to get to his father's gun kept in a locked bedroom. While fooling around, the thirteen-year-old boy accidentally shot and killed his nine-year-old friend. The tragic consequences for the families of both youngsters are inestimable. A relative of the dead child plaintively said, "With guns being glamorized so much on TV, kids will do anything just to hold a gun."[6]

These were not emotionally disturbed, psychopathic youngsters. They were a couple of kids whose parents took responsible precautions with their guns. The allure of handling the same kind of weapon seen nightly in the hands of their favorite entertainers proved fatally irresistible. The media's insistence on glamorizing guns makes a significant contribution to the high levels of homicide in this country.

Contrary to popular opinion, America's crime rate is not on the rise but has been relatively stable over the last few decades. What has changed in America is the type of crime and the likely victims of crime. Although overall crime rates have actually dropped slightly since 1991, homicide rates for certain parts of the population have escalated wildly. Children at younger and younger ages are murdering and being murdered. From 1975 to 1992, there was a 64 percent increase in the number of ten-to-fourteen-year-olds who were murdered and a 50 percent increase in the number of fifteen-to-twenty-four-year-olds.[7] These numbers are expected to increase as larger numbers of children enter adolescence. Violence is now the leading cause of death for black youth and the second leading cause of death for white youth. Until 1994, most people who were murdered were killed by someone they knew. Random violence is now more common than violence committed by aquaintances, friends, or family. Law enforcement officials find it much more difficult to solve random murders, and this adds to our growing sense of apprehension about the safety of the world we live in.

How much of this rise in violence can be attributed to the increasingly gruesome and graphic portrayals of violence in the media that have become commonplace in this country? Most researchers conservatively estimate that between 5 and 15 percent of aggressive behavior is attributable to high levels of media violence.[8] TV's influence on more serious forms of antisocial and criminal behavior such as rape and murder is even greater.[9] Epidemiologist B. S. Centerwall, writing in the *Journal of the American Medical Association*, gives evidence that "television is a causal factor behind approximately one half of the homicides committed in the United States."[10] While there may be disagreement among researchers as to the exact contribution of media violence to real-life violence, there is no disagreement that it makes a significant contribution. When we are counting bodies, effects do not have to be large to be important.

Aggression can be an instinctive response to frustration. Young babies appear to be angry when they are restrained. Take away a toddler's favorite toy and you'll see anger, sometimes even rage (in the form of a temper tantrum). Tell your teenager she can't go out with her friends because her grades have not been up to par, and you're likely to hear some door slamming. People do not like having their goals thwarted. Although frustration is a major cause of anger for many people, it is not the source of all aggression. Advances in medical research have clarified a number of biological causes of aggressive behavior. In addition, evidence has been accumulating that a predisposition toward aggressive behavior is inherited.[11]

Sociological research focuses attention on the contributions of environment—poverty, hopelessness, lack of family and community support—and availability of guns and drugs as major contributors to the high levels of violence in this country. No serious student of aggression can afford to focus only on the internal composition of the individual and ignore the contribution of social factors. *Aggression is not simply a personal issue; it is also a social issue.*

The fact remains that no one theory of aggression is able to make sense of all acts of aggression. Furthermore, no individual factor, by itself, is a good predictor of aggressive behavior. When looking at the factors that contribute to aggression we would do well to think in terms of "all of the above" rather than "either/or."

In 1960, a group of researchers, led by Leonard Eron and L. Rowell Huesmann, began investigating the effects of television violence on childhood aggression. Their studies, conducted on hundreds of children over twenty-two years, found that aggression is a characteristic that develops early in life and is resistant to change. In what was to become one of the most important studies on media violence and childhood aggression, the investigators found that not only children who were aggressive to begin with, but *all children* were made more aggressive by exposure to television violence. Children who were not particularly aggressive and who watched a lot of violent television ultimately became more aggressive than children who were naturally aggressive but whose television viewing was restricted.[12]

Since Eron and Huesmann's study, dozens of additional research studies have shown not only that aggression as a way of handling conflict is a stable characteristic, but that once established it is very difficult to modify. I've had many parents confirm these findings with comments like: "She's always had a chip on her shoulder" or "He's never been able to fight his way out of a paper bag."

Huesmann and Eron broadened and elaborated their work in the mid-1970s.[13] Later studies were designed to look not only at American children but at children in different countries as well. Gender differences were carefully considered. Studying children from age six to eleven in the United States, Australia, Finland, Israel, and Poland, the research demonstrated that the link between television violence and aggression is not limited to this country and that it affects girls as well as boys. The results of these major cross-national studies as well as practically every similar study conducted on this topic are inescapable: *Children who watch a lot of television violence are cultivating aggressive attitudes that last a lifetime.*

It is far easier to help children develop a cooperative approach to problem solving when they are young than when they are older. Parents must recognize the negative influence of early exposure to media violence and restrict their youngsters' viewing of aggressive movies and television programs. While little research has been done on the topic, it is likely that video games that reward brutality ("Rip her spine out, advance to the next level") only add to the young child's repertoire of aggressive solutions.

Some children live in homes where factors such as parental involvement, opportunities for varied cultural experiences, community standards, and the like help protect them from the negative effects of media violence. But other conditions are conducive to the learning of aggression and reinforce the effects of media violence on children. Homes in which children are subject to physical aggression, have many opportunities to observe aggression both in the home and in the community, and are reinforced for their own aggressive behavior breed children who come to assume that violent behavior is normal.

Given that researchers know so much about the effects of media violence on children, why are we so reluctant to act on their findings? Television, the movies, and video games are considered "just entertainment" and as a result are not accorded the kinds of serious consideration that we give to other factors affecting our children's emotional and physical health and well-being. We do not doubt that cigarette smoking causes lung cancer and that high cholesterol increases our chances of coronary artery disease. And even though the cigarette industry and the meat industry do their best to convince us otherwise, most of us understand that they have an economic agenda that is at odds with our best interest.

For many of us, the effects of observed violence are simply too weak and too transient to notice. The aggression-heightening impact of a violent film subsides within an hour, *unless the movie's influence is maintained by rehearsing the aggressive thoughts.*[14] This caveat is very important, because we do in fact go over events in our mind. Children in particular are likely to rehearse both in fantasy and in real life what they have seen on the screen. In other words, people may walk out of a movie like *Natural Born Killers* feeling aggressive, but unless they keep replaying the movie, or other angry thoughts associated with the movie, in their mind, they are apt to be "back to normal" in a relatively short period of time. And, of course, very few people ever respond to interpersonal conflict by attacking another person. But this does not mean that the effects of a violent film are not significant. Individual exposures to media violence are not terribly significant; it is the cumulative effects that are toxic.

A great deal of effort has gone into discovering those circumstances that most often produce aggressive behavior. Researchers have identified particular elements of media that are most likely to foster the heightened levels of aggression our society is finding increasingly difficult to tolerate.

ENVIRONMENTAL FACTORS ENCOURAGING AGGRESSION

A large body of research, much of it done by Leonard Berkowitz at the University of Wisconsin, shows that after people have witnessed screen violence, their environment plays a large role in determining whether they are likely to behave aggressively. Berkowitz and others have found that the following conditions, either in the film or in the environment, increase the likelihood that individuals will actually become aggressive themselves following exposure to media violence.[15]

1. Violence that is rewarded appears to have a powerful effect on people's aggressive behavior. Newsreel footage of looters freely carrying television sets out of ransacked stores encourages others to try to "get away with it."

2. Aggression induced by movie violence tends to be directed most strongly against people whom the viewer sees as similar to victims in the movie. In a disturbing experiment by Donnerstein and Berkowitz, male subjects were shown a movie of two men assaulting a woman.[16] Later in the experiment, these men were given an opportunity to punish a woman who had annoyed them (the woman was a colleague of the experimenters). These men delivered more severe punishment to a woman with the same name as the woman in the film. Media violence teaches about being a perpetrator but it also teaches about who is to be victimized.

3. Individuals are more likely to behave aggressively if they are angry at the time they see the aggressive film or if the film reminds them of some insult they have experienced in their own life. For example, a movie about an unfaithful wife can reactivate the rage a man felt when his own wife admitted having an affair. Berkowitz describes an "anger-aggression network" in which current feelings of anger are tied to previous feelings and memories of anger.

4. People are more strongly affected by screen violence when they believe it to be realistic rather than fictional or unreal. Newsreel footage is particularly disturbing. Timothy McVeigh, the man being held in connection with the Oklahoma City bombing as this book is being written, was said to be incensed watching the destruction of the Branch Davidian complex on television a year earlier. Newsreel footage of people who were burned and maimed following the bombing of the World Trade Center in New York is more activating than any Bruce Willis film featuring similar fictionalized bombings.

5. When cues in the environment are similar to cues on the screen, people are affected more strongly by what they see. Advertisers pay large sums of money to have their products featured in movies and on TV. They know that seeing a can of Coke on the screen encourages people to reach for a Coke when they feel thirsty. Similarly, the constant presence of guns on the screen en-courages youngsters with access to guns to pick one up in a similar situation.

It is time to end the distracting debate about whether media violence contributes to real-life violence. We are better off looking at who is at risk and how to reduce those risks. It is also time to think about the values we wish to convey to our children—both within our families and within our culture. It isn't necessary to eliminate all portrayals of violence. Adults and children are inter-ested in conflict and how to resolve it. Viewing violence can some-times educate us and illuminate the darker side of our nature. But graphic celebrations of brutal and thoughtless violence do not serve our children. Parents are charged with protecting and respecting the vulnerability of their youngsters. It is perhaps our most serious responsibility. While occasional exposure to screen violence is not likely to be damaging to the vast majority of American children, a steady diet of it promises to contribute to an increasingly violent, impulsive, and desensitized society.

6

Cognitive Development (Thinking)

These are the reactions of my three sons to the outstanding documentary *Hoop Dreams*, a chronicle of two inner-city black teens and their dreams about playing professional basketball:

> Jeremy (age 4): "It was boring. When I grow up I don't want to play basketball. I want to be a fireman."

> Michael (age 10): "I thought it was going to be boring because it didn't look like a real movie. But I liked the story about two kids who had a dream. It was tough for them because their family life wasn't so good. But their moms loved them a lot and I guess that helped. They knew they had a talent."

> Loren (age 15): "Ah, they were okay, but I can play better. No, seriously, I thought it was a pretty cool movie about what it's like to be black and try and make something of yourself when the cards are stacked against you. And these guys had talent. It makes it seem like basketball is the way out of the ghetto, but I'm not so sure that's true. Only about fifty-eight guys make it to the NBA each year."

This example illustrates that children, or adults for that matter, don't watch a movie and all walk away with the same information. We actively process, interact with, and understand what we see in ways that are particular to our age, experience, cognitive development, and level of interest.

For my youngest son, the movie held little interest because preschoolers are really not capable of seeing things from someone else's point of view. He's not interested in basketball, and therefore the movie is not interesting. He can respond only by referring to himself and his own interests. His thinking is almost entirely egocentric. This is expectable and healthy at his young age.

An enormous change takes place between age four and ten. My ten-year-old son, who in fact has no real-life interest in basketball, was surprisingly absorbed by the movie. Like his younger brother, he sees it in concrete terms as a movie about basketball. However, he is far more interested in the film because he is able to understand and empathize with the characters, even though their lives are very different from his. This ability to see things from another's point of view characterizes the thinking of middle childhood. Children of this age often meet new information and other perspectives with tremendous enthusiasm. They like having the world open up before their amazed eyes.

Finally, my teenage son demonstrates what is basically an adult level of thinking. He is able not only to consider the immediate effects on the lives of the characters, but also to construct a hypothetical future for them. The movie's characters may do well, but they may not. The adolescent knows that there is often more to a story than meets the eye. My teenager sees the concrete meaning of the movie, knows that it is about basketball, but also knows that it is addressing larger social issues of racism and limited options for black youth. His initial comment about being a better ballplayer is interesting because it illustrates why adolescents seem so terribly egocentric to adults. But this is not the egocentrism of the four-year-old who can only go as far as saying "I don't want to play basketball"; rather, his "I can play better" is the mark of the adolescent who is reflexively self-conscious and is always evaluating what his or her potential will be in the real world. Adolescent bravado hides a lot of self-doubt. In any event, it does not prevent him from being able to think about the characters in both an immediate and an abstract way.

This chapter describes the changes in cognitive development that take place from the time a child is a toddler until middle adolescence. Cognitive development covers changes in the way children think, how they reason, what they believe, and how they perceive things. Cognitive development therefore includes a large number of mental activities that undergo profound changes as a child matures.

There is no sensible way to talk about the "effects of media violence" on children unless we take into account their level of cognitive development. The five-year-old, who only takes things at face value, cannot begin to understand the television program in which the police officer is slowly and subtly revealed to be a murderer. Such a program may not be upsetting at all for the preschooler, while it might be the stuff of nightmares for the young adolescent.

Cognitive development is cumulative. The child's understanding of new experiences grows out of what he or she learned from previous experiences. Children certainly do not separate their lives into cognitive experiences, moral experiences, attachment experiences, and aggression experiences. While this book has made these distinctions for the sake of clarifying critical developmental strands, we must remember that these strands are always weaving together to create a child of whole cloth.

A child's cognitive development follows reasonably consistent patterns. Parents can make wise decisions about what their children watch if they have an understanding of their children's level of cognitive development. Some of the following theories offer particularly useful yardsticks for gauging where your child stands in his or her cognitive development.

PIAGET'S THEORY OF COGNITIVE DEVELOPMENT

> Grown-ups love figures. . . . If you were to say to the grown-ups: "I saw a beautiful house made of rosy brick, with geraniums in the windows and doves on the roof," they would not be able to get any idea of that house at all. You would have to say to them: "I saw a house that cost $20,000." Then they would exclaim: "Oh, what a pretty house that is!"
>
> They are like that. One must not hold it against them. Children should always show great forbearance toward grown-up people.[1]

This passage was written by Antoine de Saint-Exupéry in his classic book *The Little Prince*. The enduring charm of this book for both grown-ups and children alike lies in its ability to faithfully reproduce the kinds of thinking typical of childhood. Saint-Exupéry knew that young children are far more interested in things they can see and touch and hear than in the kinds of abstract information adults pursue. Behind the grown-ups' interest in figures, in this case how much the house costs, lies a set of abstract conclusions (a lot of money means the house must be beautiful, or the people who could afford to buy it must be talented or important) that the young child is totally ignorant of. Saint-Exupéry knew that children and adults speak different languages.

One of the first researchers to attempt to understand these "different languages" was Jean Piaget. A brilliant Swiss biologist, born at the turn of the century, Piaget first became interested in the question "How do we think?" when he noticed that children of similar ages frequently gave the same wrong answers on intelligence tests. Unlike other researchers, he was not interested in whether children gave right or wrong answers, but in what forms of logic and reasoning they used to come up with their answers. Eventually, Piaget came to believe that children's cognitive development proceeds in an orderly and unvarying manner. While culture may vary the timing of the sequence, the sequence itself never varies. For example, he found that children brought up in the Swiss countryside entered each stage approximately two years later than their counterparts in Geneva, but the actual sequence of development remained the same.

Piaget believed that the mental structures necessary for intellectual development are genetically determined and can develop only through maturation. A child cannot skip a stage or return to it at some later time. Children cannot be "trained" to behave or to think at a more advanced level of development. No matter how much you encourage, cajole, or even bribe your youngster, he or she will not walk, talk, or learn addition and subtraction until he or she is ready. Piaget's theories have been tested for more than fifty years, in many different countries, with generally consistent results. Some researchers claim that Piaget's stages are not as unalterable as he suggests—particularly as children approach the next developmental stage—but in general his theories of cognitive development are at the heart of any discussion of how children think. Children think differently at different ages. This is not exactly earth-shattering news to anyone who has much contact with children. But it is the nature of these changes that determines the ways in which children see, understand, and are affected by the media. Briefly stated, Piaget's stages of cognitive development are as follows.

SENSORIMOTOR STAGE (AGE BIRTH THROUGH TWO)

It is hard to know exactly how much infants "think," although current research suggests that we have underestimated their capacities. For the most part, however, newborns seem to meet the world primarily through their senses and body movements. Sucking on their bottle, their pacifier, or their toes gives them information about the world around them. Babies at this age are totally egocentric and can understand only those things that they have experienced directly. Egocentricity is normal and healthy and it will be many years before children have enough experience to see things from another person's point of view.

Children up to about age two watch relatively little television, so this age group is generally protected from media effects. It is also unlikely that babies are disturbed by much of what they see unless there is a great deal of noise and screaming or the people around them seem upset.

PREOPERATIONAL STAGE (AGE TWO THROUGH SIX)

The word "operation" in this and the following stages refers to actions and manipulations that the child is capable of performing mentally. Being able to add or subtract numbers, having an image of where the school bathroom is located, and imagining the consequences of swiping a box of cookies from the store are examples of mental operations. The child can "see" things in his or her head that aren't necessarily present in the real world at that moment.

At the preoperational stage, children are limited in the activities they can perform in their mind. However, the advent and elaboration of language during this stage make it possible for children to begin developing mental images of things. Before language develops, young children are unable to use words to help them internalize images. Very young children often become distraught when separated from their mother because they experience her as irrevocably gone when she leaves their sight. However, once language develops, children are able to easily invoke their mother's image and are therefore less upset by separations. Watch a three-year-old repeat "Mama" to her doll when her own mother leaves the room.

She is using language to help bring up her internalized image of mother.

This is an age of great curiosity. Well-parented children have come to have faith in the people around them, and as a result they are emotionally free to explore other aspects of their environment. One of the most charming features of this age is children's eagerness to construct explanations for the natural world. For example, because abstraction is still a few years off, children at this age believe that simultaneous occurrences necessarily have a cause-and-effect relationship. If it rains, it is because ten minutes ago Sally and her two friends put feathers in their hair and did a "rain dance." Although Sally's thinking is not yet logical, she has begun to reason about things she observes. She is becoming aware of cause and effect.

Play is one of the most critical aspects of this stage of development. Play helps children create a manageable version of the larger world. In children's miniaturized world of palm-size cars, small dolls, and building blocks, they gain confidence and familiarity. Youngsters experience a sense of control that builds feelings of competence and self-esteem. Eventually the cars will be life-size as will the babies and the building materials. Imaginative play paves the way for children's success at school, among peers, and ultimately in their adult life.

Make-believe nurtures both the intelligence and the soul of young children. Television, with its repetitive format and solutions, does not encourage spontaneous play. Rather, it encourages rote replication of the same banal plots and resolutions. Toys based on these same formulas further interfere with the child's creative capacity to come up with novel and interesting solutions. Bypassing creative and spontaneous play is of serious consequence for young children. Instead of buying a prefabricated Batman fortress, allow your child to construct one out of blocks or boxes. By doing this, your child learns about planning, design, construction, and physics, along with his or her fantasy play. It is a much richer experience.

CONCRETE OPERATIONS (AGE SEVEN THROUGH ELEVEN)

These are the grammar school years, a period of positively explosive intellectual growth. Children are enthralled by their newfound ability to think about things: new things, exciting things, confusing things, all in their mind. Children at this stage are developing an interior landscape that they can endlessly expand and elaborate.

The little girl who just a year or two ago had to count on her fingers to solve the simplest arithmetic problems can now add, subtract, even multiply and divide—all in her head. The young boy who recently had trouble finding his way home from around the corner can now visit a friend or go to the store, confident that he will be able to make it home on his own. He has learned how to use his mind to think about and rehearse actions that previously had to be performed in actuality. An enormous advance at this stage is the ability to "reverse operations." The reason that the eight-year-old can find his way home from the store is that he is now capable of retracing his steps in his mind.

The reason we call this stage "concrete operations" is that all the activity that goes on in children's minds relates to things that are real—what psychologists call "concrete." Children of this age can find a lost toy, picture a map of the United States, write an essay on baseball, and even rehearse for a dance recital, all in their mind. However, they would have difficulty performing these same mental gymnastics on more abstract things. They could easily write an essay on the Constitution but would have difficulty writing on the concept of equality. While thinking for children in this stage of development is becoming logical, it has not yet become abstract.

Research tells us that it is at this stage of development that children are most influenced by aggressive programming. There are several reasons why this age group is particularly vulnerable to the media. Viewing is at an all-time high; the average child watches twenty-eight hours of television per week. In terms of sheer hours, this is the period of greatest exposure. Most parents have given up what little control they previously exercised over their young child's viewing. Also, children of this age still take much of what they see literally. The development of empathy helps grammar school children begin to see things from another perspective. But this ability is just beginning, and for the most part, children of this age still see things more or less from their own point of view. Moral lessons subtly woven into a plot are frequently lost on this age group.

FORMAL OPERATIONS (AGE TWELVE THROUGH ADULTHOOD)

It is hard (sometimes very hard) to imagine that an adolescent thinks like an adult. However, in most respects, past the age of eleven or twelve, children are capable of thinking like grown-ups. At this point, young adolescents lose the basically egocentric orientation that has characterized so much of their early thinking, and they begin to think about the world in a more impersonal, abstract, and hypothetical way. Once children enter the stage Piaget called "formal operations," the nature of their thought begins to change. Children are no longer restricted to thinking about those things that are apparent. Now they can think about things that have no real substance but are only abstractions. They can think about thinking. While they may be capable of the same thought processes as adults, adolescents clearly do not have the life experience that informs thought and helps make educated guesses about the future.

With this cognitive leap comes the ability to lay aside their own point of view to appreciate the point of view of another. While teenagers are prone to constructing an invisible audience whose sole purpose is to microscopically examine their every imagined defect, they are still capable of thinking about behaviors, attitudes, and motives outside their direct realm of experience. The largest consumers of black rap music are white suburban adolescents. While the reasons for this are complex, one is certainly that teenagers are curious about how others get along in the world. At this stage, children exhibit a real thirst to reach beyond what they are accustomed to, to sample other slices of life.

Thinking during this stage becomes increasingly flexible, rational, and systematic. Children no longer search for solutions on a hit-or-miss basis. It is their lack of experience in using new mental strategies that makes adolescent thinking appear so different from adult thinking. Rather than perpetuating the myth that adolescents are basically angry and reactive, the media can encourage this age group to apply their newfound critical skills to problems they are likely to encounter in everyday life.

Piaget believed that no new mental structures emerged after the stage of formal operations. Continuing intellectual development depends on increased knowledge, depth of understanding, and experience.

OTHER THEORIES OF COGNITIVE DEVELOPMENT

While Piaget may have produced the most comprehensive theory of how children think and learn, many subsequent researchers have added valuable information to this field of study. We'll look briefly at two other theories of cognitive development because they place more emphasis on the interaction between the child and the environment, a consideration of particular importance when considering the effects of the media.

SOCIAL LEARNING THEORY

Albert Bandura's research on the ways that children learn spans four decades. Bandura began elaborating his social learning theory in the 1960s and is still studying the ways in which children learn through interaction with their environment.

Bandura observed that while very young children imitate their behaviors rather directly from important people in their environment such as parents, teachers, and peers, children older than about two engage in a much more complex learning process. Older children need to pay attention to a behavior, remember the behavior, and be motivated to reproduce it in one form or another. He called this process "modeling" (as distinct from imitation) and showed that children often produce behaviors that are novel variations on what they have observed.

Bandura's theories have clear implications for the ways in which we understand the effects of media on children. Most children simply do not go out and repeat exactly what they see on television. Hordes of children do not roam the streets performing various martial arts techniques on unsuspecting passersby. Much intervenes between what a child watches and how a child behaves. To parents who are interested in the effects of media on children these intervening variables are particularly important.

Bandura shows that children do not adopt only behaviors modeled by others, but attitudes as well. He suggests that children internalize a set of standards provided for them by important people in their lives. One of the variables that intervenes between behavior children see and whether they will model that particular behavior is their attitude, coupled with the attitudes of other important people in their life.

For parents, this only emphasizes the importance of making your beliefs known about the attitudes and values promoted in the media. Mothers who are vocal and turn away in disgust at Madonna in chains and fathers who criticize men who use intimidation to gain power help teach their children evaluative standards. In contrast, the father who repeatedly yells with enthusiasm "Kick his ass" during a sporting event also provides his children with an attitude that is likely to be internalized.

Children model behavior after their parents, but they also model the ways in which the parent evaluates behavior. Some of this is picked up through parental directives: "In this house we don't watch movies where people settle differences only by fighting." Children are quick studies, however, and if parents frequently resort to fighting or seem to enjoy aggressive media, then their children are likely to internalize these standards as well. Parents have to live their values, not simply talk about them.

SCRIPT THEORY

Some researchers believe that social behavior is controlled to a great extent by "programs" for behavior that are established early in life.[2] These programs are called "cognitive scripts," and they are basically outlines for how to act in different situations. For example, as adults we have well-established cognitive scripts that tell us how to act when we meet a new person, how to buy things in stores, how to express affection to our family, and so on. Children also have scripts, some already in place, some developing. Most children have a script for how to behave when they walk into their classroom. A ten-year-old boy may not have much of a script for talking with a girl, but within a few years he will be experimenting with many different scripts before settling on a few that suit his temperament.

Like the modeling described in social learning theory, cognitive scripts are not simply reproductions of some other person's way of handling life. While we certainly all share many aspects of familiar scripts—responding to an invitation, waiting our turn at the checkout counter, saying please and thank you—each individual is quite active in creating his or her particular ways of reacting to the environment. Scripts suggest what events are likely to happen in the environment, how a person should respond to these events, and what the likely outcome of those behaviors will be. Children who grow up in families where problems are settled by physical fighting come to regard physical force as the appropriate response to interpersonal conflict. Furthermore, their behavior is likely to be rewarded when they are seen as "tough little kids." They may develop a particular script that says "In the family, the best way to get rewarded is to fight." Unfortunately, this script may become generalized to the world at large and later produce an adolescent or adult who relies on aggression to settle conflict.

Since over time scripts become more or less automatic, it seems that the earlier children are exposed to prosocial scripts, the more they are likely to benefit. Altruistic parents are likely to value prosocial programs and to expose their children to such programs at an early age. Not surprisingly, research shows that children from altruistic homes are likely to be altruistic themselves. Scripts, both prosocial and antisocial, become particularly significant when there is little competing information available.[3]

The capacity for the media to provide scripts when the audience has little previous knowledge or alternative sources of information can be used positively or negatively. By bringing issues such as spousal abuse, rape, incest, AIDS, and cancer to the public's notice, the media have been able to provide much-needed information. They have also provided models of healthy and appropriate responses to these problems. Calls to battered women's shelters rise substantially after shows depicting spousal abuse. Doctors report increased interest in mammography following breast cancer specials. The media played a significant role in helping to reduce the number of Americans who smoke. Similarly, there has been a decrease in the rate of automobile deaths. While many factors contribute to this, such as improved auto safety and stricter drunk driving sanctions, the media's "designated driver" program is acknowledged to have played a role.

While the media have willingly taken on the responsibility of tackling some of this country's most disturbing problems, they have steadfastly refused to acknowledge their own role in the creation of social problems. They expect to be congratulated for occasional public service announcements, which are assumed to influence people's habits, at the same time that they deny the impact of incessant violent messages. In a moment of unbridled honesty, Ted Turner of the Turner Broadcasting System said before a congressional sub-committee hearing on media violence, technology, and parental empowerment: "They [network executives] are all guilty of murder as far as I can see. We all are. Me too."[4] The unremitting use of violence as a solution to interpersonal conflict does not serve us well. Suppose an adolescent finds himself confronted by a mugger demanding his wallet. The kind of knee-jerk aggressive script that television all too frequently presents to this type of situation is not likely to make the adolescent a hero; it is more likely to land him in the hospital, if not the morgue.

The media expose our children to ideas and images that are totally beyond their experience. Neil Postman, in his insightful and frightening book *The Disappearance of Childhood,* asserts that the media are contributing to the end of childhood as we know it. Postman argues that the media have made public the secrets of adulthood, thus blurring the lines between children and grown-ups. Children now are exposed to murder and rape on a daily basis during prime-time programming. For the most part, children, not capable of abstract thinking and lacking life experience, are unable to find reassurance, as adults do, by putting things "in perspective." News broadcasts show in gut-wrenching detail the terror and pain of people pulled out of train wrecks, plane wrecks, car wrecks, and exploded buildings. Postman writes:

> Indeed, it is a common enough observation, particularly favored by television executives when under attack, that whatever else may be said about television's impact on the young, today's children are better informed than any previous groups of youngsters. The metaphor usually employed is that television is a window to the world. This observation is entirely correct, but why it should be taken as a sign of progress is a mystery. . . . It means that in having access to the previously hidden fruit of adult information, they are expelled from the garden of childhood.[5]

Several years ago I treated a seven-year-old girl who had watched the horror movie *Nightmare on Elm Street* when it was shown on TV. This movie featured many scenes of young women being tortured and murdered by Freddy Krueger. The little girl was brought to my office because she was having recurrent nightmares and was preoccupied with thoughts of Freddy Krueger during the day. Her schoolwork was suffering and she was increasingly unable to play with friends, fearing that her parents might have to leave the house for a few minutes, during which time Freddy Krueger "might get me." Both her teachers and her parents confirmed that there had been no prior significant emotional problems for this young girl.

Television and movies are promiscuous. They show themselves to anyone who will look. Indeed, people are raped, murdered, and mutilated in our world. Adults know these facts and for the most part have the coping mechanisms to be able to put such horror in perspective. As Postman points out, part of what defines childhood is its innocence of some of the more unsettling aspects of adult life. It took my young patient three months of weekly office visits before she could begin to concentrate on her schoolwork. Gradually her nightmares decreased and by the end of the year she was once again able to stay alone for very short periods of time.

Seven-year-olds are on the cusp of logical thinking. This young girl had been overwhelmed by watching *Nightmare on Elm Street*. She did not yet have the cognitive skills that would have allowed her to understand that this movie was "not real" and that she was not in danger of becoming Freddy Krueger's victim. Close to a year of psychotherapy, aided by the cognitive advances that take place at around age seven, helped this child to regain her equilibrium. In the meantime, a year's worth of play, curiosity, freedom, and intellectual advancement had been compromised by her preoccupation. It is part of our responsibility as adults to ensure that children are not exposed to experiences, even fictional experiences, that are beyond their coping abilities.

7

Moral Development (Conscience)

Too often we open our newspapers to find shocking stories like this:

> Two young adolescents murdered a disabled man in Manteca, California, by kicking, stabbing, beating, and finally choking him. When asked by the police why they poured salt in the dying man's wounds, one of the boys responded, "Oh I don't know. I just seen it on TV."[1]

All parents are concerned with the moral development of their children. Few parents sit their children down in front of a television screen and hope that their sons or daughters will absorb a set of racist, misogynistic, or stereotypical attitudes. That television is banal is one thing; that television can teach our children values that run counter to traditional American values of democracy and tolerance is quite another. How much impact do the media have on the moral values transmitted to our children? Do the media bear any responsibility for the creation of the sociopathic teenagers just described?

A number of different theories have been put forward about the ways in which moral development proceeds in children. Harvard professor Lawrence Kohlberg studied the development of moral reasoning for more than thirty years. Kohlberg's theory, though it has significant limitations (his original research was conducted entirely on boys), is probably the best-known comprehensive theory of moral development.[2] Both Kohlberg and Piaget rely heavily on a cognitive basis for moral development—meaning that the changes in thinking that accompany a child's development are reflected in changes in moral reasoning.

Like cognitive development, moral development is believed to proceed in stages, each fundamentally dependent on the stage that precedes it. Critics of Kohlberg's theories, such as Albert Bandura and Carol Gilligan, place greater emphasis on the social and environmental factors affecting a child's moral development. All of these points of view have something singular and significant to add to our understanding of how children learn right from wrong. The development of moral reasoning across the life span is a fascinating and complex subject. It is not likely that any one theory is sufficient to explain all variations in moral development. So once again, parents need to see these theories as guides and to remember that each child develops in ways that are predictable as well as unique. Moral development, even more than cognitive development, does not proceed in a straight line. Children move back and forth between different stages with remarkable fluidity. The little girl who one day is willing to give an entire week's allowance to a homeless shelter may be stealing candies out of her brother's backpack the next.

KOHLBERG'S HIERARCHY OF MORAL DEVELOPMENT

Kohlberg's work is an elaboration of Piaget's research. Piaget believed that up to age two, children are basically amoral; that is, infants feel no obligation to "follow the rules," the very idea of which is meaningless to them. Kohlberg divides moral reasoning into three main stages and six substages. His main stages are preconventional morality, conventional morality, and postconventional or principled morality. He uses the word "conventional" in the sense of what is typically understood as being a "good person"—fair, honest, concerned, and well thought of.

PRECONVENTIONAL MORALITY

In this stage, from about age two to age seven or eight, dependence on authority is strong and inner controls are weak. A child's conscience is external. It is important that parents assert their authority, as children are too vulnerable and too inexperienced to know the pros and cons of different situations. If you don't like *Power*

Rangers and your four-year-old asks if he can watch, this is not the time to say "You decide." Young children depend on the adult's willingness to accept the responsibility of protecting the child by filtering the world. Children want and need their parents to set limits at this stage.

Stage 1. This stage, seen in preschool and kindergarten-age children, has a single guiding principle: *avoid punishment.* What is bad gets punished, what is good doesn't. Kohlberg calls this the "obedience and punishment orientation." If Jane spills the milk, trips over her shoelaces, hits her sibling, or steals money from her mother's pocketbook, these are all "bad" things to do. No matter if the spilled milk was unintentional and the tripping normal childhood clumsiness, they are still considered "bad" behaviors by the child if punishment was meted out by a frazzled parent. Early in this stage, children have no understanding that stealing is a more serious moral infraction than spilling milk. In a way, it's all the same to them. If it makes Mom or Dad mad, it's bad.

Stage 2. This is a pretty hedonistic stage. When he was five, my middle son found a particularly shiny quarter on my dresser and made off with it. When I asked for it back, he said, "It's mine. It's all shiny and I like shiny things, so it's mine." "Good" at this stage is defined as what one enjoys or is rewarded for.

CONVENTIONAL MORALITY

From about age seven, children are no longer completely dependent on others, their parents in particular, to define what is right and wrong. Conscience as we know it is beginning, and children know the difference between truth and lies. However, it is still largely the threat of punishment that keeps kids in line.

Stage 3. Kohlberg called this stage the "good-boy, good-girl" orientation. The child's goal at this stage is to behave in ways that will win approval and avoid disapproval. Children at this stage are motivated by rewards. This is a welcome breather for parents who seemingly overnight have children offering to clean dishes, walk the dog, or watch a younger sibling because "it's the right thing to do."

Stage 4. In this stage, the basis of moral judgments shifts away from simple disapproval toward a greater concern about dishonor and possible concrete harm to others. In a very major shift in moral reasoning, children at this stage can put aside their self-centered view of the world. They can begin making inferences and know that in some situations there is "more than meets the eye." Kohlberg calls this a "law-and-order" orientation. In reality, it is likely that this is the highest stage of moral reasoning for many adults. While in this stage people accept the responsibility of being members of society, they also are inclined to accept totalitarian thinking. This level of reasoning was evident throughout the Nuremberg trials in the defense of "just following orders."

POSTCONVENTIONAL OR PRINCIPLED MORALITY

In this stage of moral reasoning, which is rarely in evidence before middle adolescence, individuals are able to transcend conventional notions of right and wrong and focus on underlying principles. The ability to think abstractly is in full swing for many adolescents and young adults and helps them understand that there are abstract ideals that may transcend the laws of society. Participants in the civil rights movement of the 1960s who were willing to go to jail and sometimes even to die for an ideal that was in opposition to popular sentiment exhibited principled morality.

Stage 5. At this stage, there is a strong commitment to keeping society running smoothly. Individuals at this stage may understand that particular laws are arbitrary but feel that the ideal of being a law-abiding citizen is more important than whether they agree with a particular law. Kohlberg calls this a "social contract orientation." Human interdependence is fully understood at this stage. Individuals who attain this stage of moral reasoning believe that "no man is an island."

Stage 6. At this level of moral reasoning the rules of society are integrated with the dictates of conscience to produce a personal hierarchy of moral values. People at this stage recognize that sometimes the dictates of society are most important and other times the dictates of conscience must take precedence. External punishment has lost its power and has been replaced by disappointment at violating one's own moral principles.

Kohlberg's stages find considerable validation in day-to-day experiences with children. Most preschool-age children take a very egocentric view of right and wrong. For the most part, what is right is what is gratifying to the young child. It can be "right" to lie, to take someone else's possession, or to hit another child, particularly if no adult is around to mete out punishment. Young children tend to ignore the intention of an act and to consider only the result. Piaget called this "moral realism." It is the reason why so many of the moral tag lines added to Saturday morning cartoons are meaningless to young children. The preconventional child is much more capable of understanding the karate chops and exclamations of "hiyaaah" than some dreary dialogue about getting along at the end of the show. Children at this age are not capable of tying together the fighting early in a program with the message that fighting is bad. Children need to be shown, not taught, their moral messages.

Similarly, Kohlberg's stage of conventional morality is evident when we look at how children behave at school. The reason that grammar school children can sit in a classroom and learn such a large and often uninspiring body of knowledge is that they feel it is important for them to be "good kids." For the most part, school-age children are happy to get good grades and reap the approval that such efforts bring.

Children at this age are beginning to temper their moral judgments with empathy. Unfortunately, situation comedies, the most popular type of program among school-age children, are becoming increasingly dependent on snide remarks for laughs. Shows such as *Unhappily Ever After* and *Married . . . with Children* do not encourage the child's developing sense of empathy. Rather than showing family members attempting to understand each other's positions, they frequently resort to discrediting each other with crude insults and put-downs. On a recent episode of *Married . . . with Children,* I counted seven humiliating comments within the first three minutes of the program, most having to do with appearance and sexual performance. Moral development is not aided by repeated exposure to people treating each other in disrespectful and demeaning ways. Civility is not a frivolous issue. Respectful and courteous interaction is the hallmark of a smoothly running society—whether it is the microsociety of our home or the larger society of our neighborhood or country. Programs such as *Full House, Step by Step,* and *The Cosby Show* have proven that situation comedies can be entertaining, touch on some real-life dilemmas, and appeal to children without a constant barrage of disparaging and sarcastic asides.

We see evidence for Kohlberg's final stage of principled morality in some of the positions that adolescents and college-age students adopt toward social evils. There is in my community, as in many across the country at this time, a heated and emotional debate over whether condoms should be distributed to high school students. Principled morality does not necessarily suggest that children take either a pro or a con position. Kohlberg would argue that those children who can reason one way or another, based not just on what is popular, or even what is lawful, but on the greater issues of society's role toward its current and future members, are reasoning at the level of principled morality. One individual might reason that since adolescents are sexually active, condoms would work for the greater social good by preventing pregnancy and sexually transmitted diseases. Another person could argue that implicitly sanctioning sexual activity for adolescents ultimately leads to increased social problems, and therefore not distributing condoms would work for the greater social good. Kohlberg would consider each of these positions equally representative of principled morality.

Kohlberg is interested only in the process of reasoning and not with the child's ultimate conclusion. Is it really possible to separate moral reasoning from the conclusions drawn from that reasoning? What does moral reasoning mean if it is not attached to moral behavior? In one of Kohlberg's best-known research vignettes, he presents the following moral dilemma:

> In Europe, a woman was near death from a special kind of cancer. There was one drug that the doctors thought might save her. It was a form of radium that a druggist in the same town had recently discovered. The drug was expensive to make, but the druggist was charging ten times what the drug cost him to make. He paid $200 for the radium and charged $2,000 for a small dose of the drug. The sick woman's husband, Heinz, went to everyone he knew to borrow the money, but he could only get together about $1,000, which is half of what it cost. He told the druggist that his wife was dying and asked him to sell it cheaper or let him pay later. But the druggist said: "No, I discovered the drug and I'm going to make money from it." So Heinz got desperate and broke into the man's store to steal the drug for his wife. Should the husband have done that?[3]

Kohlberg then gives an example of two entirely different responses, both of which he considers equally representative of his highest stage of reasoning.

PRO: If you don't steal the drug and let your wife die, you'd always condemn yourself for it afterward. You wouldn't be blamed and you would have lived up to the outside rule of the law but you wouldn't have lived up to your standards of conscience.

CON: If you stole the drug, you wouldn't be blamed by other people but you'd condemn yourself because you wouldn't have lived up to your own conscience and standards of honesty.

Kohlberg's hierarchy is a good general way of thinking about how children's moral reasoning, just like their cognitive reasoning, progresses with age. However, it seems to me to be rather pointless to separate moral reasoning from moral behavior. Most of us would agree that "words are cheap" and actions are what counts. Research has shown that moral reasoning is in fact only weakly related to actual moral behavior.[4] In Kohlberg's example, I would be hard pressed to consider both of these respondents at the same level of moral development. Life is more valuable than profit.

GILLIGAN'S EXPANSION OF MORAL REASONING

Carol Gilligan, a colleague of Kohlberg and a researcher at Harvard for the last three decades, suggests that the moral reasoning Kohlberg observed in his male subjects is by no means characteristic of all, or even most, moral reasoning.[5] Gilligan argues that, often based along gender lines (although not exclusively), males and females have different ideas about what constitutes moral behavior. Gilligan's research illustrates that women base moral decisions primarily on principles of care and cooperation. Men, on the other hand, tend to conceptualize moral dilemmas in terms of rights and rules.

In the face of conflict, women work to preserve and enhance relationships. Men focus on determining the right rule, based on what is fair, and then meting out what is due to people in conflict. Contrary to Freud's assertion that women "show less sense of justice than men,"[6] it would appear that men and women weigh things differently when making moral decisions. Men are more affected by abstract values, women more by interpersonal relationships. This does not suggest "higher" or "lower" capacities. These two orientations can be seen as alternative or even complementary points of view by anyone who appreciates the dense complexities of moral decision making. Parents would do well to expose both their sons and their daughters to these two different ways of thinking about moral issues.

Much drama turns on the moral choices that people confront. Rather than insist that media show us only those decisions we approve of (an impossible and unhealthy demand), parents serve their children best by clarifying the consequences of different choices. A child can learn as much from a poor choice as from a good one. Media offerings benefit children when the consequences of decisions are clearly illustrated. In addition, both parents and the media can encourage children to move toward less stereotyped ways of dealing with moral dilemmas.

In the movie *Ordinary People*, a middle-class family is torn apart by the accidental death of the favored, older son and the emotional collapse of the younger son. The older boy drowns during a boating accident and his younger brother is powerless to save him. Mary Tyler Moore plays the bereaved, emotionally moribund mother who cannot break free of her sense of propriety to experience the immensity of her loss. She scolds her husband for wearing the wrong socks to their son's funeral.

Donald Sutherland, as the father, works overtime to keep his family from total disintegration. To do so he adopts many of the "feminine" values of cooperation, caring, and empathy. In the end, he is unable to reach his wife and, as she packs her bags to leave, he sits on the porch steps with his arm around his son. It is a moment of exquisite poignancy. While this movie is over fifteen years old, like all art that speaks to the heart it is ageless. It confronts some of life's most tragic moments, forcing the viewer to reconsider what makes a person "good." It mixes traditional notions of male and female characteristics and traditional modes of reasoning. Its final conclusion is that while "good" may look like community work, a well-kept house, and a conscientious discharge of responsibilities, ultimately "good" is the ability to truly care about other people. Painful as *Ordinary People* is, it is a wonderful family movie. It is not simply that we want the media to protect our children from the pain of life. But when they are old enough to confront disturbing issues, we want the media to contribute to their repertoire of coping skills in ways that will serve them well during their own inevitable pains.

BANDURA'S SOCIAL COGNITIVE THEORY

It is very hard to consider morality apart from socialization, history, and cultural context. Albert Bandura's work has focused on how socialization contributes to the development of moral reasoning. Bandura believes that children do not simply "grow" into successive stages of moral development, but are introduced and guided into different moral universes. According to Bandura, "Developmental trends obviously exist in moral reasoning and judgment as they do in everything else, but the conditions of social learning are much too varied to produce uniform results."[7]

Bandura believes that a good deal of a child's moral reasoning comes about by watching and modeling the behaviors and thinking of adults. We are social animals and a great deal of our learning is social learning. Much of it is incidental. Our children watch us take food to a homeless shelter, pick up a young child standing in the rain, or call an elderly widowed neighbor during a storm. Alternately, they see us swipe newspapers out of a box when we don't have the change or not call attention to a mistake on a bill that was in our favor. The ways in which we conduct our lives are far more significant to our children than the ways in which we say we conduct our lives.

Socialization is the process by which children internalize the values and mores of a particular culture. What is valued in one culture may not be valued and may even be disdained by another. Americans for a long time set great store on taming and controlling their natural environment. Native Americans, in contrast, believed in peaceful coexistence rather than dominance over nature. Even within our own country, which celebrates individuality, groups such as the Amish or Mormons are far more concerned with community coherence than individual rights.

Societies are reasonably consistent in protecting young children from danger so that they can be socialized at all. Parents throughout the world prevent their children from getting into trouble by physical restraint often paired with the word "no." While of course there is some variety within different cultures, young children are generally socialized with clear physical sanctions against unacceptable behavior.

As children mature, more discreet social sanctions replace physical ones as influential guides. Children's behavior is increasingly controlled by approval and disapproval, usually from parents and other adults. Explanations for what is considered appropriate and what is inappropriate help children understand what exactly about their behavior is "good" or "bad." "How would you feel if Mary hit you?" serves two important functions. First, it forces the child to reflect on her behavior and, second, it furthers empathy by pointing out the universality of human emotions. Over a period of years, school-age children are exposed to many social injunctions from parents, schools, religious institutions, and peers. While increasingly verbal, many of these injunctions still come with rewards and punishments attached: "It was a bad mistake to steal that candy bar. Now you have to go back to the store, tell them what you did, and pay them from your allowance."

Eventually, these rules for behavior are internalized and children begin, on their own, to tell the difference between right and wrong. Parents who take the time to explain the outcome of moral and behavioral choices do their children a great service. Children who are able to think through and anticipate the consequences of their choices are in a much better position than children who have always been told, "Because I'm the Mommy, that's why!" Allowing children to participate in the process of learning about what are good and bad choices encourages them to feel that the attitudes they are adopting are authentically their own. This encourages self-respect, which in turn allows children to adhere to an internalized moral code.

Consider the difference between preadolescents who are told, "I'll break your neck if I catch you smoking" and those who have read and discussed with their parents the health issues around smoking. It is the latter children who are more apt to feel that they have made their own decisions. Of course, children and teenagers will not always come up with the same conclusions that their parents have reached. Depending on a child's age and how important the issue is, parents may decide to punish the child anyway. However, it still benefits the child if the parents are able to verbalize the reasoning that led them to impose punishment: "Because you hit your baby brother you have to stay in your room for the next hour as punishment. I know he made you mad, but it's not right for big people to beat up on little people." Research has shown that parents who use and communicate higher levels of moral reasoning when punishing their children tend to have children who are also capable of higher levels of moral reasoning.

Part Three

Through the Eyes of a Child: How Children "See" the Media

8

The Cartoon Dilemma:
Ages 3, 4, and 5

GENERAL DEVELOPMENT

It's quite a stretch for an adult to see the world through the eyes of the preschool child. Young children are not little adults. They do not think like adults, act like adults, or experience things as adults do. Preschool children inhabit a world that is magical, unique, and quite distinct from that of grown-ups, teenagers, and even older children. For example:

A four-year-old will be heartbroken to discover that the tooth fairy has forgotten to leave a gift under her pillow.

Allow a three-year-old to play with a red car. In view of the child place the car behind a green filter that makes the car appear to be black. Ask the child what color the car "really" is and he will say black.

Show a four-year-old two identical tall glasses of water. As the child watches, pour the water from one into a wide, shallow glass. The child will believe that the tall glass has more water in it than the wide, shallow glass.

These few examples illustrate that a child's thinking differs qualitatively, not just quantitatively, from that of adults. It is not simply that young children have less experience than adults. The nature of their thinking and the very ways in which they experience the world are entirely different.

To make good choices about what preschoolers should watch,

we need to appreciate the nature of the young child's world. Children's beliefs that the tooth fairy is real, that cars can change color before their eyes, and that volume depends on the shape of the container are not occasional aberrations in ordinary thinking. They accurately describe the world of the preschool child, where magic is real and the laws of science as we know them don't exist. Adults usually make decisions about what is appropriate for young children based on what they themselves find offensive, as if what adults find upsetting and what children find upsetting are one and the same. This is frequently not the case. What is offensive and disturbing for children often comes as a surprise to adults.

"Why is the sky blue?" "Why do cherries have pits?" "Where does God live?" "Who is older, Grandma Edith or Abraham Lincoln?" The questions of the young child are endless and often unanswerable. Infants and toddlers come to know the world exclusively through their senses; preschoolers seek explanations. When explanations aren't apparent, preschoolers will gladly make them up to suit the situation and satisfy themselves. Many children this age believe that little people live inside the television set. This belief actually shows great cognitive advancement over the toddler, because the preschooler is searching for an explanation instead of simply taking things at face value. The preschooler is aware that some force is causing people to appear on the screen. Things don't just happen by themselves, there are reasons.

Children at this age are into everything. They are budding scientists who seem to be driven to touch and take apart everything they can get their hands on. Before you can turn around, the roll of film has been pulled out of the camera and is lying exposed on the bed. While you answer the doorbell, the television's remote control is being quietly disassembled. Mothers are often exhausted in their attempts to keep the house in order. Children at the beginning of this stage frequently appear insatiable in their quest for knowledge. The question children ask most often at this stage of development is "Why?"

While there are certainly individual differences among children, it appears that curiosity and playfulness are innate. Children do not need to be taught how to play. Bring a young child to a playground or a toy store, and if he feels secure he will play. No one ever had to teach a child how to "use" a sandbox. Researchers have shown that humans and other primates appear to have an inborn desire for discovery.[1] Adults must provide children with environments that are safe, stimulating, educational, and fun. While it can be trying at times to answer all those "Why?" questions, a youngster's enthusiasm should be cultivated. A child's level of curiosity and exploration is an important indicator of overall adjustment. By the end of this stage of development, as young children become increasingly capable of controlling themselves, things begin to quiet down. Hang in there. Try to see the world through the amazed eyes of your young child.

Preschool-age children are in a period of accelerated development. On many different fronts, we see emerging capacities for self-control and self-management. Although they were babies only a year or two ago, preschoolers can now stand on line, listen to a teacher, and play with other children without getting into pulling and hitting matches over toys. They can hold a candy bar and wait until after dinner to eat it.

Children at this stage of development are making enormous strides in the area of self-reliance. Erik Erikson, one of America's foremost developmental psychologists, called this period "initiative versus guilt." Erikson believed that children from about three to six are expanding their sense of autonomy by increasingly taking the initiative in learning about the world and about social relations. "Can I help?" and "I want to do it myself" are common requests at this stage. According to Erikson, the child who is encouraged to take on more responsibility and greater challenges is likely to develop a lifelong feeling of enthusiasm and competency. If your child wants to help you clean the car, give him a rag and thank him for his help. In contrast, the child who is challenged or criticized for his attempts to become independent is likely to feel guilty and lose faith in his abilities.

The preschool-age child's move toward greater independence is supported by a number of newly developing abilities. First of all, children of this age possess impressive physical skills. They can run, jump, climb, and manipulate objects. More and more tasks are now within their reach. They can pull on their pants, button their buttons, put away the silverware, and wash their own hair. They can climb to the top of the slide, balance on the seesaw, and ride tricycles. Watch the delight of a child who has just found out that she no longer needs her mother's push to get her swing going, that her own pumping legs can send her soaring.

Along with increasing physical abilities, preschool-age children have a host of developing cognitive skills that advance their sense of independence. Language is well developed now, so children are able to ask for what they need and put their feelings into words. They are no longer dependent on a sympathetic interpreter to have their needs met. As children become able to verbalize their wishes, they begin to see that they have the power to influence their environment. To the extent to which they are heard and their wishes treated with respect, the world becomes a reasonably benign and responsive place.

This does not mean you should always grant the wishes of your young children. On the contrary, frustration is an inevitable part of the preschoolers' life (an inevitable part of all stages of life, actually). Children of this age are up against an endless barrage of "no's": "No, you can't have ice cream before dinner." "No, you can't watch *X-Files* with your older sister." Their natural enthusiasm and curiosity propel them out into the world, while their parents try to keep them safe and healthy.

At around age four, children are beginning to develop real friendships. Preschoolers have a great deal to learn from other children, including their own siblings. Competence with peers is important not only for the fun it brings, but also because the peer group is a major arena for learning the concepts of fairness, reciprocity, and cooperation. In addition, it is a very important setting in which children learn to manage their aggression. An older sibling may ignore a younger one who calls him a "poo-poo head" and Mom may gloss over the accusation "You're the meanest person in the world." However, preschool children are not apt to find such generosity among their peers. Whether physical or verbal, expressions of aggression are more likely to be met with retaliation or exclusion than with indulgence.

In addition to an increased capacity to control aggression, preschool children are also beginning to behave in a prosocial manner. Just as controlling aggression depends on increasing self-management skills, so does prosocial behavior. "Do you want some of my candy?" means that the child is able to put aside his own desires and respond to someone else's need. The child who is able to ask this question and share his precious resources sees that there can be value in delaying his own gratification. This is the beginning of altruism.

All of these advances in the preschool child (developing and maintaining friendships, becoming more self-reliant, inferring things about the world that are not readily apparent) depend in large measure on the child's emerging self-control. These developing capacities mark a huge leap forward for the youngster and pave the way for one of the major challenges of the next stage of development—school. No preschooler exhibits these characteristics at all times and under all circumstances. Development at this point is highly variable and changeable. One day a young child is able to resolve a fight with a friend, offer her sister half of her cookie, and straighten up her room; the next day she may throw herself in a screaming heap on the floor when her mother suggests that it is bath time. This is normal. Children's controls at this time are fragile and are easily challenged by fatigue, hunger, and frustration. But overall, the child is moving in the direction of increased control.

MEDIA AND THE PRESCHOOL-AGE CHILD

There are many issues related to the preschool-age child and media, but one of them invariably invites passionate concern and disagreement. That is the issue of cartoons. Are cartoons bad for kids? Why do they need to be so violent? Are there any good ones? Can they actually harm development? Are they addicting? Don't kids know that cartoons are make-believe?

Cartoons are the most violent form of entertainment on network television today. While the average prime-time television show has approximately five acts of violence per hour, cartoons typically have closer to twenty-five acts of violence per hour.[2] It is unfortunate that our society has decided to subject its most vulnerable members to its most intensely antisocial programming.

Preschoolers see cartoons through naive eyes. The distinction between reality and fantasy is murky to a child this age, the laws of nature are unknown, and the concept of cause and effect is weak. In the eyes of a three-year-old, the sun and the moon move because of him. Certainly, then, flattened rabbits can rearrange themselves, and good guys can be immune to the kind of firepower that, in real life, would wipe out a small village. Young children's thinking is concrete, literal, and incapable of understanding symbols. Their moral code dictates that might makes right.

These basic facts of child development are often misunderstood and unappreciated by those in the broadcasting industry. Christine Hikawa, ABC's vice president for broadcast standards and practices has said, "When scholars and behavioral scientists lump *Tom and Jerry* and *Roadrunner* cartoons with movies like *I Spit on Your Grave* as being equally violent and harmful, their credibility goes out the window."[3] Statements like this, which are consistently used to justify the continuance of violent programming, show a refusal to acknowledge the developmental processes of childhood. A *Roadrunner* cartoon, with its rapid pace, continuous violence, and seductive appeal, is really very much like *I Spit on Your Grave*. They are the same experience aimed at different age groups. Both are pernicious, vacuous, and violent. It is not any single cartoon, any single movie, or any one video game that is of concern. But parents need to realize that their children are being subjected to a barrage of messages, many of them violent and stereotypical, and always commercial, that are often at odds with the moral values that parents hope to convey to their children.

Most cartoons have little to offer children. Conflicts are typically resolved by inappropriate force. The symbolism and moral endings that are included in many cartoons, probably to make parents feel that their children are learning a "good lesson," are totally lost on young children. For example, on a particular episode of *Biker Mice from Mars* that featured lots of explosions, fights, and dangerous motorcycle calisthenics, the program unbelievably ended with a "safety message" about buckling up. Such a message is retained by an adult only because of its sheer absurdity; it is not likely to be retained by a four-year-old who has barely recovered from the sensory assault of the preceding thirty minutes. Most important, the majority of today's cartoon characters do not deal with the issues that are of importance to young children.

It is during the preschool years that children begin developing the capacity to distinguish fantasy from reality. Contrary to popular opinion, this distinction is not reliably in place until a child is eight or nine years old. In a classic experiment on whether preschoolers can tell what is real from what appears to be real—called the "appearance-reality distinction"—Rheta DeVries tested a group of children age three to six.[4] She introduced them to a cat named Maynard and then put a dog mask on Maynard. She asked the children questions such as "What kind of animal is it now?" "Does

Maynard say bow-wow or meow?" and "Does Maynard like dog food or cat food?" The younger children believed that Maynard was now a dog. Simply putting a dog mask on a cat had altered reality for the three-year-olds. By the age of six, the children knew that Maynard remained a cat, that reality is not so easily changed.

Given young children's utter lack of sophistication about what constitutes reality, how are they affected by the cartoons they watch? Is it likely that youngsters will identify with and imitate cartoon characters? The answer appears to be a qualified "yes." For many young children, cartoon characters can seem real. Children have been known to imitate, sometimes with tragic consequences, the antics of their favorite characters. Teachers have reported an increase in martial arts interest, as preschoolers karate-chop their peers on the playground in imitation of *Teenage Mutant Ninja Turtles*. Parents report that their youngsters are particularly combative after watching superhero cartoons like *Mighty Morphin Power Rangers*.

Heroes (and today's technowonder equivalent, the superhero) serve an important psychological function for young children and have always been part of their socialization. In a world that is large, frightening, and well beyond the rudimentary capabilities of the young child, heroes guide and reassure. By identifying with the persistence and superior abilities of the hero, children come to feel that they too may someday be able to conquer the world, "to leap tall buildings in a single bound." Heroes provide clear rules about acceptable and unacceptable behaviors, and internalizing these rules helps the young child's developing conscience.

Children need stories that help them make sense out of the chaotic and conflicting feelings they frequently have. Most particularly, children need help sorting out their feelings of ambivalence. One moment they love their baby sister and the next moment, as mother coos and caresses the baby, they wish her dead. Contrary to adult wishful thinking, childhood is often not a sunny and saccharine time. Rather, young children are frequently awash in nameless anxieties and dark, often violent fantasies. Fairy tales, because they recognize these realities of the young child's inner life, have always been immensely popular. They speak to the issues that children care about most: sibling rivalry, ambivalence toward parents, separation anxiety, and self-actualization.

The popularity of fairy tales reminds us that children's stories do not have to be totally sanitized in order to be appropriate for young children. *Grimm's Fairy Tales* can make an adult's hair stand on end. Little Red Riding Hood and her grandmother are eaten alive by a wolf before being rescued by a hunter who slits the wolf's belly open. Both Little Red Riding Hood and the generations of children who have heard her tale learned many important lessons: Don't stray off the path, don't talk to strangers, and always follow mother's instructions. The fact that the story is told vividly, even gruesomely, does not diminish its socializing function (reading or being read to allows the child to conjure up the exact amount of "scariness" that he or she can handle). Children are aided by stories that are clear about good and evil and are ultimately optimistic. Fairy tales acknowledge the conflicts of childhood and help children manage their impulses and make good choices. Faerie Tale Theater, hosted by Shelley Duvall, puts out an excellent series of videotape versions of classic fairy tales. It's a wonderful alternative to the counterfeit heroes of Saturday morning cartoons.

Preschool children are often more frightened by fantasy programs than they are by more realistic programs. Consistency is very important to preschoolers; they are particularly frightened by things that change unpredictably from the ordinary to the grotesque. For example, children this age are far more frightened by David Banner's transformation in *The Incredible Hulk* than by the more realistically frightening movie *Jaws*. However, *The Incredible Hulk* cartoon is less upsetting than *The Incredible Hulk* drama. Many youngsters were apprehensive and even tearful when seeing the movie *Teenage Mutant Ninja Turtles*, although in cartoon form these same turtles seem only to provoke mild euphoria and a tendency to practice karate on the nearest available object. It is only very young children who seem truly frightened by cartoons. But cartoons *are* effective at boosting a child's level of aggression.

Realistic portrayals of violence, which often depend heavily on symbolic cues such as lighting and music, are often completely overlooked by the young child. By the same token, much of what is talked about on the news is less upsetting to young children than we might expect. While certainly the graphic photographs and footage are disturbing, the news is primarily verbal and children are more attentive and therefore more vulnerable to what they see rather than what they hear. This is not to suggest that young children should watch the evening news or be allowed to watch more realistic adult programs because "they won't get it anyway." I simply want to emphasize that young children are particularly vulnerable to exactly those media offerings that adults are likely to dismiss as "fantasy." *Fantasy is the world in which young children live and therefore can be most disturbing to them when violence is portrayed.*

There is, of course, another side to the debate about television programming for young children. Television has tremendous potential to educate, expand, and enrich the lives of young children. Programs such as *Sesame Street, Mister Rogers' Neighborhood,* and *Barney and Friends,* channels such as Nickelodeon, the Public Broadcasting Service (PBS), and many of Disney's movies all offer wonderful opportunities to youngsters. Research studies have shown many benefits from these offerings. Regular viewing of *Sesame Street* has been shown to accelerate academic performance in a number of ways. Research studies have shown that watching *Mister Rogers* for as little as a half hour per day for two weeks increases children's imaginativeness and positive feelings while it decreases their aggression.[5]

Although there are exceptions, the fact remains that the vast majority of children's programming, cartoons in particular, misses the boat. Why? We know a great deal about which children are most vulnerable to media violence, what kinds of programs are most damaging to children at different ages, and the potential of television to educate and socialize. Given all this information, why not simply create cartoons that take into account a child's developmental level, send prosocial messages, and are both entertaining and instructional? It seems just as easy as creating cartoons that are violent, antisocial, and mind-numbing. Besides, it would quiet down all those whining politicians, parents, and social scientists. How baffling that television executives don't seem to appreciate the opportunity.

HISTORY OF CHILDREN'S PROGRAMMING

To understand this apparent lapse in clear thinking on the part of the networks, we need to understand a bit about the history of children's television programming. In the 1970s, encouraged by activist groups such as Action for Children's Television (ACT), the Federal Communications Commission (FCC) took an active role in protecting the interests of children. It recognized the differing needs of children at various stages of development and pressured the television industry to introduce more educational programming aimed at particular ages, rather than at children in general. It regulated the amount of time networks could spend on commercials and pushed for less violent programming. The FCC clearly recognized that children are a vulnerable and unique audience when it issued a policy statement in 1974 declaring that "broadcasters have a special obligation to serve children."

This protective attitude changed rapidly under President Reagan's policies of deregulation in the 1980s. Mark Fowler, newly appointed head of the FCC, reversed earlier policy and declared that "it was time to move away from thinking about broadcasters as trustees. It was time to treat them the way almost everyone else in society does—that is, as businesses."[6] In 1984, the FCC ruled that networks could air as much commercial time as they wanted, and thus was born what is kindly called the "program-length commercial." Networks, in conjunction with toy manufacturers and other "character licensing" industries, such as makers of cereals, linens, lunchboxes, and clothing, began creating characters solely for the purpose of mass marketing. The shows *He-Man*, *Strawberry Shortcake*, *Care Bears*, and *Transformers* and their counterpart products all became enormously popular because of the joint efforts of network executives and toy manufacturers.

The magnitude of the business of selling armies of superheroes, fleets of transforming robots, and stables of long-haired ponies to little kids is staggering. In 1985, $8.5 billion worth of "character products" were sold in the toy industry alone.[7] Overly muscular, power-obsessed superheroes relying on violence, weaponry, and robots became a generically successful formula for boys. Similarly, long-haired, pastel-colored animals with splintered emotions appealed to girls. Fowler's vision of television as nothing more than a business, as "another appliance . . . a toaster with pictures,"[8] took root and flourished in the conference rooms of ad agencies, toy manufacturers, and network executives who contrived to sell the most products to the largest number of children. Needless to say, educational programming plummeted, as did programming aimed at specific age groups. Commercial children's television moved away from the educational, the developmental, and the prosocial and into the realm of business, big business, enormous business.

The Children's Ghetto: Cartoons and Consumerism

Saturday morning programming is derisively referred to as the "children's ghetto" by those in the entertainment industry. Nowhere is the statement "TV is good for 'killing time' for those who like their time dead"[9] more applicable than in these few hours of mindless trash which a majority of American children watch every week.

Cartoon programs almost without exception fall into two categories: testosterone-enhanced superheroes or pathetically witless girl surrogates like ponies or fairies. Aside from the sheer banality of these programs, several messages bear examination. Since this is a book on the effects of media violence on children, I expected to have a great deal to say about the harm that these constant displays of violence would have on young minds. Certainly, there is not much to say in favor of the excessive amounts of firepower displayed on children's cartoons. There is also a significant body of research, which we will look at more closely in the section on aggression (page 101), which suggests that viewing excessive violence makes many young children more aggressive as well as more fearful and less imaginative. When I began the hours of cartoon viewing I needed to do to write this chapter, I was prepared for too much violence.

What I was not prepared for was the astounding stupidity of the superhero cartoons (we'll get to the "girl" cartoons in a few paragraphs). In talking with many parents, I realized that few of them have put in any significant amount of time watching these shows. Granted, Saturday morning cartoons generally serve the function of parking the kids for a few hours while parents attend to other matters. However, even those parents who have made some attempt to preview what their children are watching report that usually within minutes they find themselves drifting away from the television because the programs are so unbearably crude. I suggest that all parents spend a couple of hours watching Saturday morning cartoons in order to better appreciate how poorly their children are being served. After all, we wouldn't send our children to a preschool without spending time there, nor would we hire a babysitter without an interview. With the child in this young age group watching close to twenty hours of television per week (more hours than many children are in day care) it is essential that we put some effort into monitoring what our children watch on television.

What parents are most likely to see on any of the superhero programs (*Mighty Morphin Power Rangers, V. R. Troopers, X-Men,* and so on) is that boys are expected to be fixated on ideas of power and that technology is just as likely to have run amok as to be of any benefit. Power is something that is constantly under attack and cartoon life usually consists of power gained, robbed, withdrawn, and threatened. For reasons that are unclear, many of these power negotiations deal with dire nuclear threats and the disposal of nuclear waste. The great promise of technology to aid humankind has been transformed into an equally likely force of evil, as pet rats gain mammoth proportions and unwitting scientists become walking nuclear time bombs.

Violence on these programs is singularly unconvincing. In fact, most of these programs are notable primarily for their lack of conviction. They are poorly conceived, plot is minimal (and would probably be absent were it not for the necessity of introducing new characters to sell), dialogue is ludicrous, and animation is often amateurish. The exception to this is the minute or so during which, accompanied by loud music and much atmospheric disturbance, the main characters transform themselves into superheroes.

"Girl" cartoons such as *Strawberry Shortcake, Care Bears,* and *My Little Pony* do not fare much better. While they are free of the senseless and irrelevant violence of the superhero cartoons—and this is a plus—they present a world of superficial, fragmented emotions. Cartoons for girls seem to suggest that all young girls are in need of psychotherapy. These heroines are passive, silly, and unable to identify their own feelings. Since the point of most cartoon programs is to hawk the wares of the toy manufacturers and other vendors of licensed characters, this fragmentation of emotion in girls' programming serves the same purpose as "teamwork" in boys programming. As writer and social critic Tom Engelhardt points out, "No one wants to sell just one action figure."[10] So manufacturers of licensed products produce dozens of characters for each program. Care Bear products include Love-a-Bear and Hug-a-Bear and Secret Bear, while X-Men manufacturers produce an endless stream of action figures with names like Wolverine, Krule, and Tusk.

In what small defense can be made of "girl" cartoons, they do typically acknowledge that power is not simply about the misuse of weaponry or personal dominance. Girl cartoons focus on the fact that affiliation, nurturance, and the ability to sustain interpersonal relationships are valuable skills. Unfortunately, only the wimpiest of shows tend to highlight these values. The more "powerful" girl cartoons, such as *She-Ra*, have taken on the more male-defined characteristics of artillery and intimidation. Almost without exception, cartoons miss the opportunity to present powerful role models who derive their strength from a capacity for empathy and interpersonal skill as well as a sense of adventure. Real power for both boys and girls comes from believing that one is valued and capable.

There are attempts to produce cartoons that are exciting and that feature healthier role models. Disney's entry into the field, *Gargoyles*, is a particularly interesting example. At first glance it doesn't appear very different from any other superhero cartoon, except that its animation is so much better. It's the story of a group of gargoyles who once guarded a medieval Scottish fortress and a thousand years later find themselves guarding New York City. They are alive at night, but turn to stone during the day. Goliath, the leader of the Gargoyles, has a singularly egalitarian relationship with Elisa Maza, the police officer who befriends him and the other Gargoyles. My ten-year-old son, who insisted I watch the program, billed it as "a story about outsiders." It does focus on many of the issues most pressing to children: conformity, feeling different, and intolerance.

It is too well written to need superfluous moral tags at the end of the program and this show weaves its messages into the action. But most of all, it respects children and the social problems, both major and minor, that they are likely to confront. In a particularly serious episode entitled "Deadly Force," one of the Gargoyles, pumped up after seeing a gunfight in a movie, accidentally shoots Elisa with her own police revolver. The rest of the episode focuses on the consequences of their carelessness. Elisa nearly dies, her family is grief-stricken, and the Gargoyle runs away, unable to stand the guilt he feels. It actually takes Elisa several episodes to recover from her wounds. The program has been well received and proves that children's entertainment can be both profitable and responsible.

For the most part, however, cartoons continue to reflect an adult world that clings to the relics of Stallone and Schwarzenegger as powerful men because of physical prowess, extravagant displays of firepower, and a propensity to use violence and intimidation as ways to resolve conflict. Similarly, "good" women are all too often portrayed as long-suffering victims. Children's television programming unfortunately holds a mirror to our culture. If what we see is an emphasis on power for settling conflict and an admission of how deficient we are in experiencing authentic emotions, then perhaps this is because children's television, created by adults, reflects our own compromised view of the world. Until our adult world chooses to acknowledge that both men and women can be powerful in ways that genuinely serve each other and society, we should not be surprised that children's cartoons simply reflect a balder version of this reality.

PSYCHOLOGICAL DEVELOPMENT AND THE MEDIA

ATTACHMENT

Preschool-age children are connected to their families by a very short tether. They are in a period of accelerated physical, social, and emotional development. Optimal development occurs when children's caretakers are loving, available, and firm. According to 1994 Department of Labor Statistics, over 60 percent of mothers with preschool children are working. This means that the majority of preschoolers are in day care or nursery school for part or most of every workday. While family is unquestionably the most important influence on preschoolers' lives, the outside world has begun to beckon. With their rapidly expanding cognitive and social skills, children at this age crave and benefit from new experiences.

One of the major responsibilities of parenting during this time is to encourage children's independence while protecting them from danger: "Yes, you can walk to the store with your sister, but you have to hold her hand when you cross the street." "You can ride your bike in the park, but not on the street." "I will let you go to some movies, but not *Batman*. It's just too scary for little kids." Many times every day, parents make major and minor decisions about what their youngsters can handle and what is beyond their capabilities. Because parents "dose" the world for them, children are able to have experiences that expand their world but don't overwhelm them. As will be repeated many times in this book, children who feel good about their ability to influence and manage the world and who feel secure about parental availability are likely to have high self-esteem and to be free of excessive worry.[11]

Preschool children love playacting. Mommy, daddy, teacher, doctor, police officer, and firefighter are all roles that children relish. Providing youngsters with some of the props for these roles adds mightily to their enthusiasm. Every parent has seen their child—whether boy or girl—toddling around in mom's high heels, pocketbook rakishly thrown over the shoulder, and lipstick smeared somewhere in the vicinity of the child's mouth. For most children of this age, mom is the center of the universe, and they are only too happy to grab some of her power and try it on for themselves. While their appearance suggests imitation, the dialogue of preschoolers shows that they are also engaging in a more complex process. Children at this age have begun to identify with their parents.

Psychologists understand a great deal about the process of identification, which, along with imitation, is characteristic of this stage of development. At earlier stages of development, children only imitated. Research has shown that infants as young as two to three weeks can imitate facial expressions.[12] By fourteen months of age, children can show delayed imitation of television characters.[13] But imitation is different from identification. Identification takes place at a later age and demands more of youngsters. To identify, children have to have some ability to understand the internal world of the person they are identifying with. So in addition to putting on daddy's tie and carrying his briefcase, preschool-age children will act out some of dad's attitudes. "Young man, I told you that you would be punished if you threw rocks again. Go to your room immediately," says the four-year-old to his baby brother, summoning up dad's authority and attitudes as well as his physical movements. The next time that this same four-year-old is tempted to throw rocks himself, he will summon up dad's attitude and this will help him stop himself. This child is identifying with his father, not simply imitating him.

Imitation and identification help children appropriate adult power. It is clear to the preschool-age child where the power in the house resides. Her parents no longer rush to her side at her slightest protest, and temper tantrums are generally ineffective (at least they should be) in having needs met. Toddlers' insistent "Me do it" is replaced by preschoolers' recognition that much of what gets done depends on the willingness of adults to help. At the same time, it becomes painfully clear to preschoolers that they really are not able to navigate the world alone. This is a most unsettling piece of reality. For the last year or two they have been wild with excitement at the discovery of their own will, their own beginning ability to regulate themselves. They can pour a drink, go to the toilet, and dress themselves, all unaided. They are absolutely loath to give up their newly discovered and intoxicating autonomy.

The realization that parents really run the show and call the shots sets up an interesting dilemma for preschoolers. Either they can capitulate and become babyish again, allowing their parents to take over their hard-won advances, or they can identify with their parents and incorporate parental attributes into themselves. Children invariably choose the latter solution. Instead of relinquishing their tender new "self," children enhance this self by taking on characteristics of their parents and other powerful adults in their world. Hence the constant parade of police uniforms, firefighter's gear, and superhero costumes as well as the beloved accouterments of parenthood: shoes, pocketbooks, tool belts, telephones, and briefcases.

Conflict with parents is lessened once children begin this process of identification. Four-year-olds tend to have much less conflict with their parents than notorious "terrible" two-year-olds, because four-year-olds have begun to see themselves as being like their parents. Self-control is supported because children have begun to internalize parental standards and can begin using these standards as guides to behavior. We even see the beginning of guilt as children find that their actual behavior frequently does not measure up to their newly internalized parental standards. "You go to your room right now. And don't come out until you can listen," admonishes a four-year-old girl speaking to her doll. This young girl is practicing the powerful parental role—the role that decides what is acceptable, what is not, and what the consequences of behavior are. One day this little girl is likely to send her own little girl to her room with the same admonishment, and she has begun practicing for this day years in advance. In the meantime, her admonishments to her doll remind her of her parents' rules and the kinds of behavior they expect.

AGGRESSION

There is a large body of research focusing on the effects of media violence on preschool-age children. Almost without exception this research has found that viewing violence makes children more aggressive, more restless, more fearful, and less creative. In addition, the kind of rapid pacing typically used in violent programming can limit a child's capacity for self-restraint and tolerance of the normal delays of life. No study has ever found any benefit to young children from watching violence.

Albert Bandura found that children learn to be aggressive by observing and imitating other people who are acting aggressively. If these individuals, or models, as Bandura calls them, are rewarded for their violent behavior, children are even more likely to imitate them.[14] Children learn violent behavior by observing others directly in real life and, vicariously, through the media.

Over the more than thirty years since Bandura's pioneering studies, much research as well as the observations of almost any parent supports the idea that children are learning attitudes and behaviors from the many hours they spend in front of the television. More recent work by Bandura suggests that not only are children imitating aggressive behavior, but they are also becoming more tolerant of aggression as well. Children learn how to behave from the people around them. Both science and common sense tell us that children who spend their hours immersed in a fantasy world of simple violent solutions to complex human problems are being badly schooled.

One of the most significant accomplishments of childhood is the increasing ability to delay frustration. Counting to ten, taking a walk around the block—these are strategies that adults have learned to help them control anger and not get caught up in the heat of the moment. Young children do not have this capacity and frequently find themselves grabbing another child's toy or striking out when they are angry. A study by psychologists Friedrich and Stein found that one of the most significant features of preschool children who are exposed to aggressive cartoons is a decline in their ability to tolerate delay.[15] Children with a low frustration tolerance are apt to rely on aggression as a solution to frustration. This is a poor solution, and children who continue this kind of impulsive behavior are likely to be penalized at home, in school, and by peers.

Jerome and Dorothy Singer, a husband and wife team of psychologists from Yale University, have conducted many years of research on the effects of media violence on preschool-age children. In one of their most important studies, the Singers observed aggression in a group of children beginning at age four and followed these same children through age nine.[16] Some people have argued that television doesn't make children more aggressive; aggressive children just happen to prefer more violent television programming. Studies such as the Singers' control for initial levels of aggression and see whether this is the factor that is responsible for aggressive behavior many years later. In fact, the Singers found that even when they controlled for initial levels of aggression, "later aggression in these children is strongly predicted by a combination of heavier viewing of violent TV shows, heavy preschool TV viewing and a family that emphasizes physical discipline and the assertion of power."[17] *Children who are not particularly aggressive to begin with become more aggressive as a result of their exposure to television violence.*

The Singers' research began with preschool children, an age group that is often dismissed with the mistaken assumption that "they really don't understand what they're watching." While children at this age have varying degrees of comprehension, studies such as those described here should convince us that they are being heavily influenced by what they watch. While some of the media's effects on preschool-age children are readily apparent, others may take many years to manifest themselves. We have good reason to be concerned about short-term effects—preschoolers who are heavy viewers have higher levels of aggressiveness, distractibility, and restlessness—and even more compelling reasons to be concerned about the long-term effects. The four-year-old child who is restless and aggressive after a couple of hours of Saturday morning cartoons may turn out to be the adolescent who has trouble paying attention in class and difficulty getting along with parents and peers.

Both parents and researchers tend to focus on behavior, which is, after all, easily identifiable and measurable. Children who attempt to jump over a barricade with a tricycle or who punch a younger sibling in imitation of some action hero demand our attention. Parents who see these kinds of behaviors in their children tend to take some action, at least in part because they fear for their children's safety or the family's harmony. There are, however, other aspects of media influence that I believe are just as significant, although less readily apparent. These have to do with how the media affects the attitudes of children. This topic tends to get more attention where older children are concerned. For instance, the media's influence on adolescent drinking, cigarette smoking, and sexual behavior is well recognized. But children of three, four, and five are actively developing opinions, attitudes, and values, and the media play a significant and frequently overlooked role in this area.

A number of experiments have looked at the ways in which the media can alter the attitudes of young children. Many television programs aimed at young children, superhero cartoons in particular, display aggression as a means of gaining both power and rewards. Does exposure to this attitude on television alter the way children feel about aggression? After all, it seems likely that in many households, young children are being encouraged to "get along" rather than to impose their will on others. "Don't hit," mothers are forever telling their youngsters. "Learn to share"; "You have to take turns." Most parents are not telling their preschoolers to "nuke 'em" in order to get their way.

In a clever study designed to look at whether rewarding aggression would change preschoolers' attitude toward it, youngsters were shown manipulated film sequences involving two boys named Rocky and Johnny.[18] In one version, Rocky successfully takes Johnny's toys away and is rewarded with stickers and juice. In the other version, Rocky tries to take Johnny's toys, but Johnny successfully defends his toys and beats up Rocky. Sixty percent of preschoolers who saw Rocky rewarded for his aggression expressed the desire to be like him. However, only 20 percent of preschoolers who saw Rocky punished for his aggression wanted to emulate him. *Aggression was unacceptable to these preschoolers only if the aggression was punished.* Successful, rewarded aggression, even though it was unfair, was seen as desirable.

Children's aggression needs to be acknowledged. Their emotional life is frequently in turmoil, and they are often at the mercy of intense feelings that they are incapable of understanding. The ways of the world are still far beyond their grasp. Young children rely on their parents' explanations and illustrations of what kinds of behavior are acceptable and valuable. The kinds of dilemmas that young children face daily—a sibling taking their favorite toy or a friend refusing to share a cookie—are appropriate arenas for exploring ways to resolve conflict. Shows such as *Sesame Street* and *Mister Rogers' Neighborhood* frequently deal with aggression on this level. But, media featuring violence that is excessive, gratuitous, and graphic have no place in the lives of young children.

COGNITIVE DEVELOPMENT

A mother and her three-year-old son walk briskly into their local movie theater for an afternoon showing of *Snow White*. They settle into their seats just as the lights go down. The mother can feel her young son's body stiffen in the darkness. A menacing, hooded figure with long, blood-red fingernails appears on the screen and cackles at her reflection in the mirror. The little boy closes his eyes in fear and, as the sinister music builds, lets out a terrified scream. The manager hurries over and offers a prompt refund to the embarrassed mother and sobbing child.

That mother is me, and the child is my youngest son. I use this example to show that parents and even professionals, in spite of education, experience, and the best of intentions, will occasionally make mistakes about what their children can handle. Sometimes these mistakes are the fault of the industry that has irresponsibly advertised a movie or program to appeal to children. *The Gun in Betty Lou's Handbag*, which was billed as a comedy and seen by many young children, contained violent and frightening scenes inappropriate for young children. But sometimes these mistakes are squarely the parents'. We want to see a movie that our children have been pestering us to see, so we take them along figuring, "Just this once, it can't be very harmful." *Batman*'s PG-13 rating should have alerted parents to the fact that it would not be suitable for preschoolers, but many preschoolers saw it and were very frightened by it.

Most of the mistakes that we make when we allow children to watch TV shows or movies that are upsetting to them are the result of our not appreciating children's ways of thinking. Let's take the opening example of *Snow White* and my three-year-old son to gain some understanding of preschoolers' thinking.

Depending on their individual temperament, young children have very different ways of approaching new situations. Studies on temperament identify three different groups of children: easy, slow-to-warm-up, and difficult.[19] Basically, children in the middle group take a bit longer to adapt to new situations. They need a little extra time to feel comfortable in a new environment. My third son, who is rather quiet, would fall somewhere between slow-to-warm-up and easy. He would have benefited from not being rushed into the theater and from having some extra time to think about where he was. More time would also have given me a greater opportunity to explain what would happen. "Lots of people will come into this room. You probably won't know any of them. But they all live around here and are bringing their children to the movies just like I'm bringing you." Many adults have a hard time walking into a room filled with people they don't know. For those youngsters who don't relish novel situations, a theater full of a hundred or so complete strangers is quite a challenge.

Disney makes many wonderful movies that children enjoy, cherish, and watch over and over again. So why did my three-year-old fall apart? The answer lies in the "appearance-reality distinction," discussed earlier in this chapter. This body of research looks at children at different ages and evaluates whether they can distinguish between what really is and what is deceptive in its appearance. Interestingly, a number of researchers have attempted to teach three-year-olds to make a distinction between what something appears to be and what it actually is. Children in these studies received training on the meaning of real versus apparent. For instance, the researcher would take a Charlie Brown puppet and then put the puppet inside a ghost costume saying, "Charlie Brown looks like a ghost to your eyes right now, but it is really and truly Charlie Brown."[20] Children were corrected repeatedly when they made mistakes. In spite of extensive explanations and training, and much to the surprise of the investigators, three-year-olds continued to do poorly on these tasks. While it is not entirely clear why three-year-old children cannot distinguish reality from appearance, the critical point is that they cannot. Therefore, no amount of reassurance—"It's just a movie, honey. It's not real"—is likely to convince a three-year-old that what he sees isn't real. My son's terror was justified. "What you see is what you get" for the preschooler.

Three-year-olds have a very tenuous hold on reality, one that is subject to enormous distortion and disruption. While their verbal skills are exploding, we must remember that their psychological and cognitive abilities are still very limited. By the age of six, children can easily manage simple appearance-reality tasks, but it is not until several years later that children are fluent in their ability to make this distinction. Disney makes many remarkable movies, and parents are often eager to expose their children to experiences that they found delightful in their own childhood. But three-year-olds need to be protected from even the most outlandishly unrealistic portrayals of "bad people." The wonderful world of Disney can wait until your children are four or five. At that time they can enjoy and marvel at it because they have begun to understand that not everything they see is real.

Another area in which cognitive development is taking place is in preschoolers' play. Play is serious business for children. It is here that they learn about the world, about fairness and justice, about getting along with other children, and about how to take someone else's point of view. It is in play that children cultivate inner resources of imagination, creativity, and self-reliance. Imaginative play encourages mental reflection; and mental reflection encourages the development of a personality that is empathic and self-aware.

Some research suggests that imaginative children and adults are less likely to engage in impulsive acts or in acts of gross aggression.[21] In one of the few studies of its kind, Singer and Singer studied a group of children age three to eight and tried to establish which variables inhibited or encouraged imagination in children.[22] They identified four factors as predicting imagination in children:

1. Organized daily routine
2. Less viewing of television in the preschool years
3. Limited recent viewing of realistic action television shows and less general emphasis on television in the home
4. Extent to which the mother values imaginativeness

These findings highlight the fact that television inhibits the development of imagination in young children. Play and fantasy provide children with the skills for diverting themselves from angry feelings. Play encourages children to actively master their environment. By miniaturizing the large-scale world (toy airplanes, cars, trucks, farms, people, houses, and so on), children "cut the world down to size"—a size they feel capable of handling.

Since television provides formulaic solutions for children, it inhibits their creativity. When children imitate *Teenage Mutant Ninja Turtles*, it is always with a display of karate kicks and chops. No child imitates *He-Man* without declaring, "I have the power." The point is that it is healthier for a child to try out "I've lost the power," "I don't want the power," or "I'll share the power" in addition to "I have the power." Too much television, particularly with predictable plot and resolution, robs children of the opportunity to develop different perspectives and alternative solutions.

Preschool children are in Piaget's stage of preoperational thinking. Their thinking is "black and white" and completely egocentric. The three-year-old will clap her hands over her eyes and dare you to find her. From her point of view, which is the only point of view at this stage, you can't see her because she can't see you. One of my young patients used to plug her fingers in her ears and in a louder and louder voice demand to know if I could hear her. To her, her plugged ears meant that my hearing must have been impaired as well. Children at this age have little ability to adopt a point of view other than their own.

Because their thinking is totally egocentric, preschoolers cannot distance themselves from what they watch. In the movie *Labyrinth*, an older sister, frustrated at being asked to babysit for the evening, implores goblins to take away her baby brother. They do, and she spends the rest of the movie trying to undo her wish. This movie fascinated many older children who could still remember the strength of their own wishes to get rid of a sibling but were cognitively mature enough to know that "wishing doesn't make it so." However, in my practice I saw several young children who expressed concern about this movie, fearing that angry wishes they had made toward a younger sibling might come true. For the preschooler, wishing can most certainly make it so.

Programs such as *Mister Rogers* that continually emphasize the difference between reality and fantasy ("Let's go to the neighborhood of make-believe") help children become increasingly competent at making this distinction. Like a good parent, Mr. Rogers mediates the television experience for young children, answering questions when they are likely to arise, engaging the child in a dialogue, and often restructuring new experiences and information into forms that are easily understood by children. He talks slowly, reflects on what is going on, and speaks to his young audience

directly. His kindliness is appreciated by children because he never
assumes that they know more than they do.

Fred Rogers's slow pace helps children think about what they
are learning. It is one of the few programs that has ever filled air
space with silence. After hearing a moving performance of cellist
Yo-Yo Ma, Rogers invites his young viewers to be quiet and appreciate the beauty of what they have heard. This is education at its
best—encouraging reflection and imagination, the cornerstones of
intellectual development. Children do not have to be hit over the
head to learn. On the contrary, they learn best when they are given
the opportunity to slowly incorporate new material in a setting that
respects their limitations and supports their self-esteem.

In addition to being extremely egocentric, preschoolers are
also very literal in their thinking. To a preschooler a rose is a flower,
period. It is not a symbol of love, it is not a symbol of beauty, in fact
it is not a symbol of anything. Symbols are far too abstract for
children of this age. The preschooler simply does not have enough
experience to know that sometimes things stand for ideas or concepts. Abstract concepts such as justice, duty, and fairness are quite
beyond the mental capacity of young children.

Another characteristic of preschoolers is their inability to think
in reverse. This is important because it means that the young child
does not understand that the man led off in handcuffs at the end of
a program is the same man who committed murder at the beginning of the program. As every parent knows, consequences for
children's misbehavior need to be swift and relevant: "If you throw
the candy again, I will take it away from you right now."

These examples of limitations in preschool-age children's
thinking should be kept in mind when making decisions about their
viewing fare. *Mister Rogers, Barney,* and *Sesame Street* are all excellent choices for this age group. Videotapes are often a good alternative to the more commercial television fare. Both PBS and Nickelodeon do a wonderful job of programming for young children.
Media offerings for children this age need to be kept simple, direct,
and gentle.

MORAL DEVELOPMENT

The night before I began writing this section, I found my three-
year-old playing with a Lego figure and motorcycle I had never

seen before. "Where'd you get this from, Jeremy?" I asked. "School," he answered warily, anticipating my response. "Well, if you got it at school, we'll have to bring it back there tomorrow because it doesn't belong to you." "I got it at school, but now it's mine because I took it" was his succinct response. And there of course was my opening. For the young preschooler, possession is not nine-tenths of the law, it's 100 percent.

"Fairness" at this age is identical with getting one's way. The high point of Sara's five-year-old birthday party was a colorful piñata her parents had strung up on the patio. Tired of waiting her turn on line, Sara muscled up to the front declaring, "I'm the birthday girl and it's unfair to make me wait." One of her young friends responded by pushing Sara aside and stepping into her place, saying, "No, I'm the guest. Everyone knows it's unfair to make the guest wait." Soon there was a melee of five-year-old girls, each asserting that she was being treated unfairly. Sara's parents needed to step in, restore order, and clarify that although each girl wished she could be first, this was not the same as being treated unfairly.

It is not that young children are "selfish" in any negative way; they are simply incapable of complex moral thinking, just as they are incapable of complex intellectual thinking. Youngsters at this age cannot really hold two pieces of information at the same time. Piaget called this "centration," the child's tendency to attend to only one aspect of a situation. As we saw in the beginning of this chapter, young children will believe that a short, wide glass holds less water than a tall, thin one even though they've just seen the water poured from the tall, thin glass into the short, wide one. In this example, children are able to attend to only the most prominent feature of the situation, the height of the glasses. They are unable to use other relevant information to understand the problem. Similarly, when faced with a moral dilemma like "You can't take that truck out of the store because we didn't pay for it," young children attend to the most prominent feature of the situation, their desire. In the pursuit of having their desires met, children of this age are quite willing to "lie, cheat, and steal." I have put these rather objectionable words into quotation marks to highlight the fact that their meanings are really quite different when we are talking about children this young.

Children of three, for the most part, don't understand that

manipulations such as lying are wrong. From young children's point of view, such behavior is simply a way of getting the world to conform to their wishes. The three- or four-year-old can quite innocently say, "I should have lied" when confronted with breaking the rules. "Lying" is normal and common among preschoolers.

As children move away from the issues of autonomy and separation characteristic of the two- and three-year-old, they begin work on the developmental task of accommodation, of fitting in. Four- and five-year-olds are forming friendships, learning the rules of social interaction, and are less likely to be engaged in battles with their parents. They are beginning the process of standing in someone else's shoes. As a result, their thinking about moral issues is also beginning to change. Toward the end of this stage, most children appreciate the value of getting along and understand that imposing their will on others is often ineffective. In their newfound spirit of cooperation, four- and five-year-olds look around and see that without a doubt, it is adults who hold the power. This leads them to an interesting conclusion—adults are always right. Children at this age often exhibit unquestioning obedience. "My mother says" becomes an incantation, invoking the highest authority known to the young child.

Lest we be lulled into thinking that the recalcitrant child has suddenly come to his or her senses and acknowledged the wisdom of adult authority, remember that children come to this conclusion only because adults wield more power. Four- and five-year-olds try very hard to obey adults, but it is almost entirely out of fear of punishment rather than respect for the adult's point of view.

Given that a large part of the preschool years are devoted to acknowledging parental power, it seems reasonable to suggest that parents have a particular opportunity at this time to influence their child's moral development. Parents who are involved with their children, who set limits using reason rather than power to establish their authority, and who actively communicate a set of values tend to have children with higher levels of moral development. For instance, parents who watch television with their children can enhance many of the positive effects of viewing and reduce negative effects. Research has shown that watching television with a parent increases the information children learn from educational television and helps children to understand more of what they are seeing.[23]

First of all, parents need to be willing to participate in and regulate their youngsters' television time and movie choices. The American Academy of Pediatrics recommends that children this age spend no more than two hours a day watching television. As this chapter should have made clear, children have very important social skills to develop at this time, and imaginative play is the arena where this is best accomplished. Too much television time cuts into the opportunity to play and tends to make children less imaginative, more restless, and more passive. Parents should also set up alternative activities for their youngsters. This doesn't mean that parents must be forever doing something interesting and creative with their children; few parents have the time or energy for this kind of attention. Besides, as we have seen, one of the major developmental tasks of this stage is to begin forming relationships outside of the family. Peer play as well as solitary play are both of great importance for the preschool child.

Parents also need to help their children become media literate. They need to explain that television is not "real" and that many of the solutions proposed by the media, particularly violent solutions, are unacceptable and are unworkable in real life. For example, you can explain that if one of the Power Rangers really did "nuke" his opponent, he would be placing many people in jeopardy and would be severely punished for his criminal activity. While some of this may not be clear to the three-year-old, by five or six the child is likely to understand what the parent means. It is the accumulation of these types of parental messages that impart a sense of values to children.

Many studies have shown that television can foster prosocial behavior. This effect is substantially enhanced when parents and schools provide support in the form of discussion and role playing.[24] In one study children were shown prepared videos of generous behavior and then given an opportunity to be generous to others. The exposure to the filmed example of generosity increased the children's real-life generosity.[25] *Barney and Friends* has been shown to improve children's manners as well as their vocabulary.[26] *Mister Rogers' Neighborhood* has been used in many studies and has been shown to enhance a wide range of prosocial behaviors as well as encouraging curiosity, happiness, and playfulness in young children.[27]

Most parents do not need a battery of social scientists to tell them that watching people behave well, whether in real life or in the media, helps children internalize more wholesome role models than watching people behave violently and impulsively. The fact is that television does exert a significant effect on the young child's developing mind and conscience. Parents can exercise economic clout by boycotting the advertisers of offensive programming and pushing for media literacy programs in the schools. Finally, the implementation of a true children's network, publicly funded, would go a long way toward proving that we value our children and recognize the power of the media in their lives. Such a network could be geared to the development of children at different ages and would be capable of placing responsibility before profit.

9

Middle Childhood: Ages 6, 7, and 8

GENERAL DEVELOPMENT

Children in middle childhood are having a love affair with the world. Life for children of six, seven, and eight is a challenging, exciting adventure. Transformed children who just a year or two ago depended on their mother to meet almost all of their needs now exhort and demand, "Mom, let me do it myself!"

Unlike preschoolers, middle-age children do not live solely in the "here and now," and as a result they are interested in past, present, and future. Their horizons are expanding with dazzling speed and they are enchanted by their families, their neighborhoods, their schools, other children, other countries, and outer space. The world has become their oyster.

Remarkably, Freud labeled this period of development "latency," believing that children were quietly consolidating their skills before the onslaught of adolescent sexual awakening. Unfortunately, this view of middle childhood as a period of psychological torpor has, until recently, made the social and emotional development of this period one of the least-studied topics in all of child psychology. It is true that the whirlwind pace of change that characterized infancy and the preschool years abates, physical growth slows to a few inches a year, and cognitive and social advances are perhaps less dramatic. However, middle childhood is in no way a quiet period of development. An increased interest in research in this area has begun to show us that these years are rich in changes: cognitive, moral, social, and emotional.

The family remains a major institution of socialization, although school and the peer group are becoming increasingly important. The middle-age child has three important tasks to accomplish during this developmental stage:

1. Consolidating a sense of self
2. Developing friendships
3. Academic achievement

CONSOLIDATING A SENSE OF SELF

Preschool children are apt to describe themselves as being "tall" or "skinny" or "a fast runner" or any of a number of physical characteristics. Preschoolers think of the "self" as a concrete entity and so describe their self largely in physical and tangible terms.

Middle-age children, in contrast, are beginning the process of developing a sense of self that is psychological and enduring. By the time children are eight or so, while a self-description will certainly include physical characteristics, it also includes such psychological attributes as "I'm a good person," "I'm smart," or "I like to take care of people." These more complex descriptions mirror the cognitive shift taking place at this age: the ability to think logically as well as the capacity to see things from another perspective. As always, cognitive, moral, social, and emotional development are intertwined.

While this ability to think psychologically represents a huge leap forward in sophistication, it is just the beginning of a process that will become increasingly refined throughout later childhood and adolescence. Far more sophisticated than they were just a year or two before, children of six, seven, or eight still tend to take people pretty much at face value. One mother tells the following story:

My daughter Terri and her best friend, Allison, are seven. Allison's goldfish died. My daughter asked her friend if she would like another goldfish for her birthday which was coming up in two weeks. Lip trembling, Allison said "no." Later that evening when we sat around the dinner table, my husband suggested it would be a good idea for Allison's parents to get her another fish. My daughter disagreed emphatically saying, "Allison said she didn't want another one." My older daughter Elizabeth, who is twelve, said it was a good idea to get another goldfish because "Allison's sad now, but she'll get over it."

Terri was baffled when several days later she found Allison happily talking to her new goldfish.

At age seven, Terri takes her friend at her word and does not really consider extenuating factors. She does not have enough experience with people to know that what people say is governed by a number of factors, in this case sadness and loss. It is not until about age nine that youngsters understand that motives may not be apparent and that what people say cannot always be taken literally.

Middle-age children are able to think of themselves as possessing permanent psychological characteristics. One of the most important of these characteristics is gender identity—the understanding that one is either male or female. Girls who used to play "doctor" with other girls and boys are certain they will get "boy cooties" if they so much as touch a boy. Children this age believe that it is "wrong" to behave in ways associated with the opposite sex. Play tends to be almost exclusively same-sex with very rigid rules about the circumstances under which cross-gender contact is permissible. Only about 6 percent of play during middle childhood crosses gender lines.[1]

Unfortunately, research shows that parents still have very different attitudes and expectations for their sons and daughters. Studies show that girls are given less freedom, are less likely to be encouraged to be independent, and are expected to be more nurturing and less ambitious than boys their age.[2] As we will see in the section on school achievement, lower expectations for girls have a profound influence on academic accomplishment as well as on self-esteem.

FORMING CLOSE RELATIONSHIPS WITH PEERS

Once a child enters school, the number of hours spent with peers increases dramatically. While the family, most particularly the mother, was the dominant influence on the infant and young child, now school and peers compete with the family for influence on the middle-age child.

The relationship between grown-ups and children is always

unequal in terms of power. When all else fails, parents can, and frequently do, fall back on their ultimate authority: "Because I said so, and I'm the parent." Relationships between children of approximately the same age are less about authority and more about equality; as a result, they offer children unparalleled opportunities to learn new skills and new rules of social interaction. No longer do children feel coerced into submitting to the will of those older and bigger; they are now able to negotiate to have their needs met with other children who share a similar level of status and power. "I'll play video games now if you'll skip rope with me later." Learning how to regulate aggression, how to treat people fairly, and how to offer support and loyalty are some of the skills that are advanced by friendships during middle childhood. "Being a good friend" is the theme of many television shows aimed at children, and in this area, the media have done a good job of supporting healthy attitudes and behaviors.

Beginning friendships as well as the structure of school offer children the opportunity to define themselves not only as individuals but also as part of a group. Preschoolers have very little sense of a collective identity and at best may see things as "us" versus "them." School begins to reinforce a sense of group identity revolving around shared interests, abilities, and attitudes. Children are divided into reading and math groups based on differing levels of ability and divide themselves into groups based on interest and ability such as athletics or popularity.

Children of six, seven, and eight are beginning to have the cognitive as well as the social skills to understand the nature of the group, that the group has norms and rules that are to be followed in order to maintain the privilege of membership. "No girls allowed" means exactly that, and woe to the young boy who allows a girl into the clubhouse. He is likely to be expelled, at least temporarily, from the fellowship of his young male friends.

ACADEMIC ACHIEVEMENT

From the moment the six-year-old crosses the threshold into his or her first-grade classroom, life is irrevocably changed. The child is now a full-time student. No longer is it enough to play and to keep out of trouble. New rules, new expectations, and new tasks challenge the youngster at every turn. Even the smallest details of life may be prescribed in new and often unfamiliar ways, such as where to sit, when to sit, and even how to sit. For at least the next twelve years, six hours a day, five days a week, most children will be focused on the task of learning both a body of knowledge and the rules of social interaction. It is a breathtaking task that children face, and how well they succeed at this stage has implications for the rest of their lives.

The school is a powerful agent of socialization and demands exactly those behaviors that are required of people in the work world. In the classroom, children are expected to be punctual, respectful, and organized. They are also expected to be competitive and to value achievement. They are required to follow rules, obey authority, and subordinate individual needs to the needs of the group. The school has the authority both to reward and to punish children for their compliance or noncompliance with these expectations. Obviously these requirements are in line with children's developmental capabilities. While a sixth-grade student is expected to complete and bring in homework daily, a first grader might be expected only to leave his or her pencil in the same place every day. In both cases, however, the child is being schooled in the kind of organizational skills that will eventually be called "good work habits" and that will help ensure success as he or she tackles more complex and demanding tasks, first at school and eventually in the workplace.

Because school occupies such a large role in the life of middle-age children, both academic achievement and popularity become major contributors to children's self-esteem. So it is most disturbing to have research conclude that intellectual accomplishment is differentially encouraged for boys and girls, with girls being subtly discouraged.[3] The classroom is a powerful transmitter of mainstream cultural values and norms. It would appear that girls are disadvantaged both at school and in their homes by prevailing social notions that still suggest that high achievement is not as valuable for girls as it is for boys.

MEDIA AND THE MIDDLE-AGE CHILD

The media tends to portray the middle-age child of six, seven, and eight as being precocious, spirited, inventive, and often "naughty." Most of the successful movies aimed at this age group focus on the youngsters' beginning awkward moves out of the family and the trouble that ensues as a result. Movies such as *Huck Finn*, *Peter Pan*, and *The Secret Garden* document the child's sense of both trepidation and exhilaration as they begin the journey (often literally) that will eventually lead them out of the family and into lives of their own.

Perhaps the most popular of all characters this age is Kevin, played by Macaulay Culkin in *Home Alone* and *Home Alone 2: Lost in New York*. Released by Fox in 1990 and 1992, respectively, these two movies occupy the position of ninth and nineteenth most profitable movies of all time, as of this writing. Box office gross receipts exceeded $454 million and video rentals exceeded $243 million for the two movies.[4] In both films, eight-year-old Kevin, who is tormented by his cousins and misunderstood by his overtaxed parents, is mistakenly forgotten by his family when they go on vacation. After briefly luxuriating in the fact that he is free to do as he pleases, Kevin embarks on a series of misadventures, outwitting two bumbling criminals with a combination of imagination and cunning.

The movies are both violent and disrespectful toward adults, who are portrayed as either inattentive or foolish or both. Aside from the obvious neglect of his parents, there are few adults who are capable of offering any protection to the abandoned Kevin. In fact, *Home Alone* opens with a crook posing as a police officer in order to case Kevin's house. This movie clearly says, "Don't put your money on the adults." It was enormously successful because it played to all youngsters' fantasies that they are brighter, more sophisticated, and craftier than the grown-ups who loom over them. It takes a lot of courage for small people to begin tackling the world, and their insecurity is often made bearable by a healthy dose of bravado.

Nowhere is the use of bravado more clearly seen than in this age's fascination with superheroes. Superheroes allow children to "borrow" a sense of power and mastery as well as reassure them that good triumphs against evil. Superheroes reinforce the level of moral development of middle-age children with an emphasis on being good for its own sake. While children struggle with the realization that their parents are not perfect, the superhero acts as a surrogate flawless parent.

Superheroes, like fairy tales at an earlier age and horror movies in adolescence, serve important psychological functions for the growing child. Because they reflect the psychological realities of child development, all these genres are enormously successful. In one form or another, popular stories for children, whether it's *The Three Little Pigs* or *Teenage Mutant Ninja Turtles*, tell a version of the same story. Children identify with the initial anxiety-producing situation and then find that resourcefulness and courage lead to eventual victory. Facing one bogeyman or another is a part of daily life for children and it is no small wonder that they are eager to hear over and over again that it turns out okay in the end.

Unfortunately, today's superheroes increasingly depend on violence and intimidation for their authority, rather than courage and intelligence. Unlike the early superheroes—Superman, Green Lantern, Spiderman—who battled criminals primarily with their wits and only occasionally with their hands, today's superheroes are equipped with an armamentarium worthy of the Department of Defense. "It seems that kids look at karate chops and kicks as just another way of interacting," says a seasoned first-grade teacher. "If you tell them that such behavior is not okay on the playground, they just give you this kind of puzzled look and say, 'But the Turtles do it.' " Physical dominance as portrayed by the current crop of superheroes is a whole lot of fun. Here we see the seeds of violence as a form of humor, which will find full expression many years later as older children, adolescents, and adults laugh at carnage made playful in movies like *Terminator, Beverly Hills Cop,* and *Demolition Man.*

It is not until children reach the end of this stage or the beginning of the next that they are capable of understanding that the medium of television is largely a fabrication, that it is the workings of people's imaginations. Children at this stage are still prone to imitation. Many years ago, emergency room doctors coined the phrase "Evel Knievel Syndrome" to describe children's injuries as they rode their bikes off rooftops and over cars.[5] Although the networks say they will not show things that children might imitate with disastrous results, this is simply not true. On a recent episode of *X-Men,* one of the characters stood on a railroad track, jumping aside at the last moment to avoid being killed. It is this neglect of even the most basic responsibility toward children that indicts the industry. For most of this stage, children are often unable to make accurate judgments about the reality of the programs they watch. Children cannot distinguish a toy gun from a real one until age eight or nine. Hundreds of children have been accidentally killed because they failed to recognize the lethality of a real gun.

Children are more likely to be disturbed by violence on television when the violence appears realistic, and the child identifies with either the victim or the aggressor. In one study, children were exposed to dramatized events involving either a fatal house fire or a drowning, taken from popular television programs or movies.[6] As expected, children viewing these scenes became more fearful than children viewing neutral scenes involving water and fire. More important, children who watched the frightening scenes overestimated the likelihood of such events, and their fear generalized to other related activities. "Specifically," the study noted, ". . . children who had just seen a television drama about a fatal house fire were averse to building a fire in a fireplace."[7] While children certainly need to be warned of dangers that pose a threat to their well-being, the continual exposure of young children to disturbing images does not increase their competency. On the contrary, it traumatizes them and ultimately makes them less capable.

Finally, it is important to note the differential treatment that girls and boys of this age receive in the media. In keeping with cultural stereotypes, boys are typically adventuresome, fearless, and bold. Girls tend to be quiet, compliant, and fearful. Television programs on PBS work hard at dispelling stereotypes and tend to show girls more realistically. In addition, many PBS programs do an admirable job of portraying cultural, physical, and ethnic diversity. Women, African Americans, Hispanics, Native Americans, and physically and intellectually challenged individuals are portrayed regularly and realistically. Shows like this do indeed provide children of this age with a "window on the world."

At its best, television offers children the opportunity to embark on a social and cultural journey that reaches far beyond their family and neighborhood. It has the potential to educate, to stimulate, and to encourage prosocial behavior as well as an appreciation for diversity. Hate crimes in America are on the increase. *Sesame Street*'s emphasis on black, white, and Hispanic children sharing their crayons may one day make it easier for them to share other resources.

In marked distinction to PBS, the commercial television networks are negligent in their portrayal of women and minorities. Research done in 1992 showed that CBS on its regular Saturday morning lineup, directed primarily at young children, did not include a single minority character in any regular role.[8] The researchers concluded, "If you want to see racial diversity on Saturday morning television, watch the commercials and skip the programs." Advertisers appear to have more sensitivity than programmers, undoubtedly because of greater marketing awareness. As any parent knows, kids in this age group have a significant say at the grocery store checkout counter about which brand of cereal, bubble gum, and beverage to buy.

PSYCHOLOGICAL DEVELOPMENT AND THE ROLE OF THE MEDIA

ATTACHMENT

> It's Saturday morning and seven-year-old Nicholas wants to play with his best friend, Tommy, who lives next door. As he walks out of the house, his mom reminds him that he forgot to make his bed and put away his pajamas. "How are you going to get your room straightened up and still see your friend?" asks Mom. "No sweat," says Nicholas. "I'll play with Tommy first, and I'll clean up later." "No way," says Mom. "I'm tired of looking at your messy room. Clean up first and then you can go out to play."
>
> "You're always bossing me around," grumbles Nicholas who nevertheless runs to his room, throws the quilt over his bed, and straightens his shelves. He then races out the door to play. Over his shoulder, in the general direction of his mother, he yells, "Meanie!"

This example illustrates a major shift in attachment that takes place during middle childhood. No longer is mom setting all the rules and Nicholas simply accepting or resisting her directions. Nicholas and his mother are beginning to negotiate.

Children and their parents are now involved in mutual problem solving, or what psychologist Eleanor Maccoby calls "co-regulation."[9] This more mutual relationship is possible because middle-age children are becoming increasingly competent and capable of self-control. Children at this age are very concerned with fairness and are able to understand that their parents' requests are often reasonable, and even in their children's best interest. This is not a smooth or easily accomplished process, and as the example with Nicholas illustrates, it often involves a fair amount of resistance, complaining, and even the hurling of insults on the part of the child. "Gyp," "unfair," and even "liar" are common insults at this age. However, these beginning attempts at co-regulation are paving the way for what will eventually be true cooperation. At this stage children and their parents are constructing a relationship based not on biological necessity but on mutual needs and desires.

Children can now participate in their households in real and productive ways. While many of their newly acquired skills are clearly fragile, children this age can set the table, make their bed, and take out the trash. The gradual introduction of responsibility enhances the developing child's sense of accomplishment. The acquisition of skills, along with the child's natural drive toward independence, profoundly affects the nature of the attachment between child and parent.

At the beginning of this stage of development, around age six, children are straddling two worlds. Home and family, which have occupied center stage in young children's lives, must accommodate to the reality of school and children's increasing interest in peers. By the age of eight, most children have become comfortable sharing themselves physically and emotionally with both their family and the outside world. This is not to say that family influence does not remain strong through this period. The developmental influence of the family continues to exert tremendous power over middle-age children, as it will in later childhood and on into adolescence. However, children are also working very hard at constructing identities of their own. "I'm a girl scout," "I'm a baseball player," the middle-age child proclaims proudly. While family, particularly mother, has been the center of the child's world for children, they now strive to make themselves the center of their own universe.

This change in balance in the parent-child relationship calls upon parents to lessen their control and direction and begin monitoring and guiding instead. This can be a difficult transition for parents who are used to being quite directive or who are overwhelmed. Statements like "Because I said so" and "Because I'm the mom" may have had the virtue of expediency and clarifying authority with small children, but they are generally ineffective and inappropriate with middle-age children. Just as peer relations among children are increasingly concerned with issues of fairness and equality, the parent-child relationship must also reflect this more sophisticated level of interaction.

Research has found that parents who are warm and take a

reasoning approach to discipline produce children who feel good about themselves, who are cooperative and responsible, and who have few behavior problems.[10] In contrast, a lack of parental warmth coupled with a strong reliance on physical punishment and other power-assertive techniques such as shouting tends to produce children who are aggressive, noncompliant, and likely to project blame onto others.[11] In addition, the degree of control that parents exert in relation to the amount of autonomy they encourage has a definite effect on children. Domineering and restrictive parents are found to have children who are inhibited, shy, obedient, and overly dependent.[12] At the other extreme, parents who are extremely permissive tend to have children who are disobedient and irresponsible, but also expressive and sociable.[13]

An extraordinary example of how the media can help children cope with distressing circumstances is *E.T.: The Extra-Terrestrial*, Steven Spielberg's classic film of childhood loss and reconnection. Spielberg reaches into the hearts of children who are experiencing loss and reassures them that, while perhaps temporarily disrupted, their journey towards independence need not be derailed. Elliott is the middle of three children. His parents are in the midst of a divorce. Too young to be distracted by friends like his teenage brother Michael and too old to be oblivious like his young sister Gert, Elliott is sick at heart.

When E.T., a creature from outer space, is unwittingly abandoned by his people, he seeks out Elliott. Elliott tries to convince Michael of E.T.'s existence, but he is taunted and can only reply to his brother, "Dad would believe me." Dad, of course, is nowhere to be found in the movie, and all three children struggle with their individual experiences of anger and abandonment. Finally, as the three children come to know E.T., they begin to feel both needed (as opposed to powerless, as children feel in a divorce) and reconnected. In one of the most touching scenes in the movie, Elliott and Michael are scavenging in their attic for things to help E.T. construct a telephone. Elliott finds an old shirt of his father's and the two brothers, bound in a fraternity of longing and loss, debate whether their father's shirt smells of Old Spice or Sea Breeze.

Finally, the children are able to help E.T. return home, and they learn in the process that they can attenuate their losses through compassion and the ability to internalize the people they love. Because children are able to hold within themselves images and positive feelings about their parents, they feel safe enough to spend the day at school, among peers, and eventually out in the world. I have seen many children in my practice who, in attempting to come to terms with some loss, have put to good use E.T.'s injunction "I'll always be right here" as he touches Elliott's forehead before returning to his spaceship. As is undoubtedly clear from the amount of space I've devoted to describing this movie, I feel it is an extraordinary piece of work. More important, it illustrates that the media can encourage, understand, teach, and elevate children and still turn out commercially successful products. As this book goes to press, *E.T.* is the highest-grossing film of all time, bringing in more than $628 million in box office and rental receipts.[14]

Unfortunately, the media do not always reach middle-age children with such sensitivity. Many movies emphasize parental irresponsibility and incompetence. These movies detail ineffective parenting, and young children's resultant struggle to cope with a world that is beyond their capabilities. Here we tend to see children who have been forced to abandon their childhood and shoulder the burdens that rightfully belong to adults. Psychologists term children who are engaged in this reversal of role "parentified children." As was mentioned earlier, *Home Alone* gives a prime example of a child who makes a virtue out of his parents' inattention. But unlike Kevin, most children who are neglected and forced to grow up too soon do so at great cost to their personal development and self-esteem.

AGGRESSION

Children of six, seven, and eight are making significant strides in their ability to control aggression. The emerging ability to understand consequences helps children to predict that if they hit the kid next to them, they are likely to end up in the principal's office. The socializing forces of society—school, parents, and religion—combined with increased cognitive skills help the middle-age child develop new strategies for dealing with angry feelings. This is not to say that children in this age group do not, with some regularity, indulge their angry feelings with aggressive displays of hitting or name-calling; they certainly do. Rather, middle-age children are in a period of transition. They are beginning to understand the value of self-control both because it feels good and because it brings social approval.

Research confirms that middle childhood is a critical period during which children develop characteristic levels of aggression that tend to be maintained throughout life. The more aggressive child is likely to become the more aggressive adult.[15] Therefore, the questions surrounding media violence and its long- and short-term effects on children are especially relevant to this age group.

Eron and Huesmann's comprehensive twenty-two-year study found that viewing violent television in the third grade correlated not only with aggression in the third grade but with predicting criminal behavior twenty-two years later at age thirty.[16] Although we may initially be somewhat skeptical of such grave findings, we should note that these findings have been repeated in other studies and in five different countries.[17]

Eron and Huesmann are blunt in their conclusions:

> Aggressive habits seem to be learned early in life, and once established, are resistant to change and predictive of serious adult antisocial behavior. If a child's observation of media violence promotes the learning of aggressive habits, it can have harmful lifelong consequences.[18]

Parents need to pay particular attention to violent media offerings for this age group. I emphasize this because middle childhood tends to be a relatively unconflicted period of development, and parents often allow themselves to relax a bit after the whirlwind pace of the preschool years. This lessening of parental vigilance is appropriate, and certainly middle-age children need less protection than younger children. However, children of this age still need to be safeguarded against media violence, particularly when it is realistic and easy to identify with.

Movies in which a young child is the victim of abuse and exploitation and in which adults cannot be counted on to fulfill their role as protectors of the young are far more damaging at this age than movies that are clearly based in fantasy. For example, *The Good Son* stars Macaulay Culkin as Henry, a seemingly engaging youngster who is gradually revealed to be a sadistic murderer. Henry's cousin Mark comes to stay with Henry's family following the death of Mark's mother. When it becomes increasingly apparent to Mark that Henry has killed his own baby brother and plans to kill his sister as well, he turns to adults to help him.

Unfortunately, like so many movies aimed at this age group, adults are not available to help protect youngsters. Mark's father leaves on a business trip immediately after the death of his wife. When Mark tries to tell Henry's mother that Henry is trying to kill his sister, she becomes enraged and slaps Mark. Even Mark's psychiatrist is seduced by Henry's apparent goodwill.

Unfortunately, many young children, accompanied by their parents, saw this movie in spite of its R rating. They were not expecting their *Home Alone* hero to be a serial killer. Parental responsibility and a rating system that makes clear the reasons for particular ratings would have spared many young children an extremely upsetting experience. I saw several children in my practice with recurring nightmares after viewing this film. Because there was so much to identify with in the movie (all the standard paraphernalia of middle-class childhood), children were easily drawn into a world that was familiar—and ultimately terrifying. While there is little in the way of graphic violence in this movie, middle-age children are past the point where all violence must be of the in-your-face variety to be frightening. By this age, children are becoming sensitive to the kind of psychological violence portrayed in *The Good Son*.

Movies such as *Star Trek*, although more violent, are less apt to be frightening than more realistic movies. This is because of the obvious fantasy element, which can help children at this age to feel distance from what they are watching. The adventures of the starship *Enterprise* have entertained generations because they combine action with the ever popular theme of heroism in the face of danger. *Star Trek*'s roots lie in fairy tale and myth and as a result its conclusions are typically optimistic. In addition, it is multicultural, multiethnic, and multispecies. Not a bad television or movie choice for this age group, especially because older siblings and even parents are likely to enjoy watching as well.

Graphic news reporting about violence, because of its factual nature, is likely to be particularly upsetting to children in middle childhood. Young children are exposed to ever more graphic images of death and destruction on the evening news. Several stations are attempting to deal with this problem by offering "family-sensitive" news programs that omit disturbing images. This effort is to be applauded. Although we are encouraging children in this age group to become increasingly aware of the world outside their neighborhood, we still need to protect them from graphic images that can be traumatizing.

On October 1, 1993, twelve-year-old Polly Klass was enjoying a sleep-over party with two girlfriends when she was kidnapped from her suburban home in Petaluma, California. The fact that she was abducted from her bedroom while her mother slept in the next room made this a particularly disturbing crime for children to hear about—and it was hard to avoid because of the enormous amount of national news coverage it received. Polly's smiling face became a staple on posters and news programs. Unfortunately, she was found dead several months later and images of her were repeatedly shown on television. News broadcasts juxtaposed home videotape of her laughing and dancing with her covered, dead body found off a California highway.

A study done by psychiatrist Sara Stein and colleagues looked at the effects of such extensive media coverage on children.[19] More than eleven hundred children, age eight to eighteen, in three different states were studied. Not surprisingly, the younger children (because of their inability to distance themselves) and girls (because of their identification) were particularly disturbed by these news stories. In spite of the fact that both parents and schools attempted to help children feel safer, over 80 percent of the children reported that they "sometimes" or "often" were bothered by such symptoms as bad dreams or intrusive thoughts that they could not control. The researchers wrote: "Thus, in viewing an event such as the news reporting of a child-murder, many children will be unable to comprehend the significance of distance from the crime scene, for example, or that of random threat. As a result children may not develop a reassuring sense of perspective on the crime, as adults do."

In my own practice, which was not far from the kidnapping, I saw several young girls who exhibited symptoms of post-traumatic stress disorder following Polly's kidnapping and murder. Previously healthy children, they reported sleep disturbances, concentration problems, and anxiety. One girl slept with a baseball bat next to her bed; another refused to sleep near a window. It is likely that parents underestimate the impact of disturbing images on their children. This is particularly true for real images that are seen on the nightly news.

COGNITIVE DEVELOPMENT

Mr. Jones went to a restaurant and ordered a whole pizza for dinner. When the waiter asked if he wanted it cut into six or eight pieces, Mr. Jones said: "You'd better make it six. I could never eat eight."[20]

This joke, which preschoolers find perfectly reasonable, is hilarious to the middle-age child. A great revolution in thinking is taking place. Somewhere around the age of seven, children stop thinking in terms of "black and white" and begin thinking logically. In the case of Mr. Jones and his pizza, the younger child believes that more slices means more pizza; the older child, informed by logic, knows that the amount is the same no matter how you slice it.

This cognitive revolution, which Piaget termed the stage of concrete operations, is characterized by thinking that is more efficient and more logical. Children at this stage are beginning to appreciate cause-and-effect relationships. All of this helps to make living in the world more predictable and manageable.

Middle-age children are becoming rather effective problem solvers. Compared with younger children, children of six, seven, and eight are able to think more systematically about many different pieces of information. For example, an eight-year-old at a carnival who sees a very young child crying may walk over and ask if the little child is lost. The eight-year-old is able to use what he sees (an upset toddler), what he hears (crying), the context (young children at crowded events are generally with their parents), and his own experience (being lost once and being upset) to come to the logical conclusion that the young child is lost and needs help. No longer are children bound to focus on the most obvious part of a problem. Thinking is more logical, more refined, and more elaborate. Because of this large developmental leap in cognitive skills children are now expected to be, and are capable of being, full-time students.

One of the advances during this stage in development is children's increasing capacity to predict outcomes (what Piaget termed the ability to reverse operations). This has implications for how children view media violence. The middle-age child is able to understand that the man in custody at the end of the program is being punished for his violent acts at the beginning of the program. This newly developing ability to predict outcomes and to make connections between later and earlier events helps middle-age children to appreciate consequences.

However, the middle-age child is still burdened by egocentricity. Children at this age see things primarily from their own point of view and have difficulty taking another point of view. "Children who steal food should go to jail," proclaims the middle-class seven-year-old who has no experience of going to bed hungry and who has little capacity to put himself in the shoes of a child who must steal to survive. So while thinking skills are more sophisticated and allow a greater understanding of violence and its consequences, the egocentricity of the middle-age child prevents an appreciation of the broader social consequences of violence.

Early in this stage of development, children still do not have a firm and reliable grasp on the difference between reality and fantasy. Aimee Dorr's research at Harvard and UCLA has shown that the vast majority of first and second graders are unable to explain what is "real" on television.[21] For example, six- and seven-year-old children in her study believed that actors involved in shoot-outs must wear bulletproof vests "just in case the bullets are not fake." In addition, while some children this age understood that married couples on television were not necessarily married, they also thought "they must be very good friends." Around the age of eight, children experience a major jump in knowledge about the nature of television and a reliable understanding that what is seen on television is "made up."[22]

Children at this age still have substantial cognitive limitations that are easily exploited by the media. Children who repeatedly watch television characters attempting to solve their problems by the use of violence may be storing violent scripts that, under certain conditions, will encourage them to behave violently. Behavior does not have to be performed in order to be learned, and it is under conditions of stress that our more primitive responses find expression. Media executives are fond of invoking the concept of catharsis, the notion that watching violence somehow "bleeds off" our own feelings of aggression. Unfortunately, catharsis has found no substantiation in any social science research. In spite of this, the concept refuses to die and is regularly pulled out as a justification for violent programming, typically by those who are most likely to profit from such programming.

It is much more likely that watching violent television programming has a disinhibiting effect on children's still tenuous control of aggression. "Disinhibition" is a physiological and psychological state in which defenses are lowered and behavior is more primitive. The person who has had too much to drink and is dancing the polka on his host's tabletop is said to be disinhibited. But you don't need to be a psychologist to understand disinhibition; just ask any mom whose six-year-old has pinned down his baby brother in imitation of a karate choke hold after watching *Teenage Mutant Ninja Turtles*.

MORAL DEVELOPMENT

Rachel, age seven, comes home from school and is asked by her mom to take out the garbage. With a stricken look, Rachel responds, "I'm not your servant. Do it yourself!"

Jacob, age eight, is lying on the sofa on Saturday morning watching cartoons. His mother, with impeccable tact, says, "You can watch another half hour of cartoons and then I want you to make your bed and straighten up your room." Without lifting his eyes from the television, Jacob replies, "Not today Mom. It's Saturday. Dad doesn't have to work on Saturday and neither should I. Kids have rights too, you know."

These two examples, familiar in one form or another to every parent with children in this age group, illustrate a new stage in moral reasoning. Gone is the earlier childhood belief that parents are all-knowing. Just a year or two ago, children were typically cooperative and obedient. They respected authority and generally believed they deserved whatever punishment they were given. Beginning around six or seven, children enter a stage of moral reasoning in which everyone is entitled to his or her own point of view and adults no longer have moral authority over their children. As my middle son succinctly told me at this stage, "You're not the boss of me."

Children at this age also exhibit a tremendous interest in the concept of fairness. One of the constant complaints of the middle-age child is "It's not fair." An exasperated father reports: "Every Sunday we would plan a family outing and my seven-year-old daughter would spend the entire afternoon whining, 'How come we always do what the parents want? How come we never do what the kid wants?' " This barrage would continue in spite of mom and dad's best efforts to come up with activities they thought would be appealing to their daughter, often activities the daughter had requested.

Children at this age watch, with hawklike attention, every compliment paid to a sibling ("How come you always pay attention to him and not to me?"), every piece of cake that is divided ("She got the bigger piece again"), and every privilege granted to a neighboring child ("Oh sure he's allowed to stay up late. How come nothing special ever happens in my life?"). Children at this stage see fairness as being a tit-for-tat sharing of resources. Usually the child feels that he or she has come up short.

The primary philosophy of this stage is "looking out for number one." Children at this stage of moral development are rigid, self-centered, and often cruel. This rather chilling example from Thomas Lickona's *Raising Good Children* clearly illustrates the code of vengeance often subscribed to by the middle-age child:

> A third grade teacher asked her class what would be a fair punishment for a group of teenagers who broke into the zoo in Syracuse, New York, one summer night and killed more than a dozen animals. "Shoot 'em," said several children. "Same as they did to the animals."[23]

With such a cold desire for retribution in kind, it's no wonder that this is a difficult time between siblings. No dirty look, no push, no sneer can go unpunished. Children this age may have to wait to exact their revenge, but at some point it will be payback time. Every exasperated parent knows what it feels like to say "So what if he gave you a dirty look. Can't you just let it go?" For the most part, the answer to this question is "no." The middle-age child has great difficulty letting go of real and imagined insults.

While children at this stage can appear to be particularly cruel and selfish, parents should remember that this is actually an advance over the preschooler's level of moral thinking. Children now understand that fairness is not simply following the orders of those who are more powerful. Eventually, this broadening of the concept of fairness will allow children to understand that there may be many different points of view of what is fair and that fairness may depend on whether one is looking at benefits to the individual, the family, the society, or even the world.

Television programs and movies should reinforce the moral advances of this age group. Unfortunately, the opposite is often the case, particularly in movies and programs that emphasize justified vengeance. The high body count in movies like *Terminator* and *Robocop* (which are seen by a surprisingly large number of children in this age group) suggest that murder and mayhem are heroic when the "hero" is fighting against evil. This point of view is greeted with delight by middle-age children. Movies like these are a kind of moral poison for children this age because they reinforce a sense of morality which, left unchallenged, encourages a vigilante mentality. Like the children who wanted to shoot the teenagers who killed the zoo animals, children of this age have little empathy.

Commercial television does a good job of addressing many of the concerns of the middle-age child. Friendship and family relations are the themes of many of today's most popular shows: *Step by Step, Full House, Hanging with Mr. Cooper, Home Improvement, Roseanne*, and *The Cosby Show* all deal with the kinds of real-life dilemmas that children face daily. While the twenty-two minutes of the average situation comedy do not allow for an in-depth look at more serious problems such as child abuse, substance abuse by parents, racism, or public safety, they are sufficient for problems like forgetting one's chores, lying to parents, petty theft, and loyalty to friends and family.

On one of the final episodes of the long-running situation comedy *Full House*, seven-year-old Michelle tells her father a secret that she had promised her friends she would not reveal. When her father unintentionally reveals her secret, Michelle's friends are angry with her and banish her from the group. Michelle feels betrayed by her father and abandoned by her friends. The problem is resolved when both Michelle and her dad talk about the importance of not betraying secrets. Her father encourages her to apologize and to try to work it out with her friends. She does, and is successful. Father has learned the importance of respecting his daughter's confidences, and Michelle has learned how to get help and use it effectively. Episodes like this are not trivial in the world of childhood. They are of utmost importance, and programs that address these concerns in an entertaining and useful way are extremely valuable to the middle-age child.

10

Older Childhood: Ages 9, 10, and 11

GENERAL DEVELOPMENT

It doesn't get much easier than this. Older children are enjoying a period of equilibrium that is unique and delightful. Friendly and accepting, this stage of development is a welcome breather for both parents and their children. In the words of two well-known developmental psychologists, Louise Bates Ames and Francis Ilg: "There's nobody nicer than a ten-year-old."

Remember, it's all relative, and if you're having a hard day with your particular nine-, ten-, or eleven-year-old child, just think back to the "terrible twos" or ahead to the rebellious teen years. For the most part, older children are enjoying a period of relative calm, good nature, and friendliness with peers, teachers, and family. While eleven-year-olds may be starting to move toward the edginess of early adolescence, nine- and ten-year-olds express very high levels of satisfaction with their lives in general and their families in particular.

Children at this stage of development tend to be agreeable. They are typically described as friendly, secure, outgoing, positive, and trusting. Although they certainly can be angry on occasion, these episodes usually blow over rather quickly. While the older child's spheres of interest are rapidly expanding, family is still "home base." For the nine- and ten-year-old in particular, mom and dad (if not always siblings) are pretty great people. "I have the best family" is a typically exuberant comment at this age.

Instead of the dramatic changes of the preschool years and the explosive changes of adolescence, older children are changing in more subtle ways. Relative freedom from conflict allows children of nine, ten, and eleven to elaborate a sense of self, increase social and cognitive skills, develop empathy, and refine their sense of right and wrong. The nine-year-old who can now negotiate and resolve a conflict with a friend without calling in mom to adjudicate has mastered a major task. He or she is learning to function independently—an autonomous social being in a world with other social beings. This accomplishment is no less historic than the toddler's first shaky steps and the teenager's sexual awakening.

Children at this stage of development are beginning in earnest the acquisition of adult skills. The range of tasks that older children confront is enormous: schoolwork, friendship, personal responsibility, individual talents. The list of challenges is endless, and were it not for the natural enthusiasm of children this age, it might seem overwhelming to them. Instead, it is a golden opportunity, and the secure older child embraces the chance to advance his or her sense of proficiency.

As noted in the preceding chapter, the major task of childhood is to gain experience and competence in the following three areas:

1. Consolidating a sense of self
2. Developing friendships
3. Academic achievement

The emotional, social, and cognitive challenges that older children face are similar to those confronting middle-age children. Much of Chapter 9 is relevant to older children too. Unlike the adolescent who will be confronted with challenges quite different from anything previously encountered, the older child is expanding, developing, and refining those skills and capacities already evident in middle childhood.

CONSOLIDATING A SENSE OF SELF

Children of nine, ten, and eleven are working on expanding and refining their sense of self. At this stage, children understand that, in addition to their physical self, they possess a psychological self that is enduring across time. "I'm kind of quiet, but people seem to like me. I like doing nice things for other people" is one ten-year-old girl's self-description. It is a typical comment for this age because it acknowledges both her psychological self ("kind of quiet") and her relationship to other people ("people seem to like me"). This is a long way from this same girl's self-description in pre-school: "I'm pretty tall. My hair is brown and I hate broccoli."

Children now realize that they are a single, unique person who is constantly evolving. They can consider various aspects of their experience and see them all as part of the same self. This ability to maintain a continuous sense of self in spite of the passage of time, differences in feelings, and physical change is critical to healthy emotional adjustment. As one child succinctly said, "No matter what, I've always got me."

As a child's inner self develops, he or she becomes increasingly aware of the fact that other people also have internal thoughts and feelings that may not be obvious. This awareness leads to a landmark understanding—that people can be motivated by things that are not readily apparent. At this stage children can begin to appreciate more complex story lines in the media.

As children move through elementary school, they become aware of themselves not only as individuals but also as group members. As a result of this emerging "social self," older children increasingly evaluate their own performance in comparison to others': "I'm in the highest math group," "I'm the fastest runner in the class." Researchers have found that it is not until age nine or ten that children consistently and systematically do this.[1] These social comparisons help children appreciate their uniqueness and differentiate themselves from others: "My best friend and I are both really good athletes. But he's better at soccer and I'm better at basketball." Older children deal in comparisons not because they are anxious to crow over their abilities (many children at this age do not like to be singled out) but rather comparisons help them know exactly where they stand.

In spite of the dramatic changes in self-concept that take place during childhood, researchers have found that self-esteem tends to be consistent across time.[2] This is not surprising, as we would expect the infant who was well nurtured to grow into the child who is confident and adaptable, the adolescent who is able to craft a stable and productive identity, and finally the adult who is well adjusted. This is partly the result of the child's inborn disposition, partly the result of good parenting, and partly the result of fortunate circumstances. High self-esteem is predictive of success in many areas: school, work, interpersonal relationships, and self-satisfaction. While it is not written in stone, children who feel good about themselves are likely to be successful adults.

Erik Erikson proposed that the task facing children during the elementary school years is to confront increasingly difficult social and academic challenges. He labeled this stage "industry versus inferiority"[3] and believed that those children who worked hard and succeeded in meeting these challenges developed a sense of competence and self-assurance. Conversely, children who are unable to master the tasks of childhood feel inferior and shun new activities. A vicious cycle begins when children feel bad about one thing and withdraw from other activities that might help them feel better.

Parents know that children of this age thrive when they are presented with new and challenging activities. This is the age of Little League and brownies, boy scouts, and 4-H clubs, dance lessons, karate lessons, piano lessons, and other activities that children find appealing and parents endorse.

DEVELOPING FRIENDSHIPS

As older children begin to see themselves as individuals, they are increasingly able to see their friends as complex people with unique characteristics as well. No longer are friends made because "we're in the same class" or "we live next door to each other." Older children describe their friendships as arising out of shared interests and attitudes or admiration: "We both like being kind to animals" or "She's a great dancer and that's what I want to be." Friends do not have to be exactly alike because the older child has developed a perspective which allows for different points of view: "We don't always agree, but he's a great friend anyway." Older children are able to engage in and communicate with friends in a broader and more meaningful way. Some remarkably enduring friendships are forged at this stage of development.

The newly emerging capacity to truly see things from another perspective has some rather peculiar manifestations in older children. "You're such a dweeb, Joshua," says ten-year-old Eric. "You're nothing but a princess, Laura," Elizabeth says sarcastically.

"Dweeb," "geek," "weirdo," even "bitch" are common insults that children hurl intentionally to do psychological damage to each other. This is a big change from hitting, which was the younger child's typical response to frustration. It shows the shift toward the psychological and away from the physical as the arena for inflicting pain on others. While insults appear cruel and childish, they actually represent a leap forward in children's understanding of others. Eric and Elizabeth use taunts to wound because they can stand in Joshua's and Laura's shoes and know how much the insult will hurt.

This is a particularly sensitive time in terms of teaching children about the value of prosocial solutions. Because of their increased capacity to see things from another point of view, as well as their more sophisticated psychological understanding, older children are capable of altruism. One study of fifth-grade children demonstrated that parents who value altruism and provide good models of helpful and considerate behavior have children who are also altruistic. Children at this age are particularly likely to identify with the parent of their own sex. Altruistic fathers strongly influence their sons, altruistic mothers strongly influence their daughters.[4] Research has shown that children's prosocial behavior can be increased when they are exposed to adults who behave compassionately. This is particularly true when the adults are warm, nurturing, and powerful.[5] Just as we saw that children tend to model themselves after aggressive people if they are portrayed as powerful, children will also model themselves after powerful altruistic people.

SCHOOL ACHIEVEMENT

School continues to be a major factor in the lives of older children. Children at this stage often spend more time with friends than with family members. Although family is still the major agent of socialization, it competes with school and peers for influence on the child. As usual, development is interrelated. Children who feel good about themselves are apt to do well at school and to enjoy popularity among their peers.

Older children's emphasis on comparing their performance with that of other children is encouraged by the school, which tests, grades, and places children in different groups depending on ability. Most adults have clear memories of the delight or the mortification of having their grades called out in class or posted in a public place. One grandmother told her grandson about missing a spelling word and being forced to sit with a dunce cap on her head in the row labeled "dunce alley." While such insensitive episodes are thankfully rare now, children are still very aware of their position in the social and academic hierarchy. The teacher may not call him a "dunce" but other children will not hesitate to say "Are you in the stupid group again?" The school experience has the potential to either enhance or destroy self-esteem. Research studies have repeatedly shown that classroom adjustment and academic success at this age predict mental health in adulthood.[6]

School has an enormous impact on the child's current development, as well as his or her eventual level of adjustment. It is disheartening to have research show that girls are still discriminated against in the classroom. Of all groups of children, it appears that high-achieving girls are most likely to be criticized. In a study of fifth graders, high-achieving girls received the most criticism and the least praise *from their teachers* than any other group of students.[7] Boys, when they are criticized, are reproached for misbehavior or lack of neatness. Poor performance in boys is typically attributed to a lack of effort, whereas poor performance in girls is seen as a sign of low aptitude.[8] This difference in attribution is very important because it suggests to girls that their poor performance can't be helped but is beyond their control. Boys, however, are encouraged to believe that effort can help them become higher achievers.

Carol Gilligan and her colleagues at Harvard University are studying the psychology of girls and women. Their research shows that preadolescent girls are experiencing a crisis in their lives that may be heightened by school.[9] They have observed that at about age eleven, girls reach a watershed in their psychological development. If forced to choose between their natural exuberance and society's demands that they be quiet and deferential, young girls often begin a process of distancing themselves from their true nature: "Don't beat the boys," "Don't talk too loud," "Try to be a little more feminine." Girls face an endless number of prohibitions that can dampen their enthusiasm and sense of authenticity. Couple this with the consistent, if subtle, discouragement they receive in the classroom, and it is little wonder that preadolescent girls often show a lessening of interest in academic success and an increased incidence of depression. It is important that mothers defend and encourage their daughters to remain spirited, connected, true to themselves, and academically challenged. In particular, girls this age should be allowed to express their full range of feelings. Mothers can both model and encourage their daughters to be independent, honest, and outspoken.

MEDIA AND THE OLDER CHILD

Like the middle-age child, the older child is intrigued by movies and television programs that emphasize increasing separation from family and provide the first tantalizing look at adolescence. In the coming-of-age classic *Stand by Me*, four preadolescent boys sit around their clubhouse, smoking, swearing, and insulting each other. Treated with contempt by the real adolescents in the movie, these four boys have nothing but admiration for the teenagers who despise them.

Particularly toward the latter part of this stage, children are anxious to peer into the world of adolescence, to observe its rituals of dress, language, and social behavior. They tend to view media offerings that focus on their own age group as "babyish" and beg to be allowed to watch shows like *Beverly Hills 90210*.

Peer pressure is becoming strong, and children this age are loath to admit that they still enjoy PG-rated movies or even Saturday morning cartoons. When he was eleven, my oldest son used to say he was watching cartoons "to chill," thus invoking the language of adolescence to ward off his feelings of childishness. All the same, children at this age need a break from the pressures of growing up and should not be ridiculed when they allow themselves to return to the entertainment they enjoyed at an earlier stage of development.

Developmental tasks are formidable at any age, and we all need a respite from the demands of living. Disney has had enormous success in the past few years recognizing "the child in all of us" and producing movies such as *Aladdin* and *The Little Mermaid*, which manage to engage adults as well as children. Development does not proceed in a lockstep manner. The older child who one day begs to see *Interview with the Vampire* or *Robocop* may be found watching *Bugs Bunny* the next day. This is normal behavior.

The impact of the media on this age group is very significant. In terms of the absolute number of hours spent in front of the television, eleven-year-olds watch more television than any other age group, averaging twenty-eight hours per week.[10] Twenty-three research studies conducted over twenty-six years in the United States and abroad have consistently shown that this much television viewing has a small negative effect on school achievement.[11] Interestingly, watching up to ten hours of television per week enhances achievement slightly, but most children watch far more than this. After ten hours per week of television viewing, achievement scores begin to decline. There are several explanations for this finding. It may be that parents whose children only watch ten hours per week or less are particularly active in providing other more challenging activities for their children. They may be using television to expand their children's world rather than as a babysitter. It may also be that it is only beyond ten hours a week that television begins to replace more intellectually stimulating activities such as homework or reading. This negative relationship between television viewing and academic achievement is stronger for girls than it is for boys and stronger for children of high intelligence.[12]

While boys' academic performance may be slightly less affected by the media, some studies show that their aggressive behavior is more affected.[13] When young, both girls and boys seem to be equally affected by media aggression, but after age six, as social norms become more clearly differentiated, boys show a greater effect. We can only speculate as to why boys may be more vulnerable, but part of the explanation seems to come from the content of popular media. Childhood is in large measure about the task of separating from one's family and becoming one's own person. Adventure movies and television programs are particularly appealing to children because they address these concerns: "What's it like to be on my own?" "How will I manage out in the world?" The real answers to these questions are complex and ideally involve a growing appreciation of the need for cooperation and sensitivity in human relationships. Boys in particular are frequently presented with dangerous and thoughtless answers to these questions, such as "You manage being alone in the world by being tough, aggressive, and unfeeling."

When Kevin in *Home Alone* is frightened at finding himself abandoned by his family, he dives under his bed. He coaxes himself out by saying, "Only a wimp would be hiding under the bed. I can't be a wimp, I'm the man of the house." He in fact is not the man of the house; he is only a child who under normal circumstances would be most distressed to find himself in Kevin's shoes. However, Kevin never cries or tries to enlist adult help, even when burglars break into his house. Instead he devises a series of tortures (hot irons falling on the burglars' heads, paint cans knocking them downstairs) to protect himself. Kevin is victorious and the message seems to be that if you are a crafty, little thug, then you'll be okay.

More sinister are movies that feature men of robotlike proportions who are avenging something or another. These movies need to be divided into two different categories because I believe that their effects on children are substantially different. First, movies such as *Terminator 2*, which are beloved by this age group, are clearly fantastical. Whether the hero is literally a robot, as in *Robocop*, or only figuratively, as in any Arnold Schwarzenegger movie (no, I'm not talking about his acting, only his larger than life physical self), children of this age have the cognitive capacity to understand that this is fiction, and this knowledge lessens the likelihood of identification and imitation. While I believe that these movies are not particularly in the best interest of children because they reinforce the attitude that becoming a man is in large measure about becoming sadistic, aggressive, and unfeeling, they are less disturbing and less likely to encourage imitation and identification than more realistic films.

It is the second category of violent movies that should be of greater concern to parents. These are movies such as Charles Bronson's *Death Wish*, Steven Seagal's *Hard to Kill*, and Brandon Lee's *The Crow*, where the "hero" is a regular guy caught in extraordinary circumstances. Many of the "heroes" in this genre become killers in order to avenge their women who are raped and/or murdered. It is as if every unfortunate cultural myth has been rolled into one dreadful saga: "It is okay to be violent as long as you're the good guy"; "Women can't take care of themselves and need men to protect them"; "Violence in the pursuit of justice is noble." Movies such as these reflect and magnify the worst aspects of our cultural stereotypes. They exploit many young men's budding machismo with messages that are dangerous both to themselves and to society.

One of the reasons why boys are differentially affected by the media may be that the role models they are given are so deficient, yet so very stimulating at the same time. Steven Seagal, in *Out for Justice*, is sexy, strong, macho, and, of course, a police officer. A dazzling master of the martial arts, he has palpable charisma. Unfortunately he has trouble putting together a complete sentence and the majority of his social interactions consist of breaking some part of the human body. To further confuse the issue, he says things like "Don't be a bad guy, be a good guy" as he breaks someone's arms. At a time when boys need clear models about who are the good guys and who are the bad guys, movies like *Out for Justice* muddy the moral waters.

Both movies and television programming directed at boys draw them into a world dominated by conflict, which is then resolved through the use of guns, swords, martial arts, and torture. It is the "good guys" who do most of the killing, by a ratio of more than two to one. Over and over again, young boys are presented with powerful male role models who choose force over cooperation, intimidation over mutuality, and impulsiveness over thoughtfulness. Certainly boys grapple with the issues of power and submission and dominance, and gun play, sword play, and fighting are normal expressions of this conflict. They have probably always been part of boys' play. But when the media provide so much support for violent resolutions, they cease to be simply components of symbolic play and are too often seen as viable ways to conduct one's life. There are few movies that instruct young men about how to deal with rage and loss and desperation without blowing someone's head off. In a country where young men are murdering and being murdered in record numbers, learning how to effectively handle powerful feelings becomes a matter of life and death.

Research has shown several factors that foster aggression in children once they have been exposed to television violence. These include the following:

- If the aggressive behavior is seen as justified[14]
- If there are cues in the portrayed violence that have a similarity to those in real life[15]
- If there is a similarity between the aggressor and the viewer[16]
- If violence is portrayed without consequence, such as no discernible pain, sorrow, or remorse[17]
- If violence is realistically portrayed or seen as a real event[18]

It is exactly because vigilante movies are frequently presented in a context of ordinary life that they are potentially damaging to children. The mundane backgrounds of many of these movies makes it easy to identify with the "hero." The suburban bedroom in the movie may have the same sheets as the ones on your child's bed, and the adolescent girl actress may look more or less like your daughter or the girl next door. Who wouldn't be outraged if his wife or mother or sister was raped or murdered? So while these movies encourage children to identify with the "hero," they repeatedly come to a savage and unacceptable conclusion: that the appropriate response to violence is more violence. Just as girls are so poorly served by media that reinforce passivity, dependence, and lowered expectations for achievement, boys are poorly served by media that reinforce insensitivity, competition, and aggression.

PSYCHOLOGICAL DEVELOPMENT AND THE MEDIA

ATTACHMENT

While family is still of primary importance to the older child, other strong ties are being developed. Children of this age spend more time with friends than with family. School takes up a large portion of their day. Older children are no longer interested only in being "good kids." They now want to be good students, good friends, good athletes, good dancers, and so on. Accomplishment does not revolve only around furthering one's success in the family, but involves furthering one's personal success as well. Of course these domains have considerable overlap. For instance, children who are successful at school are generally appreciated at home for their academic achievement.

Children at this developmental stage are increasingly capable of taking care of themselves, both physically and psychologically. They frequently resent babysitters and feel quite capable of being alone in the house for a couple of hours. Toward the end of this stage, some children are even beginning to babysit outside of their home.

Parents need to shift their parenting styles as their youngsters become increasingly capable and independent. Children of this age need to be allowed greater freedom to explore their developing capacities; they also need protection and supervision to make sure they don't get in over their heads. Parents at this stage should be guiding more and directing less. Older children have a point of view, and it is important that parents communicate respect for their children's developing perspective, even if they don't always agree with it.

Older children are forming opinions and prejudices that often last a lifetime. The media are powerful communicators of cultural values. As we have seen from Gerbner's work, television cultivates attitudes that not only are at variance with reality but actually contribute to violence and victimization.[19] Parents who have fallen victim to what Gerbner calls a "mean world syndrome" undoubtedly convey their insecurities and apprehensions to their children. Singer and Singer studied this syndrome in children. Their research supports Gerbner's findings that heavy viewers of television violence experience the world as a particularly frightening and unfriendly place: "Our data provide some indication that, even when various controls are taken into account, heavy TV viewing is significantly associated with elementary school children's later aggressive behavior, restlessness, and belief in a 'mean and scary world.' "[20]

AGGRESSION

Older children are exposed to extremely high levels of media violence. Current estimates are that 15 percent of all television material is violent. With the average child this age watching close to four hours of television per day, he or she sees thirty-six minutes of violent crimes such as rape and murder each day. The child who is a moderate viewer of prime time television is entertained by about fifteen murders a week, not counting cartoons or the news.[21] All of this seems temperate when compared with the 81 violent deaths in *Robocop* or the 264 violent deaths in *Die Hard*. Scientists have come to understand a great deal about how this steady diet of media violence affects older children.

In many ways, the television has become "personified" in that it has taken over the role of society's storyteller. It is frequently referred to as the "third parent" or an "uncertified teacher." It is not "just entertainment," as people in the media are fond of saying, because it creates and elaborates attitudes just as much as it reflects them. Gerbner points out, "For the first time in human history, most of the stories about people, life and values are told not by parents, schools, churches, or others in the community who have something to tell but by a group of distant conglomerates that have something to sell."[22] The sheer number of hours that children spend watching television ensures its status as a communicator of the social order. As one of my sons explained, "If they can say 'it sucks' on television, why can't I say it at home? It's just an ordinary word now." The media in large measure have come to define what is appropriate and acceptable in our society.

There are differences between boys and girls in their readiness to model fictionalized aggression. One of the factors that encourages imitation is identification, so it is not surprising that boys are more likely to imitate aggressive behavior. Men outnumber women three to one in prime-time television and six to one in action movies and programs—a genre aimed at this age group. Same-sex modeling is stronger than cross-sex modeling. In addition, girls generally see television as less realistic than boys do.[23] As we have seen, believing that the violence is realistic and justified is one of the conditions most likely to encourage imitation.

While girls may be less likely to model aggressive behavior after movie and television characters, they are also learning something about aggression from the screen. Unfortunately, what they often learn is that girls and women are the frequent recipients of male abuse.

In the movie *Dirty Harry*, one of the original male-vigilante-as-hero movies, there are only five extremely brief scenes that include women: one wife, one secretary, two sexually promiscuous naked women, and one dead naked teenage girl. While this movie was made twenty-five years ago, its view of girls and women is remarkably similar to today's MTV videos. Women and girls are sexual accessories to the real "action," which is about men showing their power in various ways, typically aggressive, sadistic, and narcissistic. Women have very limited roles in the kinds of action movies that children of this age find so appealing, and when they appear they are frequently portrayed as victims.

In reality, most victims of male aggression are other men. The media's persistent distortion of this social reality adds to young girls' sense of vulnerability. Excellent movies such as *Flirting* and *A Little Princess* attempt to present more realistic models to girls and encourage their strivings toward independence and competency. Even Disney, with *Pocahontas*, has finally made a movie in which the heroine honors commitments other than falling in love with some handsome prince. However, even movies that portray spirited women, such as *Thelma and Louise*, often have a subtle but poisonous subtext: Independent females end up dead.

Should parents restrict viewing of aggressive programs and movies for children of this age? Yes, of course. At this age, as throughout childhood, parents are in large measure responsible for what kinds of experiences their children are exposed to. In the best of all possible worlds, television is an activity with a purpose. While there is a certain fondness for saying that television should not be a babysitter, there are in fact good and bad babysitters: babysitters who take our kids out, show them the world, and help them develop and babysitters who are passive and do not engage our kids. We want television to be the former kind, and, when it is, calling it a babysitter is no insult. Children and their parents should look over television listings at the beginning of the week and make decisions about specific programs. Not all programs and movies that children watch must be "educational" or "elevating." As the film critic Roger Ebert has said, "Most movies are not for any one thing, of course. Some are to make us think, some to make us feel, some to take us away from our problems, some to help us examine them." However, we should ensure that our children are not consistently exposed to messages that are at odds with our values.

Jerry Mander, in his popular book *Four Arguments for the Elimination of Television*, argues that television is such a hopeless enterprise that it should be eliminated.[24] I disagree. Television and the movies still provide significant experiences for older children that are both entertaining and informative. *Home Improvement, Step by Step, The Cosby Show*, and even *Roseanne* reinforce family values in the truest sense—that an open, loving, and cooperative family is the surest launching pad out into the world. *Star Wars* and *Star Trek* take kids to outer space; *E.T.* and *Huck Finn* take them to inner space and the territory of loneliness, divorce, and friendship. *Aladdin* takes them to Arabia, and *White Fang* to the Yukon. *Mister Rogers* has taken them to the symphony, and *Sesame Street* has taken them to Israel, Spain, and China. When it is successful, the media expand the world of children by bringing rich experiences into their living rooms and their lives. At its best, it encourages curiosity and an appreciation of diversity. The potential of the media to enrich children's lives should not be underestimated.

Television has its greatest negative effects on those children whose parents are not involved in their viewing and who have few friends.[25] To lessen television's influence, parents can use the opportunity of watching with their children as a jumping-off point to discuss issues such as conflict resolution, the use and misuse of power, and cultural stereotypes. Open-ended questions such as "Did that story make sense to you?" "What made you care about the characters?" "Can you think of other solutions to the problem?" encourage the older child to use expanded social and cognitive skills and begin thinking about a variety of solutions and consequences.

COGNITIVE DEVELOPMENT

Jennifer, age eleven, comes home from school preoccupied and downcast. Her mother asks if anything is wrong. "I had a fight with Amy," says Jennifer and retreats to her room. Lying on her bed, Jennifer goes over the day's events. Her birthday is next week, and she and Amy were going to the mall after school to shop for a present. At the last minute Amy ditched her, saying, "I gotta do my homework, my parents are really on my back." "You never keep your word," said Jennifer before she took off in a huff. All the way home Jennifer felt bad. She realized she was disappointed because last year none of her friends remembered her birthday. Besides, her own English grades weren't so hot lately and her own parents were breathing down her neck. She telephones Amy. "Can we go shopping on Saturday instead?" she asks.

This everyday example illustrates the tremendous progress in thinking that has been made by the older child. While the preschooler would have called her friend a "poo-poo head" and the younger elementary school child would have looked around for another friend, the older child has the capacity to think about her situation with insight and empathy. In spite of her disappointment, Jennifer is able to reflect on her feelings and to see that they have several causes. She is angry at her friend, but she's also been disappointed in the past and understands that this adds to her current feelings of betrayal. She is also experiencing parental pressure and knows that it can be stressful. Jennifer is able to empathize with her friend in spite of being disappointed. This lessening of egocentricity is one of the great accomplishments of this stage of development. As a result, Jennifer is better able to feel for her friend even when her own wishes are being thwarted. Jennifer is able to stand in Amy's shoes.

Children at this stage of development may be most vulnerable to the effects of media violence because, although their ability to think and empathize is great, their store of experience is still relatively limited. While the very young child may not be frightened by a hijacking recounted on the news because he is too young to understand what is being said, and the teenager may be concerned but still knows that hijackings are rare, the child of nine, ten, and eleven knows just enough to be frightened but not enough to have much perspective.

Television is exerting a particularly potent effect on children during these years. They are watching a great deal of television, with a lessening and often an absence of parental supervision. During this stage of development, long-term interests are emerging, and lifelong attitudes as well as patterns of behavior are being cultivated. What are children watching?

For one thing, far too many children at this age are watching "slasher" movies. These movies, which include *Nightmare on Elm Street* and *Friday the Thirteenth*, are often referred to as "splatterfests" by the critics. While these movies are discussed in greater detail in Chapter 11, they deserve mention here because they are seen so frequently by children in this age group. In a poll conducted by *TV Guide*, an unbelievable 89 percent of eleven-year-old children have seen the R-rated *Nightmare on Elm Street* (I can't bring myself to comment on the fact that this same poll found that 20 percent of children under the age of five have seen this movie).[26] Slasher movies are among the most disturbing and inappropriate movies available for consumption by children. In my clinical experience, Freddy Krueger of *Nightmare on Elm Street* is the single greatest media-created source of nightmares for young children. He is a child molester and murderer; he is disfigured and cruel and, worst of all, he inhabits the dreams of children. A slew of child psychologists could not have come up with a more perfectly terrifying character if they tried (except maybe Chucky in *Child's Play*, where a youngster's favorite toy, in the safety of his own home, turns out to be a serial killer).

Older children, however, seem able to get away from Freddy and his likes all too easily. Ask any eleven-year-old if he is frightened by Freddy Krueger and the response is likely to be an indulgent and jaded "What's the matter with you? It's a movie!" By the age of eleven or so, the unremitting barrage of violent images that children have been exposed to for the past decade has done its job. Children have become so desensitized, so accustomed to fictionalized violent imagery, that they no longer find it disturbing.

It is frightening enough to understand that media violence is encouraging some children to incorporate violent solutions into their everyday behavior. It is perhaps even more frightening to confront the fact that even larger numbers of children are becoming tolerant of these solutions. Ronald Drabman, in a series of experiments on media violence and desensitization, tested the hypothesis that "viewing violence under the guise of entertainment may increase one's tolerance of aggression that occurs in the real world and thus make one less willing to aid when he witnesses such behavior in his own life."[27]

Drabman conducted many studies on children at this developmental stage. Typically he divided children into two groups, those exposed to a violent program and those who saw either no program or a neutral program. What he found was that older children who had seen the violent program were more likely to ignore the distress of children in trouble and, if they did respond, to respond more slowly than those who had not seen the violent program.

Unfortunately, much of what children this age are exposed to by the media works at cross-purposes to their developmental advances, such as an increased ability to think critically and with empathy. Parents would do well to look for media offerings that encourage newly emerging critical skills and help develop an understanding of different perspectives. True prosocial behavior is emerging during this stage of development and deserves to be encouraged. Often this can be done through comedy—children this age watch more situation comedies than any other form of television. *The Mask*, *Ace Ventura*, and *Dumb and Dumber* are all very funny, and also showcase the kind of "hero" that children can identify with, sometimes uncertain, often bumbling, but always with his heart in the right place. Comedies can be good alternatives to the mind-numbing excesses of violence often targeted for this age group.

MORAL DEVELOPMENT

Moral development is accelerating at this stage because of the child's newly emerging capacity for true and ongoing empathy. A deepening sensitivity to other people, coupled with an increasingly well developed conscience, helps the child of nine, ten, and eleven want to please others.

However, children at this age also have a strong commitment to their own values. "I was going to cheat on the math test, but my conscience would have bothered me," says a ten-year-old boy. "Nobody saw me take the blouse, but inside of me I knew it was wrong, so I put it back," says an eleven-year-old girl. These children are giving evidence of a conscience that needs no external enforcement. Conscience is no longer only the fear of a punishing parent but has become "a voice deep inside." Psychologists and psychiatrists talk about superego development, and parents say, "He really seems to know right from wrong for himself now." It is a landmark in moral development.

Parents and the media have a special opportunity during this stage to help children further their moral development. Children are particularly accommodating at this age and many are interested in the idea of what makes a "good person." They are curious about moral values such as responsibility and honesty. All parents want to see their children enter adolescence with a sense of independence and an honest and responsible conscience.

There are many outstanding movies and television programs that encourage moral development as well as provide wonderful entertainment for children. George Lucas's *Star Wars*, *Return of the Jedi*, and *The Empire Strikes Back* were all blockbusters, the third, fourth, and eighth highest ranking movies of all time in terms of gross receipts.[28] These films continue to be avidly consumed, on video, by a new generation of children. While hardly breaking thematic ground, these movies have enthralled both children and adults for close to twenty years.

There are several reasons why these movies are so beloved by children. Like all good fairy tales, they take place "long ago, in a galaxy far, far away." This device allows children both to participate in the story and to watch it from afar. *Star Wars* is the archetypal "journey" story, and it is this journey out of the family and into one's own life that is the major task of childhood. Luke Skywalker, with his ordinary demeanor and air of confusion and insecurity, is easy for children to identify with. He is an ordinary young man called on to perform extraordinary feats as he confronts the Forces of the Evil Empire led by Darth Vader. Instructed by archetypal wise man Obi-Wan Kenobi (Luke's own parents are dead, as is the tradition in fairy tales), Luke learns to draw on his own moral and intuitive strength. "May The Force be with you" has now reassured two generations of young children that somewhere inside of them is the ability to go out into the world, survive, and even triumph.

These are movies that, despite all their spectacular fight scenes, contain a minimum of violence and virtually no bloodshed. In spite of the battleships, lasers, and assorted extraordinary hardware, it is the people who concern us most. At the theater kids "oohed" and "aahed" over the fight scenes, but in my office they were most concerned with Luke's struggles. Would he be able to lead the Rebel forces? Was Darth Vader his father, and if he was, how could Luke kill him? Could Yoda really teach him to use The Force? In spite of thrilling intergalactic fights, fantastic aliens, and spectacular special effects, *Star Wars* is a very psychological movie. It defines issues (how to face the dangers of the world) and presents solutions (develop internal strength and moral conviction) in a format that is breathtaking and compelling for children in this age group. It is moviemaking for children at its finest.

11

Early Adolescence: Ages 12, 13, and 14

In their search for a new sense of continuity and sameness, adolescents have to refight many of the battles of earlier years, even though to do so they must artificially appoint perfectly well-meaning people to play the roles of adversaries.

ERIK ERIKSON, *Childhood and Society*

GENERAL DEVELOPMENT

Being a young teenager is not easy.

Neither, for that matter, is living with a young teenager. No other period of development generates as much fear and anxiety in parents as the new adolescent. Surly, confused, oppositional, and often withdrawn, the early adolescent often seems an unfortunate replacement for the easygoing and cooperative child of the previous developmental stage.

Adolescence is demanding and difficult. It is a time of accelerated physical, sexual, social, cognitive, and emotional development. One of life's greatest challenges is being navigated—the transition from childhood to adulthood.

Physical and hormonal changes are noticeable, often painfully so. Early pubertal changes—pubic hair, breasts, and menarche for girls, increased genital size, facial and body hair for boys—are both anticipated and dreaded. Adults often forget the confusion felt by adolescents as they shed their childhood bodies. A twelve-year-old girl is unable to complete her homework because she spends three hours in the bathroom trying to figure out how to insert a tampon. A thirteen-year-old boy finds himself unable to concentrate in school fearful that his erection will be noticed if he is called to the blackboard. While physical changes are the most conspicuous, they are really only the tip of the adolescent iceberg. Changes in peer relationships, family relationships, cognitive abilities, self-concept, and social roles all conspire to keep the young adolescent off-center and preoccupied.

Coupled with the unrelenting physical changes of early adolescence is the need for remarkable emotional adjustment. Perhaps the most noticeable shift occurs around issues of autonomy and self-determination. The anthem of adolescence has many variations, but essentially it is some form of "Leave me alone," "Don't tell me what to do," "You can't run my life anymore." Children who just a few months ago were cheerful and compliant suddenly are resentful and provocative. While the notion that adolescence must include *extremely* high levels of parent-child conflict in order for the child to become fully independent has been discredited, there is little disagreement that mild to moderate levels of parent-child conflict, particularly in early adolescence, are typical.[1] Parents are being forced to step aside and are most frequently replaced by the adolescent's peers.

For many parents, this conflict and withdrawal is particularly painful, coming at a time when middle age is imposing its own developmental challenges. In a knowing moment on *My So-Called Life*, fifteen-year-old Angela is out with her attractive, middle-aged mother. A good-looking man smiles at them and her mother brightens, thinking the attention was meant for her. Her face collapses imperceptibly as she realizes that he is actually admiring her daughter. Mothers who enjoyed shopping trips with their daughters for years now find those same daughters stricken at the thought of being seen together in the same mall. One thirteen-year-old boy instructed his father to only use his first name when introducing himself, lest someone suspect that the two were related. These can be powerful blows to parents who previously enjoyed a close and friendly relationship with their children. Although painful for both parents and teens, such poignant displays of self-doubt are reasonably short-lived.

While it is true that the young adolescent experiences periods of increased conflict, the cultural commonplace that "teenagers are crazy" has been shown to be an inaccurate and potentially dangerous misconception. Both the professional and popular perspective has encouraged the point of view that adolescence is a period of disequilibrium unmatched in the human life cycle. The term *sturm und drang*, or "storm and stress," was popularized in 1904 by G. Stanley Hall, the father of American psychology, to describe adolescence. No less an authority than Anna Freud wrote: "The differential diagnosis between adolescent upsets and true pathology becomes a difficult task."

Research over the past three decades has helped to clarify what is and what is not expectable adolescent behavior. Although early adolescence is a time of particular sensitivity and rather characteristic behaviors (withdrawal, moodiness, self-absorption), the vast majority of young teenagers pass through this stage of development without exhibiting major psychological or emotional disorders. As a group, adolescents have no more and no less emotional illness than any other age group. Approximately 20 percent of all teenagers suffer from clinical-level symptoms—that is, symptoms such as anxiety or depression that are of significant severity and duration to warrant a diagnosis and treatment.[2] This rate is comparable to adult rates of emotional illness.[3]

Teenagers can be moody, anxious, and depressed. They tend to suffer from feelings of self-doubt and inferiority. However, should these feelings be intense and unremitting, it is likely that the teenager needs psychological help. Teenagers do not "grow out of" true depression or anxiety disorders any more than adults do.

Although not emotionally ill, adolescents can appear idiosyncratic to adults because of their constant attempts to define and refine their identities. Low-riding "skater pants," dark hooded sweatshirts, and pierced noses all seem foreign and a bit forbidding to parents. However, adults need to be cautious and not overinterpret these superficial signs of nonconformity. Although certain aspects of dress or appearance, such as "wearing colors" to show gang affiliation, can signal real danger, the vast majority of adolescent indulgences in dress and appearance are harmless and short-lived. This does not mean that parents have to like or sanction all adolescent excesses. One of the major developmental tasks of adolescence is to develop a new and enduring identity. Many hats must be tried on before the teenager finds one that fits.

Pick your battles carefully. Save the showdown for the body piercing, skip the haircut.

MEDIA AND THE EARLY ADOLESCENT

Teenagers have been given a bad rap by the media. They are portrayed alternately as sullen, withdrawn misanthropes or violent, testosterone-driven deviants. The rebellious, alienated teenager has become a cinematic icon ever since James Dean perfected adolescent angst in *Rebel Without a Cause* some forty years ago. Why have we chosen to see adolescents as being more troubled (and troubling) than they actually are? When Marlon Brando was asked in *The Wild One*, "What are you rebelling against" and replied, "Whadda ya got?" he set the standard for teenagers as defiant individuals in constant conflict with family and society. This theme has been elaborated in some of the most popular films of the last four decades, beginning with *The Wild One* (1953) and *Rebel Without a Cause* (1955) and continuing through *West Side Story* (1961), *A Clockwork Orange* (1971), *Saturday Night Fever* (1977), *Purple Rain* (1984), and *Sid and Nancy* (1986) and ending with more recent films like *My Own Private Idaho* (1991) and *Kids* (1995).

While movies have tended to focus on adolescents as wild, troubled, and estranged, television has presented them as one-dimensional and sanitized. From Wally and the Beaver on *Leave It to Beaver* and David and Ricky Nelson on *Ozzie and Harriet* to Samantha on *Who's the Boss* and D.J. on *Full House*, television teenagers have been primarily concerned with their looks, shopping, and borrowing the family car. It is only recently that television programs such as *The Wonder Years*, *Beverly Hills 90210*, and *My So-Called Life* have looked at the more serious and pressing issues that adolescents face: drug abuse, teen pregnancy, and violence as well as the less dramatic but equally important issues of self-esteem, school performance, and peer acceptance.

By neglecting to present varied, appropriate, and relevant role models for teens, both society as a whole and the media in particular have failed miserably in their responsibility to this age group. Without healthy and clearly defined roles, young adolescents are extremely vulnerable to the media, which tend to provide clear but undesirable roles and standards. In the long tradition of vigilante-as-hero movies, Jean-Claude Van Damme in *Cyborg*, Sylvester Stallone in *Rambo*, and Arnold Schwarzenegger in *Terminator* present romanticized and sanitized versions of mass murderers who are doing the right thing and suffer no remorse or doubt. Equally troubling is the affectionate treatment of cannibalism, sadism, and psychopathy in movies like *Silence of the Lambs, Demolition Man*, and *Natural Born Killers*. Clearer yet more antisocial role models are hard to imagine. In *Heat*, a particularly confusing movie starring two of our most popular actors, Al Pacino and Robert De Niro, the boundary between good and evil is completely dissolved. Cops and killers are one and the same, and De Niro makes being a mass murderer look appealing, even heroic. In the best of all possible worlds, young adolescents would not be exposed to these mostly R-rated movies. But in fact, advertising is heavily targeted toward teenagers, there are few appealing alternatives, and parents too frequently feel that they have little control over what their teenagers watch.

The task of adolescence is to begin creating a new adult. There are periods of intense exhilaration as well as abiding anxiety and depression both for teenagers and their families. Power relationships that were carefully forged over the past twelve years are obsolete. Parents are often at a loss as to how to relate to this "new" family member. Unfortunately, parents frequently fall back on trying to reassert their previous authority and as a result become overly restrictive. Typically, this parenting approach backfires. Authoritarian households are found to have higher rates of delinquency than more democratic households.[4] The adolescent's task is to develop an emerging identity; the parent's task is to allow greater and greater freedom without sacrificing the child's physical safety or mental health.

One of the most common ways that adolescents work on their emerging identity is by spending a significant amount of time daydreaming. Teenagers of twelve, thirteen, and fourteen spend inordinate amounts of time in their rooms. Intrusion is discouraged by a variety of signs, locks, and offensive posters. While staring into space, teenagers are crafting the individuals they are about to become: "How do I look?" "Will I make a fool of myself?" "What will I be when I'm older?" "Am I any good?" and so on. Early adolescence is a period of intense self-doubt. It is by addressing these commonplace concerns of young adolescents and offering them creative, healthy solutions that the media can become an ally in their development.

Teenagers are avid media consumers. Ninety-eight percent of all households in the United States have at least one television (with the average home having 2.25 TVs), and young teenagers spend, on average, twenty-six hours per week watching television. Seventy-five percent of American homes have VCRs, and teenagers make up a disproportionately large audience for the six million videos that are rented daily. Sixty percent of American homes have CD players, and teenagers make up 25 percent of all record, CD and tape sales: This translates into adolescents spending over $3 billion a year on rock and roll music. Teenagers obviously represent an enormous potential audience for advertisers. With teenagers spending $89 billion per year, some $3 billion on athletic shoes alone, they become a significant and (unfortunately) vulnerable consumer group.[5] Their value to advertisers is, of course, enhanced by the fact that they have so many years in front of them to be loyal consumers.

The potential magnitude of the adolescent's buying power is a fact not lost on those companies who are in the business of selling addiction. Name recognition and product identification take place at younger and younger ages, as even small children come to recognize cartoon characters and animals like Joe Camel and Spuds McKenzie. Much of the advertising in the cigarette and alcohol industry is aimed at those issues to which adolescents are most vulnerable: peer pressure, independence, rebellion, and personal acceptability.

The Marlboro man, one of the most successful campaigns in advertising history, reflects America's romance with the cowboy— the rugged individualist who answers to no one. In *Breaking Away*, an angry, young Dennis Quaid points to a Marlboro advertisement and says, "That's where to be. Wyoming. Prairie, mountains, nobody around." The pitch here is to the adolescent's desire to be free, particularly free of parental demands. The product itself of course brings addiction and therefore a lessening rather than an increase in freedom. Virginia Slims runs a particularly shameless advertising campaign tying female liberation not only to cigarette smoking but to weight loss as well. Liberation in this case appears to be the right to give yourself a life-threatening illness. Adolescent girls are the only group that shows an increase in cigarette consumption. It is estimated that 20 percent of young women suffer from an eating disorder.

While the overselling of consumer goods to American adolescents may be inappropriate and troubling, it is the selling of addiction that is potentially lethal. In an article entitled "The Selling of Addiction to Women," Carol Moog writes:

> It's one thing for a woman to purchase too many cosmetics or jeans in a convoluted effort to gain love and acceptance by measuring up to Madison Avenue. At that point she's buying into the cultural myth brought to us through the wonders of advertising, that women must be young, ingenuous, gorgeous and innocuous. But what about when she's being lured with products which are dangerous, even lethal, and addictive? The stakes are much higher, and the trade-off for a woman isn't just a genuine sense of self, it may be her life.[6]

As a clinical psychologist, I must add that a "genuine sense of self" is critical in order to lead a healthy and productive life. While perhaps not as immediately life-threatening as cigarette and alcohol abuse, a poor self-image can be just as dangerous, potentially leading to anorexia, bulimia, unnecessary cosmetic surgery, and depression.

There have been some gains in raising the awareness of adolescents about the dangers of smoking and alcohol abuse. Not surprisingly, these gains have come as a result of efforts outside the tobacco and alcohol industries. In 1988, Harvard University's School of Public Health launched a major campaign to educate the public, via the media, about substance abuse. This program received strong support from the entertainment industry. In response to Harvard's program, ABC's popular sitcom *Growing Pains* aired an episode entitled "Second Chance." In this episode, a close friend of the show's teenage lead character is seriously injured in a car accident after having "just a few drinks." The young adolescent vows to take full advantage of his second chance and lead his life more carefully and thoughtfully. Unexpectedly, he dies. The show's producers decided to have the character die in order to "break the typical sense of denial by young people that they're anything but immortal."[7]

Cigarettes are the most heavily advertised product in the United States, and alcohol is second. One out of every six deaths in America is attributable to cigarette smoking. Nearly half of all violent deaths—automobile accidents, suicide, and homicide—are al-cohol-related. Alcohol problems cost our nation more than $70 billion per year.[8] A large percentage of people begin smoking and drinking in early adolescence, encouraged by the seductive and deceptive images of advertisers. Our society's tolerance of drug peddling aimed at adolescents is unconscionable. Targeting our youth for addiction should not be tolerated any more than allowing billboards encouraging heroin use or advertisements for crack co-caine on the sides of buses. Parents need to make it known to the networks and studios that they will not support programming that encourages or glamorizes addiction. They must help their teen-agers recognize the ways in which the media's appealing portrayals of cigarettes, drugs, and alcohol are designed to manipulate young people into a lifetime of drug use and abuse.

PSYCHOLOGICAL DEVELOPMENT AND THE MEDIA

ATTACHMENT

"Would you like to go to the movies with Dad and me?"

"No!" (Said with the kind of emphasis usually reserved for the unthinkable.)

"Why not?"

"I'm not that kind of person."

"What kind?"

"The kind of dweeb who would spend Saturday night with his parents."

In this typical interchange, the young adolescent can make it perfectly clear what kind of person he isn't; the much more difficult task is knowing what kind of person he *is*. Adolescents know that they are shedding their childhood but haven't yet evolved into the person they will ultimately become. They have not had the time or the experience to generate a new self. The creation of this new self is the task of the teenage years.

The young adolescent's moves toward independence are often erratic and tumultuous. While there is great striving toward be-coming an individual, there is also a great sense of sadness for the loss of childhood security. The day my eighth-grade son had to fill out a schedule for high school, I found him in tears on his bed. "I feel like it's too soon for my childhood to be over," he said in a moment of rare vulnerability. Although it is exactly this process of separation, of "growing up," that is the hallmark of successful parenting, it is often met with both joy and sadness for parent and child alike.

Becoming an adult demands becoming independent of one's parents. This demand is at the heart of much of the conflict between young adolescents and their parents. To some degree, adolescents need to reject their families in order to forge their own identity. Parents are challenged, ignored, and endlessly criticized during early adolescence. Those parents who understand the reasons and the temporary nature of this disruption in family relations are in a much better position to help their children (and themselves) pass through this demanding and often difficult period.

It is important that parents not take their young adolescents' squawking too personally: "You're so uncool." "What do you know?" "I refuse to be seen with such weird-looking people" (this said by a teenager wearing pants with a crotch around his knees and green hair). No matter how good and close a relationship you have had with your child, no matter how liberal or conservative or apolitical your point of view is, no matter how well you dress, or how much you know, your adolescent is driven to find fault with you. It helps teenagers to know that grown-ups have faults. Painfully aware of their own shortcomings, adolescents find solace in the fact that one does not have to be perfect in order to be an adult.

Being critical of their parents also allows adolescents to consider other adult points of view: "My coach said . . . ," "My teacher said. . . ." While parents may feel displaced by their teenagers' sudden reliance on other sources of authority, it is an important advance for teenagers to expand their horizons and draw from other role models.

Teenagers, like the toddlers they were some ten years earlier, are essentially explorers. The media make available new places, different people, other points of view, and fresh experiences. Nothing is so foreign or so remote that it cannot be brought into the teenager's world via the television or the movie screen. Early adolescence is a crucial turning point in development; attitudes that will be carried into adulthood are being formed and consolidated. Media become a large source of information for this age group, as they rely less on parents and more on outside information for developing a worldview. Therefore, the media's potential for encouraging prosocial attitudes, as well as their potential to cultivate and enhance antisocial attitudes, continues to be significant at this age.

It is not that young adolescents need to be shielded from conflict and violence. On the contrary, these are issues that are relevant to this age group. What specific kinds of effects do the media have on adolescents? In what ways are their behaviors and attitudes being influenced? How can the media help young teenagers in their struggle to separate from family and forge a healthy and prosocial identity? Where have the media been successful in their attempts? Where have they failed? How can parents help adolescents to become thoughtful consumers of the media?

Certainly "coming of age" movies such as *The Breakfast Club, Stand by Me,* and *This Boy's Life* have been successful both in terms of entertaining young adolescents and in addressing their concerns. Movies that realistically portray young adolescents' struggles with attachment and separation from family are particularly useful to this age group. Adolescents benefit from being exposed to the consequences of different courses of action. Movies and television provide an opportunity to witness, from a safe distance, the results of different life choices. It is not realistic, or even desirable, for adolescents to always make good choices. Often there is just as much to learn from the fictional adolescent who makes a poor choice as from the one who makes the "right choice." What matters is that adolescents begin to appreciate the complexity of life.

Personal Best is a movie about two young women runners who are competing for a spot on the U.S. Olympic team. It tackles the question of intimacy versus individual achievement. The two women fall in love with each other but find that their intense competition precludes a completely open heart. It is a moving and natural movie that was enjoyed by many adolescent girls. While dealing with complex issues such as identity and homosexuality, it poses questions, provokes thought, and suggests answers. It does not preach or demean. It is a movie that takes seriously the issues of adolescence and young adulthood, does not trivialize these concerns, and encourages thought. These are the hallmarks of good moviemaking for this age. Other fine movies include *Ordinary People, Dead Poets Society, School Ties,* and *What's Eating Gilbert Grape?,* which prove that adolescents can be successfully engaged, entertained, and educated all at once.

Parents frequently feel that they have little control over their young teenagers' viewing choices. Certainly their authority is different than it was when their children were younger. Parents now need to appreciate the power of influence as opposed to control. Influence takes more time and more tact than "Because I say so." However, the judicious use of influence provides young adolescents with a model for a more respectful and adult way of dealing with others. Contrary to popular belief, study after study has shown that adolescents crave more, not less, discussion with their parents.[9]

Watch what your teenager watches and then encourage discussion. Listen. Set limits when you feel strongly.

AGGRESSION

Adolescents make up a disproportionately large percentage of both the victims of aggression and the perpetrators of aggression. Firearms are the leading cause of death of black teenagers and the second leading cause of death of white teenagers. One out of every four teenage deaths is caused by a gun.[10] The issue of how young adolescents experience and deal with their aggression takes on an added sense of urgency given these distressing statistics.

We are in the midst of a crisis. We are losing an insupportable number of young lives because too many teenagers are incapable of working out the interpersonal conflicts that are an inevitable part of everyday life. The media, because they bear responsibility for glamorizing violence and offering easy solutions to difficult problems and because they have the power to shape both individual and social perspectives, should begin to use their influence to preserve this country's youth.

One of the greatest concerns that parents have about their young adolescents is their tendency to act impulsively. In fact, young adolescents are under the influence of many new and powerful feelings. There is an emergence of sexual feelings and physical sensations that are both exciting and confusing. Adolescents can find themselves in trouble if they feel overwhelmed by these new feelings. Many agencies of society recognize this developmental challenge and try to aid adolescents in their efforts to think before they act.

Sex education classes teach the wisdom of waiting for a degree of emotional as well as physical maturity before becoming sexually active. Driver's education classes teach the need for responsibility and the necessity of following the law if one is to be accorded the adult privilege of driving. Drug education classes teach that seemingly minor decisions of the moment can have far-reaching consequences. Over and over, adolescents are reminded that decisions such as "I'll just smoke this one cigarette" can have consequences that they do not yet have the experience to envision. This doesn't mean that most young adolescents will never try that cigarette. What is probably of greater importance is that adults and major agencies of society are clear that they expect adolescents to think about the consequences of their actions.

If the media have failed in their responsibility to young adolescents, and I believe they have, it is in large measure because of their lack of emphasis on consequences. Killings may be everywhere, but funerals are rarely seen, and the devastating grief of real loss is rarely acknowledged. In *Total Recall*, Arnold Schwarzenegger puts a gun to his wife's forehead, pulls the trigger, and deadpans, "Consider that a divorce." In the movie she is an agent who has double-crossed him, and so his retaliation is "justified." But the audience, composed largely of teenagers, is left laughing at murder and one of this country's most serious social problems, spousal abuse.

Similarly, hugely popular television programs such as *Cops* blur the boundaries between violence as real-life tragedy and violence as entertainment. The program opens with the infectious popular song "Bad Boys." Viewers are still tapping their feet as the first incident of child abuse, spousal abuse, or drug abuse unfolds on the screen. The police and the judicial system work to protect people from the same experiences that we allow into our homes nightly. Violence is no longer something to be horrified at; it has become something we turn to for entertainment and relaxation.

One of the greatest tasks of adolescence is learning to be able to control impulses so the process of planning for the future can begin in earnest. When President Clinton was on MTV in the spring of 1994, he exhorted millions of teenagers and young adults to begin thinking about the future in terms of years, not days or weeks. His emphasis was well placed. The media can be a powerful ally in helping young adolescents appreciate the wisdom of delaying gratification. Over and over, in ways that are sensible and appealing, young adolescents need to be taught the skills that will help them work out differences of opinion verbally rather than with a weapon and to anticipate that today's actions may affect their future. Without this ability, young teenagers in our society are all too often finding that they don't have a future at all.

The largest audience for "slasher" movies—spectacles of exceptional gore and gruesomeness—is young adolescents. It should be noted that these are R-rated movies that are so disproportionately consumed by young teenagers, a fact that illustrates the limited value of a rating system that is only marginally enforced in theaters and not enforced at all in most video stores.

Typically, teenagers in slasher movies are murdered with graphic sadism by an unstoppable male psychopath. Affectionately called "slice and dice" movies by film critics, the best known of this genre include the *Nightmare on Elm Street* series and the *Friday the Thirteenth* series. Extraordinary only for the amount of horrifying violence shown, slasher movies invariably link sexuality and aggression and pander to adolescents' desire for stimulation. As any parent who has yelled "Lower that music!" can attest, adolescents seem to crave mind-numbing levels of stimulation. This overstimulation probably provides a welcome relief from young adolescents' rumination about themselves. Slasher movies exploit this vulnerability without offering solutions that adolescents can use to lessen their preoccupations. They teach adolescents nothing about how to live in the world and are devastatingly pessimistic.

The most disturbing aspect of these teen exploitation films is the welding of violence and sex. For many young adolescents, Freddy Krueger of *Nightmare on Elm Street* is their first experience with soft-core erotica. It is a most unwelcome introduction to sex. For instance, in *Nightmare on Elm Street*, a young girl is killed right after having sex with her boyfriend. Her flimsy nightgown is shredded by Freddy's knifelike fingers until she is soaked in blood. Moments later, Freddy returns to another teenage girl, naked in the bathtub; his hand rises between her spread legs before she too is murdered. And on and on it goes, with young women being mutilated, decapitated, exsanguinated, and disemboweled. I urge every parent to watch one of these movies. Sickening as the experience is, it will introduce you to what many children—perhaps even your children—can watch without batting an eyelash.

Although most teenagers do not engage in sexual intercourse until later in adolescence, attitudes about sexual intercourse, as well as about the opposite sex in general, are being formed in early adolescence. Parents, schools, and the media are in positions of influence if they can reach young adolescents before they begin acting on their sexual impulses. The schools have long recognized this and begin sex education classes years before teenagers become sexually active. One of the most critical aspects of this education is to help adolescents become aware of the potential for their abuse and exploitation once they become sexually active. Since we live in an age where the lack of communication about sexual matters can have deadly consequences (at least 20 percent of all AIDS patients contracted the disease in their adolescence),[11] adolescents need to truly understand the responsibility they assume when they become sexually active.

Movies and television programs that do not emphasize the serious consequences of unprotected sex or abusive relationships (sexual or not) are acting irresponsibly. MTV, which shows videos ad nauseam in which women are portrayed as nothing more than sexual objects, is irresponsible in a way that no amount of brief public service messages can counter. Although MTV insists that it has "standards" to determine what videos are allowed on television, repeated calls to its offices for a copy of these standards were ignored.

In his provocative analysis of MTV videos, Professor Sut Jhally points out that the essential role of women in many rock videos is simply to be looked at as objects.[12] To that end, women are often presented as body parts: breasts or legs. This refusal to take women seriously and insistence on focusing on them as body parts rather than full human beings represents the first step toward dehumanization. Research tells us that it is exactly this capacity to dehumanize women that leads men to hold increasingly tolerant attitudes toward rape.[13]

When physical abuse or sexual abuse is glamorized, we are putting our children at risk. In America today, a child is abused every thirteen seconds, born to a teenage mother every fifty-nine seconds, arrested for a violent crime every five minutes, and killed every two hours.[14] It is estimated that some form of violence takes place in one out of every three households. One out of every four women is subject to some form of sexual attack during her life.[15] The epidemic of violence among America's youth has become so severe and so threatening that the surgeon general has declared violence one of our most serious public health problems.

It is our responsibility as parents to protect our children, but it is also important for teenagers to see that having strong values is an integral part of living one's life well. We can fulfill our responsibility by not allowing our children to view things that we find patently offensive and by refusing to economically support sexist, racist, and other unacceptable media offerings. My young adolescent fought long and hard against my Guns and Roses prohibition. The group's smash hit album *Use Your Illusion 1* had multiple references to homosexuals as faggots and women as bitches. As parents we all make decisions about which lines can be crossed and which cannot. Clearly these lines change along with the development of our children. Everything may be open for discussion; not everything is open to compromise.

COGNITIVE DEVELOPMENT

Young adolescents are in the middle of the second great revolution in thinking—the ability to think abstractly. Adolescent thinking approaches the level of adult thinking. Teenagers are long past seeing things only in "black and white." They are able to understand symbols and to see that people may have motives that are not readily apparent. They can think about the past, the present, and the future. Their thinking is no longer limited to their own point of view. They can begin to make formal, logical arguments. This is what Piaget termed the stage of "formal operations." Young adolescents are sophisticated thinkers, a fact that their teachers can vouch for.

But rather than appearing to be capable of complex, adult thinking at home, young teenagers often appear to their parents to be ornery, hypercritical, and rigid in their thinking.

"Do you think it was right of Lauren to leave her girlfriend at the mall and go off with James instead?" mom asks.

"How should I know? Besides, what do you know about friends?" her daughter replies.

"Well, I was just wondering what you thought."

"That's the trouble with you, you're always trying to figure out what I'm thinking. Sometimes your girlfriends are the most important thing, but sometimes they're not."

Here we have some hallmarks of a typical early adolescent conversation. Mom ends up feeling criticized, while her daughter feels intruded on. But if some of the crankiness of the adolescent can be ignored, this example shows that the real issue she is struggling with is one of relativity, of competing allegiance, of moral judgment. The younger child would have had a simple yes or no answer. The adolescent struggles with more complicated realities.

Adolescents are great debaters. They argue about their clothes, their allowance, their homework, their curfew, their responsibilities, and just about anything else that can possibly be argued about. While this can certainly become irksome for parents who are tired and harried, it is a testimony to the young adolescent's growing intellectual prowess.

The adolescent mind takes nothing for granted, a necessary precursor to the ability to think clearly and scientifically. Allow your adolescent to flex his or her intellectual muscles. Young teenagers are full of ideas, and to the extent that they are free to indulge their thinking at home, parents are in a better position to monitor and encourage their intellectual development.

Adolescents are manufacturing their future selves. In the arena of thought, this means crafting a position on everything from their homework schedule to nuclear disarmament. Parents need to control their shock when their thirteen-year-old announces at the dinner table, "I don't understand why they don't legalize marijuana; everyone knows pot can't really hurt you" or "I wish they would hand out condoms at school, lots of kids are 'doing it' anyway." First of all, adolescents at this age are given to hyperbole. Do not prematurely cut off communication with your teenager; learn to take adolescent exaggeration with a grain of salt.

Teenagers need a safe place in which to practice their burgeoning intellectual skills. A healthy home provides young adolescents with both a laboratory and a launching pad from which to securely catapult themselves into adulthood. Home becomes a training ground in which young adolescents can develop positions, resist coercion, and become independent thinkers. Encouraging debate and discussion at home lays the groundwork for young adults who think independently, who can resist the pressure of the crowd, and who are able to stand by moral decisions even if they are unpopular. Few parents would quarrel with these goals for their children.

One aspect of adolescent thinking that parents often find irritating is that although their young philosophers may have all kinds of lofty ideas about how to solve the world's problems, these ideas seem to find little application in their daily life: "It is disgusting that we don't recycle. You guys are probably the only people in the world who don't care that our planet is being destroyed by garbage and consumerism." Could this be the same child who leaves a trail of litter at the fast-food restaurant or is insulted when you suggest he walk or ride his bike rather than be driven someplace? Young adolescents are new to the world of ideas. The connection between theory and practice is fragile and will take many years to solidify. The idealism of adolescence is a precursor to social action. Don't expect too much practical application from your teenagers yet, but encourage thinking about social issues. Teach action through your own involvement in good causes.

Adolescents generally like television programs and movies that make them think about physical danger, separation and individuation, identity, commitment, and success. The movie *Wild Hearts Can't Be Broken* tells the story of Sonora, a strong-willed, orphaned adolescent who runs away from an unsympathetic aunt rather than become a ward of the state. Through the force of her persistence and her love of horses, she is able to realize her ambition of becoming a "diving lady." She joins a traveling circus and rides horses off a forty-foot tower into a pool of water. Sonora is blinded in an accident when her horse stumbles, sending her crashing into the pool. Driven by determination and love for her work, she eventually returns to performing even though she has been repeatedly cautioned that she can never ride again.

This movie addresses many of the themes of adolescence: separation from family, finding one's own identity, and overcoming physical danger. The film teaches more about real courage, the ability to push oneself to the maximum as an act of love, than all the macho posturing of a movie like *Cliffhanger*, which purports to be about courage but is really about the mindless myth that links masculinity and violence. While we would prefer our young teenagers to always view the more realistic and prosocial film, it is not likely that this will always be the case. There is an element of rebellion in adolescent tastes and, as one of my teenage patients pointed out, "If grown-ups all hated *Bambi*, that's probably what I'd want to see."

So, while young teenagers can be encouraged to see movies that are more instructional and optimistic and can be prohibited from seeing movies that are at complete variance with family values, there is a wide swath of movies that are neither. Taken individually, teenage favorites such as *Beverly Hills Cop*, *Die Hard*, and *Terminator* probably do little to either advance or inhibit adolescent thinking. As a steady diet, however, I would argue that they present adolescents with a worldview that is pessimistic and cynical, and that endorses violence and impulsivity. They appeal to young adolescents' lowest level of thinking rather than encouraging abstract and complex thought.

What these movies *can* provide is an opportunity for parents to discuss violent solutions as a way of resolving interpersonal differences. Talk with your teenagers about what they see. Encourage your adolescents to challenge the point of view of the movie; explore why the audience has become so sympathetic to a murderer. In what ways has the movie or program manipulated its audience and how does it accomplish this? It's an opportunity for adolescents to actively think about what they are viewing instead of simply being passive recipients, and it's an opportunity for you to help guide their newly emerging abilities to think and analyze.

MORAL DEVELOPMENT

Along with the revolution in thinking that young adolescents are experiencing is a revolution in moral development. Young adolescents are able to appreciate that people and their motives are complicated. They understand that morality can be relative and endlessly ponder questions like "If your life depended on it, could you eat human flesh?" or "If you knew you could save the lives of many people, would you kill one evil person?" These questions are alluring to young adolescents because they go beyond the kind of "black and white" answers that were previously so satisfying to them as children.

The hallmark of this stage of moral development is an increased capacity for caring and cooperation. Young adolescents are able to consider the point of view of the group, whether it be their peer group, parents, school, or society at large. Unlike younger children, adolescents want to be good, not only to please those in authority or because they have something to gain, but because they now have an internalized image of a "good person" and strive to live up to it. They benefit from living up to this image in two ways:

They think well of themselves (self-approval), and others think well of them (social approval). Together, these two types of approval can boost self-esteem and help young adolescents create a more altruistic and responsible sense of self.

Just as we saw the demise of "black and white" thinking in young adolescence, so do we see the end of severe moral judgment. At this stage, teenagers are more forgiving and flexible in their moral judgment because they are able to consider extenuating circumstances and to understand that people's motives can be quite complex. As opposed to the philosophy of "every man for himself," young adolescents can embrace a more benevolent and unselfish "all for one and one for all." Mercy begins to temper justice: "Mike is smoking pot. It's a tough time for him because his mom is sick"; "I gave Susan a dollar. She was crying because she lost her allowance. You know how forgetful little kids can be."

Given this significant shift in moral reasoning, why do young adolescents seem so hideously critical of their families? Reading about the compassion of the young adolescent in the previous paragraph may make some parents think I am writing about a totally different creature than the one they have living in their home. Compassion? Mercy? Often it seems like young adolescents are engaged in full-blown, take-no-prisoners, verbal warfare with their own family. "You guys are just hopeless" or "Please wait outside so no one sees you" is hardly the height of tolerance or charity. What is this crazy dichotomy that allows young adolescents to empathize with friends' major flaws while at the same time being so hypervigilant and critical of their family's minor or imagined flaws?

During the childhood years, it is primarily parents who supply the role models for appropriate, caring behavior. This changes in adolescence, when the demands of creating an individual separate from the family force a temporary withdrawal and even a renunciation of family attitudes, behaviors, and values. The peer group often replaces the family as the most important transmitter of attitudes and behavior. At this stage, being accepted by other kids becomes a full-time job and often a preoccupation. Adolescents will give up a lifelong interest if a friend declares it "uncool." Most young adolescents are desperately unhappy with their looks, their personality, their family, and often their life in general. Projecting some of their hypercritical self-evaluation onto the family helps maintain a level of equilibrium. The assaultive, critical comments and questions adolescents pose to their families—"What do you know?"; "I can't believe how dorky you look?"; "Please don't let anyone see you"—are all reflections of the insecurity adolescents feel about themselves. Rephrased, these comments really mean "What do I know?"; "Am I really a dork?"; "These horrible pimples on my face—I wish I was invisible."

Even though there may be conflict between parents and young teenagers, this does not reflect an undoing of the previous twelve years of childrearing. If parents have been successful in laying the foundation of clear moral values in early childhood, their young adolescents are better able to benefit from exposure to different values and to withstand the pressure of their peers when those values conflict with their own. For many of the reasons that have been discussed in this chapter (the need to break away from family, the development of a new sense of self, the reliance on friends), adolescence is a period of marked vulnerability to peer pressure and conformist thinking. "Everyone's doing it" is a remarkably powerful justification for most young adolescents. Social approval often takes precedence over conscience.

Parents need to help their young adolescents feel good about themselves by maintaining a healthy and positive relationship with the family and by providing acceptance and love in the face of adolescent insecurity. They need to further their young adolescents' moral development by actively modeling what they believe to be moral behavior. This is no time for "Do as I say, not as I do." Adolescents are very critical of hypocrisy. Finally, parents need to balance their teenagers' need for independence with adult experience and judgment. A good rule of thumb is to say "yes" when you can and "no" when you must.

Movies and television programs that deal with common adolescent issues such as autonomy, separation-individuation, commitment, and career and that emphasize the often painful process of self-evaluation are helpful to young adolescents. While *Beverly Hills 90210* depicts older teens, it tends to be watched by younger ones who are looking for clues as to "what's next." Although this program overemphasizes some of the dramatic elements of adolescence such as sex and drugs and underemphasizes the more ordinary dilemmas such as grades and self-esteem, it does portray the adolescent's struggle to consider consequences and forge a personal sense of right and wrong. The issue of going against the crowd is repeatedly considered, and support is largely given to those who are able to "march to their own drummer." This perspective is very helpful and probably of greater significance than the actual content of each episode. It communicates that a major task of adolescence is to "be one's own person"—to consider and feel comfortable with one's point of view, one's judgment and sense of morality, whether or not this is the popular point of view. Programs like this appeal to young adolescents' higher level of reasoning and recognize the complexity of this stage of development.

Many excellent movies have attempted to deal with the complex moral issues and dilemmas that adolescents face without trivializing their struggles. In *This Boy's Life*, Ellen Barkin and Leonardo DiCaprio play a mother and her young adolescent son down on their luck. In an effort to provide stability for herself and a male role model for her son, she marries an unhappy and abusive man. As he is increasingly tormented by his sadistic stepfather, the boy begins to plan his escape from both his family and the leaden town they live in (appropriately named Concrete). He edges toward juvenile delinquency, changes his grades, and writes fake letters of recommendation to get into an eastern prep school. While some of his behavior is "wrong," it is understandable. Dilemmas like the ones presented in the movie—Is it ever okay to hit a parent? Are there situations in which lying and cheating are reasonable responses?—help the young adolescent think about right and wrong as being complicated and situational issues rather than simple and absolute ones.

While young adolescents are busily engaged in developing attitudes and behaviors toward the opposite sex, every effort should be made to communicate that respect is the underpinning of all successful relationships. Gangsta rap lyrics that demean women and encourage violence against them promote the idea that abuse of women is admirable. While a superficial reading of this kind of music suggests that only black gangsta rappers hold such reactionary beliefs, adolescents are well aware that records are produced and distributed by large corporate machines. It is this complicity of the adult world in packaging and popularizing abuse of women, as well as violence in general, that is ultimately most damaging. Rich, powerful, mostly white men in suits tolerate and promote the dehumanization of women. This lesson is not lost on young adolescents.

MTV, the most conspicuous purveyor of adolescent stupefaction, insists on reducing the complexities of life to banal, misogynistic, and myopic music videos. Rather than encouraging adolescents' more advanced level of cognitive and moral development, MTV plays to the remnant of the child in every teenager who demands stimulation at the expense of reflection. Tom Freston, chief executive officer of MTV, when asked to describe what kinds of qualities it takes to run MTV, revealingly said, "Shallowness and the ability to fake sincerity."[16]

The cornerstone of moral development is the ability to truly empathize with someone else's point of view. Movies and television programs that dehumanize the other, that show women or minorities as less than full human beings, work against the evolution of moral development. For all of their brief public service messages on rape, MTV cannot undo the hours of propaganda showing women in dog collars, on leashes, and as sexual objects in their music videos. Poignant poems about violence as part of their Enough Is Enough campaign are not likely to reduce the impact of the hours of glamorization of violence in gangsta rap. To take a moral position against these infringements on human rights and either censor or censure them would be a powerful statement to their primarily young adolescent audience. (Parents need to take a moral position against these violations to human rights.) Parents must be clear about the unacceptability of all forms of media which support and glamorize human rights violations.

12

Adolescence:
Ages 15, 16, 17, and 18

GENERAL DEVELOPMENT

Early adolescence is a time for distinguishing oneself from one's parents. Middle and later adolescence is a time for distinguishing oneself from the crowd. As we saw in the previous chapter, early adolescence is marked by turmoil, overidentification with peers, and high levels of conformity. Young teenagers fight mightily against their parents in an effort to begin forging an identity of their own. As teenagers move along in adolescence and begin to feel less vulnerable to the pull of childhood, they begin a process of experimentation and exploration that eventually will lead to a new and stable sense of self. To do this, teenagers invent and reinvent themselves on a regular basis.

Fifteen-year-old Katie has been involved in gymnastics since she was seven. She attended class twice a week for almost eight years and consistently ranked high in the competitions she insisted on entering. At times her parents worried that gymnastics was "consuming" her life and suggested that she might find other activities interesting as well. These suggestions were always met with vehement denial and tears. "There is nothing in the world I like better than gymnastics" was Katie's unequivocal response. Three weeks after her fifteenth birthday, Katie announced that she was no longer interested in pursuing gymnastics and criticized her parents for "making it my whole life."

Clean-cut sixteen-year-old Seth was captain of the junior varsity football team. He was an outstanding and aggressive athlete who had participated in team sports for many years. He had always aspired to be on the varsity team, and his excellent performance in his sophomore year assured him a place on the varsity team the following year. Over the summer, his parents noticed that he began growing his hair out and even had a small earring put in his newly pierced ear. While he continued to play football, his parents often heard him criticizing the "aggressive" nature of his teammates. He signed up for elective courses in poetry and journalism. He did, however, eagerly accept the college football scholarship that was offered to him.

Parents of younger adolescents often feel that they are living in a war zone with their new teenagers. Parents of older teenagers often feel more bewildered than attacked. Erik Erikson coined the term "identity crisis"[1] to help clarify and define this period of development. While "crisis" may be misunderstood to mean catastrophe or emergency, Erikson did not see this as a pathological state. He understood that adolescents who are experiencing an "identity crisis" are in a normal stage of development, but one that is of singular importance. It is out of this "crisis" that a coherent and stable adult identity will emerge.

The development of an identity, of a sense of self, is a process that takes place over decades. Throughout childhood and early adolescence, young people are forging a sense of self that undergoes continual and radical change. These changes take place as children get feedback from themselves and their environment. My athletic oldest son "knew" he was going to play for the NBA when he was in elementary school, "thought" he would play for the NBA in junior high school, and in high school started thinking about law school, "just in case" he didn't make it to the NBA. Interests, competencies, and opportunities wax and wane over many years.

The challenge of adolescence is to assemble different pieces of the self into a working whole that serves both the individual and society. Inquiry and experimentation are critical to this period of development, as they allow teenagers to try on many different identities before settling on one that is consistent with their abilities, nature, and opportunities. While parents may be baffled by the fact that fastidious, conservative, fashion-conscious Suzy suddenly lives in a room that resembles a garbage dump, buys her clothes at the Salvation Army, and is out protesting animal rights violations, Suzy is in fact "taking care of business." Without this period of exploration, Suzy would face significant psychological risk.

Erikson identified two unfortunate outcomes that can result when teenagers are not able to go through this normal process of exploration. The first of these he called "identity foreclosure," to describe the kind of teenager who continues to see things only through the eyes of others. Most typically, this would be the eyes of his parents, but it could also be the eyes of other important peers or adults such as his gang or his religious leaders. He goes to church every week because that's what his parents expect, he plans on being a lawyer because "all the men in this family are lawyers," and his criteria for dating are whether or not his parents would "approve" of his choice in girls. Instead of developing an identity of his own, he has adopted the identity provided him by others.

In effect, this child has completely bypassed adolescence. He has sidestepped the developmental task of identity formation, and it is likely that this strategy will ultimately produce an individual who suffers from deep feelings of emptiness and depression. Although it is essential that parental and community values be communicated to adolescents, teenagers must also have an active and vigorous role in forging their own identities. It is not something we can simply lift from those around us, no matter how well intentioned they are.

The second, more generally recognized consequence of a poorly navigated adolescence is what Erikson termed "negative identity." As in identity foreclosure, parental overinvolvement plays a major role in the formation of a negative identity. The family who is considered a pillar of the community finds itself with a provocative, "druggie" adolescent. An upper-middle-class family finds that its teenager has "renounced materialism" and is joining a cult. Of course, many adolescents go through periods of opposing their parents' point of view. It is only when adolescents feel no choice but to solidify their opposition in the face of parental overinvolvement that true negative identity takes place. Once again, this is a poor conclusion to the process of developing a unique identity. Teenagers often need to "de-identify" with their families for a period of time. However, the task of identity formation is aided when teenagers feel free to explore their options in the context of family support. Parents who are *overinvolved* in the lives of their teenagers run the risk of limiting their children's healthy options. *Ideally, a supportive and respectful family is the critical context in which teenagers can work on the major task of identity formation.*

Adolescents are solidifying the gains they made in middle childhood when they worked hard at mastering different and increasingly complex tasks. Teenagers have to connect the abilities and talents they developed in childhood to realistic adult goals. Here we see the importance of the middle years when much effort went into developing skills and learning information. The adolescent now has to reconcile his private image of himself with how the world views him, and he knows the world is larger and often less gentle than his family has been. While his parents have only admired his crabbed piano playing, he has heard others play who are more talented, and he is better able to see "where he stands" in the world. It is not enough that he's a good listener or a talented writer. The teenager wants to know how to translate his abilities into skills that will serve him in the "real world." The good listener could be a psychiatrist or a sound technician in the movies. The good English student could be a journalist or a teacher. Adolescence is a time to experiment with how one's abilities will be of service in adulthood.

As we saw earlier in this chapter, with Katie and Seth, adolescence is not necessarily a period when skills that were evident in youth are polished and accepted. Although some teenagers may continue to pursue long-standing interests, others seem eager to disassociate themselves from earlier interests. Identities are embraced and discarded with equal zeal. One day the teenager is a Democrat and the next he's a Republican. Jocks become poets and poets become jocks. Good girls become fast girls, and fast girls become nuns. Great passions well up and just as frequently dry up. While parents are often telling their teenagers to "play the field" when it comes to dating, because they recognize the hazards of cutting off social options too early, so do teenagers need to "play the field" when it comes to political ideas, moral choices, academic interests, and outside activities.

Parents need to keep in mind that adolescence is often a period in which there is actually less, not more, than meets the eye. Although teenagers like to think of themselves as outrageously different from their parents and from each other, there is an almost comic quality to the similarities of their differences. Erikson called this a "uniformity of differing." Teenagers who abhor the conformity of their blue-jean- and blazer-clad suburban parents all wear their baseball caps backwards and their flannel shirts covering their uniformly bottom-sagging pants. But by the end of adolescence, individual differences in dress, manner, interest, and activities are clearly visible.

There's a final point that I would like to make in this section on general adolescent development. As a psychologist, I am often asked by parents exactly "how much rope" they should give their adolescents. My answer has always been "enough so they don't hang themselves." The issue of setting limits with teenagers runs through this and the previous chapter. Give your teenager enough opportunity to try out different identities, different ideas, and different activities. Don't be overinvolved or critical of your teenagers' changes of heart, lest you interfere with their ability to develop a healthy sense of self. But as parents we also want to be sure that our children are protected from real danger. It's one thing to allow your teenage son to hang out with a couple of kids who smoke; it's quite another if he starts selling drugs. Your daughter's dressing like Madonna is acceptable; her sleeping with half the football team is not. How are parents to gauge when their adolescent's exploration is healthy, when it is flirting with danger, and when it demands intervention? The following is a brief list of what I consider to be the most frequent adolescent danger signs.

REGULAR DRUG OR ALCOHOL USE

Approximately 90 percent of all high school seniors say that they have had some experience with alcohol. This number has been constant for quite some time.[2] While it is very difficult to say where experimentation stops and abuse begins, it is likely that teenagers who use drugs or alcohol over time and more than occasionally are at risk. In addition, the frequent use of these substances is generally tied to other problems such as depression, low self-esteem, and risk-taking behaviors. If parental injunctions prove useless, then professional intervention is mandatory. Alcohol is involved in an extremely high percentage of adolescent deaths.

PROMISCUITY

Sexual intercourse among adolescents is prevalent. By age fifteen, approximately 25 percent of adolescents are sexually active. Two years later, by age seventeen, approximately half of all teenagers are sexually active. By age nineteen, 70 percent of girls and 80 percent of boys are sexually active. In general, boys become active about one year earlier than girls, and black youths are more sexually active at younger ages than their white or Hispanic counterparts.[3] Sexual activity among adolescents is surprisingly monogamous, with 50 percent of sexually experienced adolescent girls having sex with only one partner, and another 35 percent having sex with two or three partners. These statistics make clear the distinction between being sexually active and sexually promiscuous. Most teenagers at some point during their adolescence will become sexually active, but the vast majority do not become promiscuous. Sexual promiscuity, like drug and alcohol abuse, is correlated with an array of psychological problems such as low self-esteem, depression, and a prior history of sexual abuse. Because adolescents have become one of the fastest growing groups of HIV-infected individuals, responsible sex has become a matter of life and death.

TEENAGE DEPRESSION AND SUICIDE

While the suicide rate for adults has remained relatively constant for the last thirty years, it has quadrupled for adolescents age fifteen to nineteen. The suicide rate for adolescent boys is twice as high as for girls. White adolescents are twice as likely to commit suicide as black or Hispanic adolescents. The increased availability of firearms is believed to contribute dramatically to the increase in successful suicide attempts, since youthful suicide is often an impulsive gesture made possible by the lethality of readily available guns.

It is my experience that adolescent depression is one of the most overlooked and misdiagnosed psychiatric illnesses. Too often, the clinical symptoms of depression—apathy, withdrawal, hopelessness, and often aggression—are considered part of the normal *sturm und drang* of adolescence and are not taken seriously. Teenagers who exhibit these kinds of behavior for more than brief periods of time should be evaluated for depression. Untreated depression places adolescents at risk for early death whether by suicide or by increasing the likelihood of engaging in risk-taking behaviors such as drinking and driving.

MEDIA AND THE ADOLESCENT

I wouldn't mind thinking I was somebody.
Mike in *Breaking Away*

This simple statement, spoken by an adolescent who feels his future options are limited, illustrates the longing and hopefulness of all teenagers. If, at the end of adolescence, teenagers feel like they are "somebody," then the developmental tasks of adolescence have been successfully resolved. These young people will carry into adulthood an enduring sense of self. Those adolescents who enter adulthood feeling like "nobody," however, are at risk for leading lives that are nonproductive, unsatisfying, and frequently antisocial.

While this is not a book about the sociology of adolescence, it is impossible to write about teenagers while ignoring the crisis that American youth are experiencing. The role of media and their effects on adolescents can be understood only if we realize that our teenagers are confronting unprecedented social problems. While the reasons for these problems are complex and not likely to be easily solved, the media's contribution to the problems of teenage violence, pregnancy, drug and alcohol abuse, and hopelessness are well documented and substantial.

It would be preposterous to claim that all these social ills are caused by the media. But to ignore the role of the media in contributing to these dreadful statistics is to ignore one of the most potent influences in the lives of teenagers. Children who watch *Sesame Street* can increase their cognitive skills; those who watch *Mister Rogers* have been shown to exhibit more compassionate behavior. Adults have learned to buckle up, quit smoking, and begin exercising, largely from massive public health campaigns presented through the media. Advertisers spend millions of dollars each year to "educate" us about the virtues of their various soaps, detergents, and deodorants, knowing that a successful ad campaign can change the way we think and what we buy. So certainly adolescents, with their thirst for information and taste for experimentation, are also likely to learn from the media. Don Roberts, chair of the Department of Communication at Stanford University, aptly summarized the hard reality of media influence on adolescents: "The issue is not whether mass media affect adolescent perceptions, beliefs, behaviors. Rather, it is one of society's judging how many adolescents need to be put at risk, in what way, before various corrective actions are viewed as necessary and justified."[4]

Adolescents turn to the media for many different reasons. They are plagued by concerns about identity, are actively seeking information about the adult world they will soon enter, and need significant amounts of time to "do nothing" in order to work on their internal preoccupations. The media provide relief, information, and distraction. Are the media honestly meeting these needs or are they in large measure exploiting a vulnerable market?

The media have glamorized the portrayal of guns so completely that adolescents brought into emergency rooms with gunshot wounds are amazed to find that they are in pain. Guns have become as ubiquitous a symbol of adult power as packs of cigarettes were in previous decades. It is the throwaway lines of casual violence like "Make my day" and "Are you feeling lucky, punk?" that have become part of the common lexicon. There is not a single studio head in this country who is not aware of the exploding homicide rate for adolescents. These captains of industry have all been shown the connection between media portrayals of violence and real-world violence. Their continued dismissal of these facts is criminal.

Teenagers, for the most part, do not need protection from the realities of life. On the contrary, they need as much information and education as possible. *Dead Poets Society* deals with suicide, *Boyz N the Hood* deals with homicide, *Schindler's List* documents genocide. Responsible movies such as these do not hesitate to confront and explore the kinds of difficult topics that interest adolescents. But they provide a historical context, emphasize complexity, explore alternatives, and show teenagers the consequences of actions that may limit or even destroy future opportunities. They are important movies for teenagers to see.

Of course, one of the purposes of media is to provide distraction, a way of "kicking back" and forgetting about one's problems. We all need "downtime." Action movies are exciting and engrossing and as a result allow us to turn our attention away from our own difficulties. This is a perfectly reasonable function of entertainment. Horror movies can also serve a psychological function for adolescents. They are a rite of passage that allows teenagers, at a safe distance, to "dare" to be unafraid and willing to confront demons. They hold the same attraction that fairy tales hold for younger children. They are preparation for going out into a world that contains many frightening unknowns. They also help adolescent males, the major consumers of action and horror movies, to lessen the psychological grip of mother by proving that they are "man enough" to manage on their own.

Evil has its attractions—from fire-breathing dragons and evil stepmothers to serial killers; people at all ages are interested in the darker aspects of humanity. This is because we all carry within ourselves thoughts and fantasies that are cruel and violent. It is naive and dangerous to deny the duality of human nature. But it is the socializing agents of society—family, school, religious institutions, and mass media—that are charged with the responsibility of helping children and adolescents understand and control their aggressive impulses.

At the risk of being repetitious, I will say again that no one movie or television program, no matter how violent, is likely to be damaging to reasonably healthy adolescents. The problem lies in the fact that violence is the rule rather than the exception. While boys do benefit from the man-as-dragon-slayer story, it is only one of many stories they need to hear. They also need man-as-father, man-as-nurturer, man-as-healer, and man-as-peacemaker stories if they are to enter adulthood truly equipped for the varied responsibilities they will find there. Unfortunately, outstanding television programs such as *My So-Called Life*, which dealt with serious and common adolescent problems, are often short-lived on network television. Teenagers have become so habituated to extreme violence that they lack the patience and insight needed to appreciate even marginally more demanding programs.

In spite of the industry's claim that it is only giving the public what they want, research shows that it is action, not violence, that appeals to audiences. The surprise summer hit of 1994, *Speed*, with Keanu Reeves, while not an intellectually demanding movie, managed to be thrilling while maintaining a minimal body count. *Apollo 13* was a gripping and fascinating history lesson, loudly applauded by the group of teenagers sitting next to me in the theater. *Crimson Tide* provided a good dose of action and suspense and still managed to pose questions particularly appealing to adolescents: Where does one's greatest responsibility lie? What constitutes betrayal? How to decide between one's conscience and the dictates of society? All of these movies were popular with adolescents, and they're good examples of the fact that audiences can be entertained and even riveted without being soaked in blood. Entertainment executives might consider these types of action movies as absorbing, responsible and profitable alternatives to movies featuring gratuitous violence.

ATTACHMENT

Every time I speak to a group of parents with high school–age kids, I'm asked the same question: "At this age, what can a parent possibly do to restrict a teenager's viewing choices?" The question is unfortunate on two counts. First, restriction is not the major issue. No one who is realistic would suggest that a teenager's viewing can be restricted in the same way as a younger child's can. Second, the question has a kind of implied despair about being able to control adolescents at all. Both of these misunderstandings stem from popular misconceptions about attachment between parents and teenagers.

There is no question that the nature of the tie between parents and adolescents has undergone a radical change. No longer are parents repositories of wisdom, filling up eager young vessels with their knowledge, life experience, and sense of morality. Teenagers are eager to construct an identity of their own, one far less dependent on their parents, and more in line with their own strengths and weaknesses. As we have seen, this means several years of exploration and experimentation with everything from clothes and mannerisms to ideas and identities. Studies show that most teenagers crave more time with their parents. Equally surprising, once adolescence is over, most children grow up to be more or less like their parents.

How can parents reconstruct a relationship with their adolescents that includes advice and guidance but is not seen as intrusive or controlling? First, parents need to call on the natural curiosity and intellectual expansion that teenagers are experiencing. Rather than repeated admonitions about the "garbage" kids are watching, parents serve their teenagers well by asking open-ended questions such as "What made her tolerate his abuse?" "What was he feeling that made him believe that the only solution was violence?" The media present myriad opportunities for parents to help their adolescents think about and formulate opinions on different issues.

The O. J. Simpson trial, which took place during much of the writing of this book, provided many opportunities to talk with my two older sons about violence, spousal abuse, sports, hero worship, and friendship. Parental pronouncements such as "What a pig" may make parents' values known, but they do not expand teenagers' thought processes. Teenagers need to know where their parents stand but also have opportunities to think through a problem and come to their own conclusions. Ask questions, discuss, even be provocative. Talk to your teenager!

One of the extraordinary events taking place at this time is the teenager's discovery of love and sex. While emotional reliance on parents is diminishing, the adolescent is finding new support and nurturance in intimate relationships with peers. These relationships can be sexual or not, heterosexual or homosexual. They become part of the process by which the adolescent comes to define his or her identity. Erik Erikson describes this stage with great insight:

> This initiates the stage of "falling in love," which is by no means entirely, or even primarily, a sexual matter—except where the mores demand it. To a considerable extent adolescent love is an attempt to arrive at a definition of one's identity by projecting one's diffused ego image on another and by seeing it thus reflected and gradually clarified. This is why so much of young love is conversation.[5]

It is unfortunate that the media choose to ignore this reality of adolescent development. Conversation, discussion, and endless thinking are large components of adolescent life that are virtually ignored in favor of sexual adventure. While sexual issues are critical as never before, and will be discussed at length later in this chapter, let's focus for a moment on the equally compelling emotional aspect of adolescent love. As parents, we know that it can be hard to remember parts of our adolescence, but we all remember our first broken heart. The emotional investment that teenagers make in each other is perhaps unparalleled. Although couples break up frequently and seem to treat each other with apparent indifference, the truth is that these foundered relationships can be excruciatingly painful to the adolescent.

One of the reasons *My So-Called Life* was so well liked by many adolescents was that it acknowledged the primacy of adolescent emotional connection, not just sexual activity. The producers of that program made a sound decision by having their fifteen-year-old central character, Angela, remain a virgin. This device allowed the show to circumvent many of the mandatory sexual escapades of television characters and instead focus on psychological development. While sex certainly came up as a subject, it was mainly talked about, not acted upon. Characters were given the opportunity to plumb some of the conflict and ambivalence characteristic of adolescents.

There is a wonderful movie called *The Man in the Moon*, a beautifully drawn portrait of two sisters, one on the verge of adolescence, the other closer to adulthood. The movie chronicles their shifting intimacy with each other as well as their equally passionate love for a local boy. This movie provided a particularly telling opportunity for me to witness the power of treating adolescents with respect. Moments after I began watching, my teenage son wandered into the room. I was certain that this movie, about two girls, set in some dusty small town in the 1950s, would provoke disinterest at best, sarcasm at worst. But he sat and began watching with me, pulled in by the honest portrayal of adolescent hope, longing, and confusion. This is a movie totally devoid of the usual devices to grab and hold our attention. It takes place entirely in the dialogue and body movements of its characters. We sat spellbound on the couch, woven into this family whose lives were so different from our own. But we each recognize the language of the heart when it is spoken clearly and directly. When the movie was over, my fifteen-year-old, Rambo-loving son said, "That was the best movie I ever saw." We frequently underestimate our teenagers. They deserve, and profit from, being spoken to directly, honestly, and with dignity.

TEENAGERS AND SEX IN THE MEDIA

The basis of all successful human relationships is respect and affection. Teenagers should be encouraged to see programs and movies that acknowledge that fact. It is unfortunate that teenagers frequently feel pushed into sexual activity before they have a firm grasp on the emotional underpinnings of human connection. The media have failed to show that real human connection comes out of emotional intimacy, not just sexual intimacy. Overall, the media portray sex as glamorous, spontaneous, and, most dangerously, risk free.

Learning about sex is different for teens than any other kind of social learning because the information comes not through participation and observation but from each other—and much of it turns out to be false. Teenagers watch each other skateboard and then try it themselves. Even such things as "how to talk to girls" are things that teenage boys watch in a variety of contexts (how dad talks to mom, how big brother talks to his girlfriend) and then gradually participate in at the level they find comfortable. Sex, however, is not something that teenagers learn through observation. The actual act of intercourse is rarely a public event.

When it comes to disseminating sexual information, parents, schools, and religious institutions vary greatly in their willingness and comfort level. Parental denial plays a large part in limiting access to sexual information as teenagers have sex at younger and younger ages. This trend has potentially devastating implications for our society, for it is well documented that younger teenagers are less likely to be well informed about birth control and disease prevention and are more likely to engage in unprotected sex than older teens.

Since adolescence is a time of lessened parental control, greater access to media, and few competing sources of information about sex, it is no surprise that the media play a very important role in the sexual socialization of teenagers. Unfortunately, little of what teenagers see about sex in the media is thoughtful or respectful. Instead, teenagers are exposed to a sexual world heavy on violence and other assertions of power and low on love and commitment. MTV has immersed adolescents in a world where sexual activity is primarily the province of hormonally flooded males with little concern for their female partners. Consequences of sexual activity are virtually nonexistent and the few mentions of contraception that exist are often paired with emotional indifference. Snoop Doggy Dog may have a "pocketful of rubbers" for the "bitches in the living room,"[6] but he has nothing meaningful to teach adolescents about the joys and responsibilities of love.

The media have been grossly negligent in their portrayals of sex and its consequences. Approximately 85 percent of all sexual relationships on television are between unmarried or uncommitted couples.[7] The media are content to stick with the subject of "screwing around" rather than struggle with the far more complex issue of human intimacy. Watching television and movies, one would think that sex stops at the altar.

While preparing this book, I watched many dozens of the most popular teenage movies, and I never saw a reasoned and intelligent discussion of birth control. According to most stories told by the media, intercourse and pregnancy are unrelated. Can we measure the percentage of the million babies born to teenagers each year who in some measure owe their existence to such repeated irresponsible portrayals of teenage sex? Probably not. Like violence, teenage pregnancy is the endpoint of many individual and social factors. But there is absolutely no doubt that the media portrayals, *on the whole*, have been derelict in informing teenagers about the consequences of sexual activity.

As we have seen earlier in this book, aggression as a style of dealing with conflict is something that is learned early in childhood and learned well. It is in fact quite difficult to modify aggression once it is the preferred way of handling problems. By adolescence, most children have a reasonably consistent way of handling interpersonal conflict. It is unlikely that media violence can turn a previously cooperative and peaceful child into a mid-adolescent criminal. That kind of damage is probably done earlier in life by any number of social and individual factors.

Although crimes are being committed by younger and younger individuals, it is still adolescence that contains a disproportionate number of both perpetrators and victims. With very few exceptions, seven-year-olds don't rape and murder; seventeen-year olds do. In her powerful book *Boys Will Be Boys*, Myriam Miedzian looks at the many factors in our society that contribute to boys developing a sense of self that relies heavily on aggressive posturing: "Many of the values of the masculine mystique, such as toughness, dominance, repression of empathy, extreme competitiveness, play a major role in criminal and domestic violence and underlie the thinking and policy decisions of many of our political leaders."[8] The book forces the realization that it is usually not "aggression" that is being studied, but male aggression. The vast majority of crimes are committed by men, and so we need to pay particular attention to the messages that both parents and the media send to boys.

The media have failed to provide teenage boys with role models that are worthy of imitation. Conversely, why is it that males seem particularly attracted to media messages that stress intimidation and the abuse of power as ways to navigate the world? Boys are far more affected by male role models than by female role models, while girls are equally affected by both. Women in the media are typically portrayed as being less aggressive and more socially conscious than men. Perhaps it is the acceptance of female role models that confers a protective factor on girls, making them less vulnerable to the aggressive, macho images that suffuse popular culture. Boys desperately need a wider range of male models, some of whom incorporate the more traditional female values of cooperation and sensitivity. It would be of great benefit for adolescent boys to see male characters who are attractive without being violent. Unfortunately, male characters who are presented as gentle are frequently also portrayed as defective or crazy, as in *Edward Scissorhands* or *Don Juan Demarco*.

It is a peculiarity of our culture that exposure to sexual material is considered more damaging to children than exposure to violence. The Puritan aversion to sex still evident in our culture results in some truly extraordinary contradictions. In 1995, *NYPD Blue* caused a stir by breaking the nudity code on television. For the first time, a major television program allowed one of its stars to bare his buttocks. No matter that we had seen decades of shootings, knifings, rapes, and mutilations. Jimmy Smits was shown bare-assed. Personally, I would rather have my children see someone's butt hanging out than his brains hanging out. Call me a romantic.

We have decided, against all scientific evidence, that it is sex, not violence, that we need to shield our youth from. Tom Cruise saying "fuck" twice in *Rain Man* is in no way the equivalent of John Travolta blowing someone's brains out in *Pulp Fiction* (both R-rated movies). The effects of these two movies on children are considerably different, and that difference is not adequately acknowledged under the current rating system. While there is a value to ratings that reflect what the hypothetical "average American parent" would consider appropriate for his or her child, there is also value in considering what research has to tell us about what is damaging to children and teens. The rating system would be far more useful to parents if it acknowledged different developmental stages and gave additional information about why films received their particular rating.

Total Recall, Terminator, Die Hard, and *Robocop* all feature gratuitous violence and often combine sexual and aggressive messages. Is it true that the sexual content is what is most damaging? After all, adolescent boys, heavy consumers of media violence, are having their first sexual experiences and are formulating attitudes toward women that they will carry for a lifetime. Edward Donnerstein, one of this country's leading authorities on pornography and a member of Surgeon General C. Everett Koop's Task Force on Pornography, has spent decades studying the effects of pornography and violence. In 1987, Donnerstein and his colleagues published *The Question of Pornography: Research Findings and Policy Implications.*[9] They write in their preface:

> It is perhaps ironic, but we did not write this book because of our concern about the prevalence of sexually explicit materials in American society. Rather, we were concerned that so much attention was being paid to the possibly damaging consequences of exposure to pornography, that more pervasive and more troubling combinations of sex and aggression in the media were being ignored. We contend that the violence against women in some types of R-rated films shown in neighborhood theaters and on cable TV far exceeds that portrayed in even the most graphic pornography.

One of the chapters in the book, entitled "Is It the Sex or Is It the Violence?," attempts to bring decades of scientific research to bear on answering this question. Typical of many studies cited, a series of studies by Donnerstein and colleagues shows that it is violence, or a combination of sex and violence, but not sex alone, that tends to encourage callous attitudes toward women.[10] For example, in one of the experiments, a group of college-age males were shown one of three edited versions of the same movie. In the sexually aggressive version, the woman was tied up, threatened with a gun, and raped. In the aggression-only version, the sex was deleted; and in the sex-only version, the aggression was deleted.

After viewing the movie, the men were asked to complete questionnaires measuring their attitudes toward rape, their willingness to use force against women, and their willingness to rape if not caught. In the sex-only group, only 11 percent of the men indicated some likelihood that they would commit rape. In the sex and violence group, 25 percent indicated some likelihood, and *in the violence-only group, fully 50 percent of the men indicated some likelihood that they would rape a woman.* The researchers conclude the chapter by saying, "We risk the possibility that many members of our society, particularly young viewers, will evolve into less sensitive and responsive individuals as a result, at least partly, of repeated exposure to violent media, particularly sexually violent media. Such a possibility should be alarming, if not to law makers, at least to policy makers responsible for rating motion pictures and thus to limiting young people's access to sexually violent depictions."[11]

Knowing as much as we do about the effects of sexually violent entertainment, we must, as parents, respond. At the very least, we must work to ensure that our teenage boys understand that such attitudes and behavior are reprehensible. Mothers need to command respect from their sons, and fathers need to be involved in lessening the impact of degrading messages by discussing the realities of love, sex, and aggression with their sons. The high levels of sexual abuse in our society suggest that sexual violence is not committed by a few deviant men. Rather, it is a common and too frequently acceptable way of exercising control over women.

COGNITIVE DEVELOPMENT

Adolescents undergo a revolution in thinking that began at about age eleven. Younger children can appreciate different points of view as long as they are familiar and testable. Adolescents can entertain multiple perspectives about things that are hypothetical and outside their realm of experience. Piaget called this the stage of "formal operations." For example, a sixteen-year-old can think about what it would be like to stay out late and have fun, and at the same time he can appreciate that his parents might worry and even eventually call the police. As they develop this ability to foresee consequences, adolescents are capable of making more informed choices than younger children. Not all fifteen-year-olds think like adults, and not all adults reach the stage of formal operations. In general, however, adolescence is a period in which reasoning shifts from being based on the obvious to being based on an awareness of complexity.

This more advanced appreciation of life has an important bearing on how adolescents understand the media. Adolescents like to think; ideally, the media would aid them in the development of a more sophisticated worldview. Schools acknowledge adolescents' more advanced ways of thinking and substitute essay questions for true/false or multiple-choice questions on exams. Students are encouraged to present arguments, often at odds from their own point of view, because they can now make a cogent case from someone else's perspective. The feminist may have to argue against abortion, the school liberal may have to outline why social programs should be eliminated.

Television as a medium is ill suited to advancing the kind of intellectual growth necessary to produce reflective adults. Neil Postman, in his classic book *The Disappearance of Childhood*, points out that electronic media, by their very nature, encourage a childish worldview.[12] Just as childhood is characterized by a desire for instant gratification and minimal thoughtfulness, so does television lure us into a world that is fast, vapid, and without consequences. Television that jumps from *Roseanne* to a Calvin Klein sexual fantasy to genocide in Croatia with equal enthusiasm and emphasis does not allow for the kinds of distinctions necessary to develop a sense of context and meaning.

One of the tasks of adolescence is to develop a sense of historical continuity and context. Adolescents need to feel that they are part of the ongoing human process. The isolation of adolescence is lessened when teenagers can glimpse themselves at work, with a family, as part of a community. This is why teenagers are so interested in movies and television programs that deal with careers, relationships, and social issues. Popular movies such as *Reality Bites* help muddled adolescents feel that eventually they will be able to figure out how to work and how to love.

While movies can occasionally take the time to tackle complex problems, television usually cannot. This is most evident on the news. Adolescents watch the news more frequently than they did when they were younger. Although they often feel that they are watching a more "grown-up" form of television, the fact is that the news is just another way of packaging entertainment. Murder, missing whales, and special reports on hair loss alternate with inane and seductive commercials. The adolescent's newly acquired cognitive skills are never called upon. There is nothing in the news that is not understood, and all too often seen, by the average ten-year-old. While some thoughtful news programs, such as the *McNeil-Lehrer Report*, suggest the complexity of domestic and world problems, these programs are rarely watched by adolescents. Postman uses the news, probably because it is often considered the most "serious" of television offerings, to illustrate how little illumination is generally found on television:

> This way of defining the "news" achieves two interesting effects. First, it makes it difficult to think about an event, and second, it makes it difficult to feel about an event. By thinking, I mean having the time and motivation to ask oneself: What is the meaning of such an event? What is its history? What are the reasons for it? How does it fit into what I know about the world? By feeling, I mean the normal human responses to murder, rape, fire, bribery and general mayhem. . . . The point is, of course, that all events on TV come completely devoid of historical continuity or any other context, and in such fragmented and rapid succession that they wash over our minds in an undifferentiated stream. This is television as narcosis, dulling to both sense and sensibility.[13]

In effect, the media, particularly television, fail to provide adolescents with experiences that would help develop their thinking and aid their sense of coming into a reasonable world. Once again, this lack presents greater problems for some adolescents than for others. Teenagers whose parents encourage careful thinking, both by modeling reflective thinking and by expecting their teenagers to do likewise, are encouraging intellectual development. The problem is not that teenagers are exposed to occasional doses of vapid, overstimulating, anti-intellectual junk. The problem is that, too often, that's pretty much all they're exposed to.

MORAL DEVELOPMENT

Six neighborhood boys decided to indulge in the teenage ritual of a beer in the bushes before the school dance. Three of the boys were caught by the school's vice principal, and three escaped. The police were called and, while none of the three were charged, they were suspended from school for a week. I was asked by the high school administration to talk with the boys and their families. The next week provided a crash course for me in the vicissitudes of teenage morality.

The three boys who were caught were uniformly remorseful. However, their reasons for being remorseful were remarkably different. Two were extremely concerned with the fact that they would be punished and might lose their "good kid" status. One of the boys was far more concerned that "it was stupid to break the rules. I know better than that." More interesting than these differences was the fact that two of the boys who weren't caught showed no re-morse at all. They were quite articulate about the fact that the school couldn't "prove" anything once they had left the campus. The third felt that he had "broken his parent's trust" and should be punished. What is interesting about these different responses is that they illustrate both the strength and the weakness of Kohlberg's theories of moral reasoning.

Clearly these six teenagers experienced a moral dilemma and showed very different ways of thinking about their predicament. All six of these students were honored at an assembly the following week for outstanding academic achievement, so the issue of intelli-gence is insignificant here. In fact, the example does a good job of illustrating Kohlberg's contention that moral reasoning lags behind cognitive advances. These six boys, who all showed the highest levels of academic achievement, varied in their moral reasoning across all of Kohlberg's stages, showing how fluid and situational moral reasoning can be.

What is probably most important for teenagers is that they are exposed to the process by which people make moral judgments and decisions. To some degree, the content of what is seen is less impor-tant than the modeling of moral reasoning. Retribution-type mov-ies of the Van Damme/Seagal/Schwarzenegger/Stallone genre are damaging to adolescents less because of the violence they show and more because of the kind of primitive eye-for-an-eye philosophy that lies behind the heroes' decisions. Typically, the male hero in these movies does not struggle with issues of principled morality. Teenagers' ability to make moral decisions based on social rather than individual needs is sorely tested by vigilante movies.

Some movies do engage adolescents' newly emerging level of moral reasoning. A movie like *Quiz Show* not only is entertaining but also forces viewers to grapple with the fact that moral decisions are difficult and corruptible. It is a particularly appealing movie for adolescents because it concedes that temptation is not easily turned away (a fact that adolescents are all too familiar with), while at the same time fully exploring the consequences of submitting to seduc-tion. This outstanding movie, directed by Robert Redford, chroni-cles the quiz show scandal of the 1950s. Audiences believed that they were watching contestants on shows like *Twenty-One* and *The $64,000 Question* struggle to answer difficult questions in order to win money. In fact, what they were watching was a carefully choreographed deception. Contestants who were likely to boost advertisers' products were fed correct answers. Charles Van Doren, an engaging, attractive English professor, is seduced by the opportunity, but eventually finds himself in the middle of congressional hearings. While the toll on the individuals involved in this scandal is high and Van Doren never teaches again, the machinery behind the duplicity, the advertisers, and the network remain untouched.

This movie provides a wonderful opportunity to discuss with adolescents what goes on "behind the scenes" of the programs and movies they watch. While Charles Van Doren's charade in the 1950s seems more pathetic than criminal, it sowed the seeds for today's pocketbook journalism and propaganda passing for documentary. Richard Goodwin, the congressional investigator who uncovers the scandal, says, "I thought I was going to get television. The truth is television is going to get us." This is real meat for adolescents to chew on. While cheating on quiz show questions might seem puerile to adolescents whose media heroes are more recently tried for murder and molestation, *Quiz Show* never seems outdated. Movies like this, which don't rely on violence and formulas, are often overlooked by adolescents. It is unfortunate because although most adolescents will never be involved in real violence, they all will be faced with the kinds of moral decisions that *Quiz Show* so carefully considers.

Unfortunately, television and cinema aimed at this age group rarely take the time to engage adolescents' new reflective capacities. Instead, adolescents are portrayed struggling with the most dramatic and highly charged aspects of life. Ghetto teens struggle to stay alive and arm themselves adequately; suburban teens deal with cutthroat competition, peer pressure, and existential angst. Themes tend to focus on the delinquent, the tragic, and the dramatic. Some of these films do teenagers a service by highlighting the most difficult aspects of adolescence. But it is not enough to draw attention to a problem; the media must also present solutions that are safe, appealing, and useful.

Teenagers certainly need to consider issues that affect their lives, both the dramatic and the ordinary. Media that encourage adolescents to consider their future as well as their present and that support the integration of individual principles with social demands are of great service. They act as allies of those other powerful agents of socialization—family, school, religion—which strive toward producing men and women of conscience.

Part Four

Where Do We Go
from Here?

13

Suggestions, Solutions, and Directions for Parents

It is relatively easy to identify a problem as major as media violence and its effects on youth. It is even reasonably easy to describe such a problem; evaluate existing research, draw from personal and professional experience, and consult the experts. But it is extraordinarily difficult to come up with suggestions and solutions that have any "teeth" in them. The usual platitudes of "reducing violence" and "safeguarding our children" are sentiments that are unlikely to be challenged, but they are also sentiments that have produced little measurable change. This chapter will look at the opportunities available to us for affecting meaningful change in how the media teach, persuade, and seduce our children.

There is no question that children learn from the television shows and movies they watch. Children are continuously learning from their environment. Much of this learning is incidental, things they "just pick up" as opposed to things they are intentionally taught. They learn from parents, teachers, peers, siblings, and the general culture as well. But the media send their messages to our children for far more hours each week than any other institution. Children spend thirty and sometimes even forty or fifty hours a week with different forms of electronic media—television, movies, video games, computer games, and music. Compared with the few minutes a day spent alone with their fathers, the forty or so minutes spent alone with their mothers, and the six hours of school (which is in session only ten months of the year), it becomes clear that

media and television in particular are accounting for disproportionate amounts of children's time.[1] Non–school related reading clocks
in at less than ten minutes a day. Electronic media's emphasis on
the fast, the flashy, and the nonreflective is squeezing out more
important experiences of relatedness, the development of communication skills, and thoughtfulness.

Those within the entertainment industry who maintain that
they are "only entertainers" insult our intelligence. While they are
entertainers, the power of their media has made them much more.
They are storytellers in a culture that has become so fragmented
that the traditional communicators of cultural values are often absent. Economic pressures and job insecurity mean that harried,
overtaxed families have less time to spend with their children.
Americans who have been great believers in technology have found,
to their surprise, that rather than having more leisure time, they
feel that they have less.

In my conversations with dozens of media executives while
preparing this book, the most common response to criticism was
"If you don't like it, turn it off." Repeatedly they made the point
that parents, not media executives, are in charge of their children.
Certainly, parents are a child's first line of defense against cor-
rupting influences. But eventually, I began to feel that telling parents to shut off the TV set was like telling them not to use seat
belts. As parents, we of course have the responsibility to drive carefully, and if everyone drove carefully then perhaps we wouldn't
need seat belts. But we know that we can't control the drunken
driver who is barreling down on the wrong side of the road, and so
we demand reasonable protection from those who profit from the
cars we buy. We do our best to protect our children by buckling
them in, even if we have impeccable driving records.

Evidence tells us that the media bear some responsibility for
this country's increase in violence, particularly for the glamorization of guns. Just as consumers have demanded that automobile
manufacturers take some responsibility for the potential lethality of
their product, so should we demand that those in the entertainment
industry provide safeguards for their youngest consumers. We do
not ask that cars be banned in spite of their enormous contribution
to premature death. And while it has become de rigueur for anyone
suggesting restriction to be called a censor, the fact is that few
people are advocating censorship. Parents want, need, and are enti-

tled to as much help and information as possible about the programs and movies their children are watching.

There is no question that the media send moral messages to our children. What I mean by this is that the media are continually telling stories that suggest what are "good" ways to lead one's life and what are "bad" ways; what choices are likely to be rewarded and which to fail. The function of all art is to describe and illuminate the nature of the human condition. We are most drawn to those things that not only recognize our struggles but in some way point us toward solutions. I would assume that anyone who is reading this book is doing so in the hopes of having suggestions or solutions revealed. The messages of the media, both obvious and often embedded, significantly affect how children come to understand right and wrong.

Extended families, which previously spread the hard task of childrearing among a group of adults, no longer live in the same house. Often they do not live in the same town or even the same state. Matriarchs, patriarchs, shamans, and religious leaders, all those previously charged with the responsibility of handing down a set of values from one generation to the next, never considered themselves "just entertainers." They understood the grave responsibility of their task, and if they were clever and entertaining in the telling of their tales, so much the better. Responsibility comes with power, and, unlike Charles Barkley's "I am not a role model" commercial for Nike, people who were in positions of authority were expected to accept their responsibility.

As long as entertainment executives continue to ignore the scientific research that shows, clearly and unequivocally, that they are a major socializing force on American youth, we are unlikely to see much change in what our children are exposed to. Entertainment is "show *business,*" not "show culture," "show art," or "show education." As one major network executive remarked to me, "My allegiance is to my corporation, my sponsors, my characters, and then to the children." This listing of priorities is not accidental. Television is a business, and its product is the audience it delivers to advertisers. Children by necessity are the last priority in a business that, as it is currently constituted, owes allegiance to corporate America, not to America's children. David Walsh, in his thought-provoking book *Selling Out America's Children*, argues that we are a country that has put profits before values with disastrous effects.[2]

Nowhere is this more evident than in the media. The point is not to put the entertainment industry out of business by insisting on commercially unattractive programming, but to draw attention to the fact that commercial ventures can have a conscience as well as make money.

Overall, the media do a very poor job of representing the complex, diverse nature of various groups in this country. A study carried out by Children Now, a nonpartisan policy and advocacy organization for children, looked at the ways in which television depicts children.[3] The study found that only 10 percent of television shows featured children dealing with major social issues such as racism or safety, and a mere 2 percent featured children dealing with major family issues such as child abuse. In a country in which one in three children live in single-parent homes and where murder is the leading cause of death of large segments of our young population, the media are in a position to teach children more effective ways of coping with a host of social problems. Certainly a major function of television is to entertain, but programs as varied as _Mister Rogers' Neighborhood, Party of Five,_ and _My So-Called Life_ and movies as diverse as _Lion King, Flirting,_ and _Hoop Dreams_ have tackled difficult social and personal issues with great success. In the words of Walt Disney, it is possible "to educate entertainingly and entertain educationally."

At an important conference of media executives, writers, academics, and child advocacy groups, I had the opportunity to talk at length with a man named Dick Wolf.[4] He is currently the president of Wolf Films in association with Universal Television. He began his television career writing for _Hill Street Blues,_ which earned him an Emmy nomination. He has written and produced several of our most popular television shows, including _Miami Vice_ and _Law and Order._ He is a man at the top of his profession who was brave enough to face a rather hostile audience. I was determined to get his perspective on whether the media were fulfilling their moral obligations to this country's children. Mr. Wolf was generous with his time and cordial in answering my questions.

One of the comments that Mr. Wolf had made during his talk was that he did not allow his own children to watch many of the shows he produced. He said this without hesitation, and it stunned me that such an obviously articulate person could miss the irony in his statement. After all, if he didn't consider it appropriate for _his_ children, why was it appropriate for mine or for the many children who are denied parental supervision because of unfortunate circumstances of one kind or another? We talked about this in some detail, and he took the position that it is parents' responsibility to monitor their children's activities. "I know this can make me sound like a jerk, but it's just not my responsibility," he said.

Now I hardly believe that we should have twenty-four hours a day of *Barney* or *Mister Rogers*. Certainly I'm interested in having good-quality programming for people of all ages. And *Law and Order* is as good as it gets—a dramatic, responsible, well-written adult program. But his disowning of responsibility, the knee-jerk "tell parents to shut it off" response bothered me. Television is ubiquitous and in fact has been quite successful in circumventing parental disapproval. My four-year-old is not allowed to watch *Power Rangers*, but half his preschool class come to school wearing various forms of licensed Power Ranger clothing. McDonald's features them on its placemats. The morning I began writing this chapter, I noticed them cavorting up the side of my Quaker oatmeal box. This is no simple matter of turning off the television and being done with the problem. The commercial enterprises associated with our most popular programming make it naive to suggest that parental supervision is all that is required.

Mr. Wolf said, "My responsibility is to be an entertainer." He felt a great deal of accountability toward the sponsors of his program. He felt that his job is "to tell the truth" but felt no accountability toward the overarching problems of society. Just as I was internally polishing my position that the captains of this industry are either profoundly dishonest about the impact of their work or singularly allergic to self-reflection, Mr. Wolf happened to mention that he had written the screenplays for two movies that he felt dealt with some of the moral questions I was raising. Neither movie was particularly successful financially. One of them was *School Ties*, a movie about anti-Semitism, mentioned earlier in this book as an example of moviemaking at its best—entertaining, reflective, socially conscious, and honest. My jaw dropped, and with some pleasure Mr. Wolf chided, "What are you going to do with that?"

What I did with "that" was to spend many weeks thinking. How was it possible that this same person who clearly could speak in a language that I found redeeming and valuable to youth could also fail to be willing to acknowledge his unique responsibility for the images and stories shown to those same young people? It would be easier to come up with a group of damning quotes from executives who produce irresponsible programs. But over and over I heard from some of the producers whose work I had come to respect most—Dick Wolf from *Law and Order*, Charles Rosin from *Beverly Hills 90210*, Greg Weisman from *Gargoyles*—that they were just trying to tell a good story.

My conversations with all these producers were revealing and instructive. I came to have a greater appreciation of the complexity of the industry and the competing demands on those who work in broadcasting. I easily fell into a trap when Mr. Wolf suggested that we block all violent images from the air between 3:00 and 6:00 P.M. Anticipating my approval, he pointed out that CNN has only a single transponder, meaning that it broadcasts simultaneously to the East and West Coasts, and therefore its blackout time would be six, not three, hours. How could its producers possibly change the nature of their programming (which is largely devoted to world affairs with a heavy dose of violent images) for such a long period of time? Who would support the station for the services that are deemed so critical at other times—coverage of wars, disasters, and the like?

As Mr. Wolf succinctly said, "Can we cut to the chase? There are no easy answers." People who work in the entertainment industry have multiple allegiances: to their craft, their corporation, their conscience, their advertisers, and their audiences. Parents, however, have a simpler agenda—they want to protect their children from unhealthy influences. We want to make sure that our children don't believe that aggression is a useful way to settle interpersonal conflict, and we want all the help we can get in educating our children about the responsibilities that go along with sexual activity and drug and alcohol use. We want our children to grow up to be "good" people. We care less about whether our children are entertained and more about their character, the choices they make in life, and, most important, their safety.

As the figures throughout this book make clear, there is a crisis going on in America, and violence is only one symptom of a deeper and more pervasive problem. We have become a country of many rights and few responsibilities. Parents charge the media with irresponsibility while the media charge back that parents are the ones who are being irresponsible.

I would like to offer suggestions for changes that parents can make. This is because, in the final analysis, it is parents, not media executives, not Madison Avenue, and not corporate America, who are most concerned with the welfare of their children. The responsibility of raising, protecting, and educating children has always been the family's. Obviously, the family has never functioned alone but is set within a larger context of both a particular social group and society at large.

We can effect change by working together, not by working at odds with each other. Even if we protect our children, monitor what they watch, and instill what we believe to be good values, they are still at substantial risk in a world that worships affluence and glorifies violence. A stray bullet fired by a hopeless adolescent whose desire for a product outweighs his appreciation of life can find my child or yours. We are not only parents, we are also citizens of the world. This message is rarely shown on television, which focuses on individual achievement and personal happiness. It is a message we must fully appreciate ourselves before we can communicate it to our children.

WHAT PARENTS CAN DO

It would be wonderful if parents could all march to Hollywood and demand better programming for their children. Galvanizing the entertainment industry would seem to be the most efficient way of making sweeping changes in the nature of children's television. However, it seems unlikely that we will be seeing "television violence can be hazardous to your health" warnings on our screens any time in the near future.

How can we encourage programming that meets the developmental needs of children and is in accordance with most parents' values? Surveys show that in spite of the diversity of opinion in this country, there is actually a great deal of consensus on what "good values" are. Loyalty, responsibility, family, integrity, and courage are all high on the list of values that parents say they want to see in their children. There are few who would quibble with these values. In 1992, top leaders of youth and education groups, under the guidance of the Josephson Institute, met to formulate a character education program.[5] They named six values that they believe define good character. Called the "Six Pillars of Character," they are trustworthiness, respect, responsibility, fairness, caring, and citizenship. So it seems that parents, educators, youth leaders, and ethics scholars all pretty much agree on the character traits that produce "good" human beings and therefore a more vital and resilient society. How are we failing to communicate those values to our children? And how can we use the media to reinforce those values we consider important rather than supplant them with confusing and often antisocial messages?

The following list of suggestions, all supported by research as well as by common sense, is intended as a guide for parents who would like to lessen the negative effects and encourage the positive effects of media for their children.

WATCH TELEVISION WITH YOUR CHILDREN

Research studies have repeatedly shown that parents are not particularly interested in what their children watch. The majority of parents do not monitor their children's television viewing. The most frequent interventions parents make with regard to television are rules about how late their children can stay up and watch. It is unrealistic to expect parents to watch everything their children watch. However, in order to take a stand about television viewing or movies, we have to see enough to have a leg to stand on. I suggest that parents spend a week or two getting an idea of what their children are watching. Are your children channel surfing out of boredom? Is their viewing more selective, and what kinds of selections are they making? A steady diet of situation comedies is different from a steady diet of adventure and action shows. And even within these genres there are substantial differences. *Full House* is a far cry from *Married . . . with Children*. Situation comedies are, by far, the most frequently watched programs for children of all ages. Children need help discriminating between humor that entertains and teaches and humor that insults and humiliates.

What children watch depends on many factors, including age, gender, interest, and what's available. Unlike almost all other forms of entertainment, television viewing tends to be a nonselective ritual. Kids with spare time turn it on not to view a particular program but to kill time. This is a particularly poor use of television because it encourages indiscriminate viewing.

Once parents are familiar with what their children are watching, at what times, and under what circumstances (boredom? relaxation? background noise?) they can develop a plan to help their children avoid the worst of what TV offers and enjoy the best.

Aside from arming ourselves with information about what our kids see, watching with our children serves their development in a number of well-documented ways.

Watching with children increases comprehension. Several researchers studied children over a two-year period and found that when parents watch with their children, *and actively discuss and explain* what they're viewing, the youngsters' understanding of television content improves.[6] Parental involvement also improves children's judgments about reality and fantasy, increases prosocial behavior, and lessens the desire to watch television altogether. These findings were particularly compelling for boys. This may be because girls' verbal abilities are evident earlier, and they may need less explanation in order to understand the programs they watch.

Simply sitting in the same room with a child while he or she watches television is not likely to be beneficial. Parents need to comment, explain, and interpret in an active process of interaction with their children. The media, television in particular, pour into our homes and into the minds of our children. Without parents helping children sort out and understand the many messages that are delivered, children are vulnerable to misunderstanding much of what they see.

Watching with children decreases stereotypical thinking. The power of television to provide children with stereotypes is greatest when children have few other sources of information. Stereotypes, like aggression, are learned early and are difficult to correct.[7] When my nine-year-old son saw the movie *Dances with Wolves*, he was fascinated by hearing the language of the Sioux. "I never really thought about it. I guess I thought they just spoke English," he said. The message most of us grew up with was that cowboys are good guys and Indians are bad guys. Recently there have been some efforts to correct these stereotypes, often equally unrealistic in their portrayal of Native American culture. Kevin Costner's movie was the first time that many children in this country had any exposure to a sympathetic but unsentimental view of Native American life. Parents watching this movie with their children were given a tremendous opportunity to talk about the ways in which the media promote ideas about groups of people and how often these ideas are inaccurate. Movies like this can be a wonderful jumping-off place for discussions, for trips to a museum, and especially for further reading on the subject.

Watching with children increases prosocial behavior. A number of studies have shown that watching television programs with prosocial messages increases cooperation, sensitivity, and caring among children. *Mister Rogers' Neighborhood* is a program that has been scrupulously studied by social scientists, who find that as little as two weeks of watching this program helps preschoolers to be more cooperative, nurturing, and better able to express their feelings.[8] It also helps children to "follow the rules," stick with a task, and tolerate frustration. *Barney and Friends,* written by a team of early childhood education specialists, has been shown to enhance not only cognitive development but emotional and social development as well.[9] With the show's attention to safety issues, Barney has taught children as young as two to warn family members about house fires. Other studies have shown that even older children and adolescents are positively influenced by prosocial portrayals.[10]

Researchers have found that while children tend to learn aggression simply by watching it, they learn prosocial behavior far more effectively when it is combined with additional reinforcements such as role-playing and discussion.[11] While rivers of ink have been written on the effects of media violence on children, there has been barely a trickle of interest in the effects of prosocial television. This is unfortunate because *prosocial portrayals have a potentially larger effect on children than antisocial portrayals.*[12] Parents need to choose more prosocial programming and encourage their children to adopt the prosocial behaviors they see. Exposing children to prosocial programs and helping them interpret what they see is one way to diminish the enduring power of early aggressive television messages. In addition, prosocial messages nurture a sense of optimism, which is critical for children's healthy psychological development.

SHUT IT OFF

A colleague of mine who researches children's reactions to traumatic news reports relates this telling story. She received a phone call from a woman, agitated and tearful. The sobbing woman said that she and her daughter were watching news coverage showing the recently found body of a murdered young girl. They tried switching channels, but the image of the young girl's body was everywhere. Her daughter was terribly upset, and the two of them were crying. What should she do? "Shut it off," my colleague said gently.

Television is not a permanent part of our environment. It comes by invitation into our homes, and should be shut off when it is not serving a useful purpose.

PUT CHILDREN ON A TELEVISION DIET

Parents are usually reluctant to interfere with their children's viewing habits for several reasons. Television has become an easy and effective babysitter for parents who are strained both emotionally and financially. For many people, it is "just entertainment" and they remain unconvinced of its damaging potential.

Many media effects are weak and short-lived. While people have certainly noticed that they may feel elated or angry or disturbed after a movie, they also notice that these feelings tend to dissipate rather rapidly. But because children watch enormous amounts of television, even short-term effects become extremely important.

The American Academy of Pediatrics recommends that children's viewing be restricted to two hours per day or less. Many other organizations and researchers working on this issue have come to the same conclusion. Children who are heavy viewers of television tend to do more poorly than their light-viewing peers on a number of different measures, as we saw earlier in this book.

Watch a couple hours of children's television, either on Saturday morning or after school. Don't pay attention to the programs (an easy task), but do pay attention to the commercials. What is striking is that it seems there are only two things that children buy—or, more accurately, two things that children can nag their parents to buy for them. One is toys, which has been discussed at length in Chapter 8. The other is sugar-coated cereal or some closely related type of junk food. According to children's commercials, America's youth somehow subsist on a diet of Fruit Loops, soda, bubble gum, Hostess cupcakes, and Cheetos. The connection between heavy viewing of television and obesity has been well documented.[13]

One way to limit the amount of television that children watch is to put them on a television diet, modeled after a food diet. The analogy allows us to recognize that it is more complex than simply turning off the bad stuff and only watching good stuff. Diets make us aware that we have different kinds of needs. Mostly we eat for nutrition, but sometimes we eat for pleasure and sometimes we eat for comfort.

Similarly, our children ought to be using television primarily to educate and inform (this doesn't mean only "educational TV," with its connotation of one too many animal specials) by watching programs that stimulate their thinking. There are a host of amusing, informative programs for kids to watch, and parents need to become familiar with them. I was pleasantly surprised to find a half dozen remarkable new programs for my four-year-old, many of them on PBS. *Mister Rogers*, *Barney*, and *Sesame Street* are perennial favorites, as well they should be. Shows such as *Rugrats*, *The Magic School Bus*, *Reading Rainbow*, *Lambchops Playalong*, and *Bobby's World* give young children a wider choice than ever before of wholesome entertainment. For grammar school children, there's *Beakman's World*, *Nick News*, *Carmen Sandiego*, *Animaniacs*, *Full House*, and *Family Matters*. Young adolescents and teens can be both entertained and occasionally even educated by shows like *Home Improvement*, *Star Trek: Deep Space Nine*, *Beverly Hills 90210*, *The Secret World of Alex Mack*, *Lois and Clark: The New Adventures of Superman*, *Boy Meets World*, and *Party of Five*. These lists are in no way exhaustive; they are just a way of pointing out that there are many good programs available to children of all ages.

Recently my whole family was stuck in a miserable hotel in a rainstorm over Christmas vacation. The local theater was showing the movie *Dumb and Dumber* and all of us—ages four, ten, fifteen, forty-six, and forty-nine—went to see it. We all laughed a lot. Was this a great movie? Not at all, although being able to entertain such a diverse group of people is an impressive accomplishment. But mostly, it was a kind of mindless adventure that was fun and pleasant for the whole family. A jelly donut for the mind. Sometimes kids want to kick back, put their minds in neutral, and watch entertaining but uninspiring pap. That's okay as long as it's not tainted. We don't always want to read "serious" literature; there are times when *People* magazine hits the spot. An occasional candy bar is fine, a steady diet of junk food isn't. As parents, we don't hesitate to oversee that our children are eating properly; we need to be equally attentive to their media diet.

TEACH CHILDREN TO WATCH WITH A PURPOSE

Television is a vehicle, a means to an end; it is not a way of life. Many children sit for hours at a time, mindlessly channel surfing their way through life, as opposed to living it. Children need to be taught that the television, just like every other appliance in the house, has a specific function. We do not leave the hair dryer on once our hair is dry, or the toaster on once the toast has popped up. We recognize the specific uses of these appliances and know when to shut them off. Our children need to be similarly educated about television.

One way to begin teaching this is to sit with our children and go over the programs they are interested in seeing. Look at *TV Guide* or your local television listings and make decisions about what your children's television week will look like. Some parents are quite successful at holding their children to a number of choices that they agree on. Others find that accommodations and changes can be made over the course of the week. Either way, the exercise of sitting down together and making decisions about what children will watch teaches a very valuable lesson. It teaches children that television viewing is a directed activity. Allowing even young children to participate in this exercise makes it clear from the beginning of their relationship with television that *television is not a device that we passively allow to fill up dead space; rather, it is a source of entertainment and education that we actively pursue.* Parents need to help their children become consumers of media, making thoughtful and economical choices about programs that are of real interest to them. Often that means thinking about our own choices as well.

Provide other cultural opportunities. It is interesting but not surprising to note that one of the groups most negatively affected by heavy television viewing is economically advantaged children. Children from lower socioeconomic families benefit from the "window on the world" that television can sometimes provide. But children who watch a lot of television in spite of being economically advantaged tend to fall behind others in their peer group who spend time enjoying a range of cultural activities.

Television is one medium. Theater, opera, ballet, reading, and museums all provide other opportunities for kids to appreciate that the world offers many different forms of entertainment and enlightenment. All of my children were particularly fond of *Peter and the Wolf* when they were young. We went to *Peter and the Wolf* concerts and read *Peter and the Wolf* books, and even put on our own *Peter and the Wolf* dramas. This move from passive enjoyment to active imaginative play is optimal for children. Each of my children, in his turn, constructed different wolves: sly ones, evil ones, greedy ones. Each relied on his particular personality and breadth of imagination to construct individual and singular images. Play, which is the work of childhood, is the foundation for a lifetime of rich, flexible, and imaginative thinking.

Many youth organizations supply healthy and active alternatives to the television habit. Church or synagogue youth groups have traditionally provided a place for preteens and teens to spend time involved with each other as well as with community service projects. Similarly, organizations such as the YMCA offer a broad range of programs focusing on both individual and social development. Outward Bound has provided more than 200,000 teenagers with the opportunity to experience the outdoors in ways that are exciting and promote self-confidence and self-esteem. Participation in organizations such as these decreases your children's television viewing time and sense of boredom and also help connect them to others with similar interests and to the community at large.

Hobbies and sports are important and healthy activities for children. My teenage son's television viewing was cut in half when he discovered the guitar. Life is not a spectator sport, and children should be encouraged to be active in things that interest them. Being involved with a child's particular hobby encourages family cohesion and shows that parents value participation rather than passivity.

INSIST ON READING

Reading offers the human mind unparalleled opportunities for expansion, diversion, and reflection. Studies have shown that children who watch a great deal of television read less than their light-viewing counterparts.[14] Television does not displace all activities, but it tends to replace those activities that have a similar purpose such as entertainment, relief from boredom, and increasing knowledge. For example, we don't go to the movies instead of going to the bathroom, or eating or sleeping for that matter. But kids do watch television instead of playing or reading or drawing.

In *Amusing Ourselves to Death*, Neil Postman traces the rise of literacy in America and its replacement with mass electronic media in our current century.[15] From the title of his book, it is safe to assume that he does not see this as a change for the better. Postman notes that to the founding fathers of this country the idea of citizenship was inconceivable without sophisticated literacy. He cites historians who have pointed out that while certain voting restrictions were "flexible," the ability to read was nonnegotiable. Literacy rates, which were quite high in colonial America, were one of the reasons America rose to greatness. Being able to read encourages objective, rational, and critical thinking.

Greater and greater technological advances do not *necessarily* mean greater understanding and advancement of the human condition. Children in particular need to slowly construct an understanding of the world based on experience and reflection. A father recently complained to me that when he took his fourteen-year-old son to San Francisco's Exploratorium, a hands-on multimedia learning environment, his son seemed interested only in those things that "dazzled" him. Exhibits with flashing lights and loud music held his attention, while he completely ignored quieter and more complex exhibits. "If it's not as exciting as television, it just doesn't interest him," complained the father. I believe that this father had good reason to be concerned. Learning about life, whether through classroom academics, social interaction, or personal development, is a slow and demanding process. Children who sit back and say "Entertain me" are bound to run into difficulty when they face the more rigorous tasks of learning that are always part of academic achievement. Reading, because it moves at a slower pace than almost all television programs, from *Sesame Street* to *Cops*, allows children to develop a more thoughtful, integrated, and personal style of learning.

USE ECONOMIC POWER

In the media industry, one letter is generally acknowledged to represent the opinion of many thousands of people. Network executives say that short, reasoned letters are the most likely to be taken seriously, and hastily written postcards or long ranting letters are typically ignored. Parents who want their voices heard by media executives must take the time to state their position forcefully and clearly. Huge corporations such as Johnson and Johnson, General Motors, and Ralston Purina have all canceled commercials on shows when public pressure made these decisions financially prudent. Pepsico canceled a $5 million commercial featuring Madonna after her music video *Like a Prayer* (featuring burning crosses, sexual scenes with saints, and stigmata) offended large segments of the population.[16] A one-woman campaign by an angry Michigan mother who objected to the "blatant exploitation of women, sex, and anti-family attitudes" on *Married . . . with Children* prompted Procter & Gamble, Kimberly Clark, and McDonald's to cancel advertising on the top-rated Fox series.[17]

With a few exceptions, most notably PBS, the media are quite simply businesses. Television has only one product, and contrary to popular opinion, that product is not the shows that are produced; it is not even the products that are advertised. *Television's one product is you—the audience that is delivered to an advertiser.* And it is exactly at this intersection, where the audience meets the advertiser, that parents are most likely to influence what is on television. I can assure you, after spending many hours interviewing network executives, that changes in programming will not come about because parents don't like violence; they will not come about because those in power feel a responsibility to use their power wisely; and if the last thirty years of effort are at all predictive, they will not come about through government regulation. Rather, any changes that come about in the entertainment industry will come about because someone's wallet was either fattened or flattened.

BE AN ACTIVIST

Studies show that children grow up to be more like their parents than different from them. We teach our children how to live by the ways in which we live our own lives. When I began researching this book, my children were less than thrilled with my "sticking my nose into other people's business." My teenage son perfected keeping just the right amount of distance between us so that no one would guess that we were related. I spoke with managers of fast-food restaurants, bookstores, toy stores, video stores, and record stores, asking questions, expressing concern, and frequently making known that I would not support an establishment that exploited the vulnerabilities of children. We walked out of places from Toys 'R Us to Waldenbooks (both suppliers of Power Rangers paraphernalia), with my children alternately confused, amused, and embarrassed.

However, as my research proceeded, my two older children became increasingly interested in what I was so worked up about. My older son decided to do his year-long social issues project on media violence and even tolerated my speaking to his high school assembly (no mean feat for a fifteen year old!).

A week before I completed writing this book, my ten-year-old came home from a river rafting trip in Oregon. Jumping out of the car, he thrust a wrinkled McDonald's placemat in front of me. It was a picture of the six Power Rangers, each reciting a few disingenuous words of wisdom: "So find something you care about and make it happen!" "It takes time to be good at anything. Use the power of determination to see you through." My son said, "I knew you'd hate this." Pointing to "With the power of education, you can think your way out of the toughest problems," he laughed and said, "And if that doesn't work, you can always kick some butt is what they really mean." Crumpling the placemat, he threw it in the garbage can. "Not even little kids are that stupid," he added over his sunburned shoulder.

Involve your children as you become involved. Set a good example for them.

PETITION SCHOOLS FOR MEDIA LITERACY PROGRAMS

Education serves many purposes, but first and foremost it provides children with the skills they will eventually need to deal with a large and complex world. We want our children to learn math not only because it promotes a type of conceptual thinking, but also because in the future they will have to add up grocery bills and balance a checkbook. We want our children to learn how to read not only because it will provide them with a lifetime of rich enjoyment, but also because they will one day need to read a map, a medical report, or a mortgage contract.

It is incredible that, given the amount of time our children spend with electronic media, most schools do not have media literacy programs. While schools may bring their pupils to see particularly powerful and historically important movies such as *Schindler's List* or *Gandhi*, they tend to ignore the day-to-day influence of the media. This is a serious mistake. Parents who work at providing every educational advantage fail to realize that their children are being denied an essential part of their education when media literacy is not part of a school's curriculum.

Children who scream and cry for cheap plastic toys or demand a nutritionally bankrupt cereal because it carries the name of their favorite superheroes are being conned by the most sophisticated propaganda machine the world has ever known—Madison Avenue. Girls who want to grow up to be as thin and pathetically dependent as the models they see on television and boys who think that physical prowess and intimidation are attractive and acceptable uses of power have all been exposed to repeated images that suggest that these are normal and desirable ways to live one's life.

Media literacy, by clarifying the ways in which the media exploit and manipulate their audiences, helps children understand the nature of what they are seeing. This understanding makes them less susceptible to these manipulations. Critical viewing skills—that is, the ability to understand and to "read" the media—have become as necessary as knowing how to read a textbook. Former U.S. Commissioner of Education Ernest Boyer says, "It is no longer enough simply to read and write. Students must also become literate in the understanding of visual images. Our children must learn how to spot a stereotype, isolate a social cliché, and distinguish facts from propaganda, analysis from banter, and important news from coverage."[18] Parents need to actively encourage schools to add media literacy courses and to make certain that the importance of media is acknowledged by weaving it throughout the school's curriculum.

REESTABLISH A PARENT-CHILD GRADIENT

What I mean by a parent-child gradient is that there is an inherent difference in authority and stature between children and adults. We may think of this gradient as a diagonal line with parents on the high end and children on the lower end. This does not suggest that children are inferior to adults. However, by virtue of their age and experience, adults occupy a very different position in the hierarchy of the family than children do. Common sense tells us that a critical part of the job of parenting is for parents to be able to maintain their position of authority and credibility. When a parent's legitimate authority is compromised or abandoned, families falter.

One of the things that has been most noticeable in my clinical practice over the last fifteen years is the degree to which parental authority has been eroded. Many of us who were coming of age in the 1960s are now parents with children, often adolescents. Unfortunately, the '60s zeitgeist of "do your own thing" has permeated our parenting. Families are not simply collections of people, each doing his or her "own thing." Families are by necessity interdependent; they function most effectively when there is a division of labor. Out of the '60s came the recognition that this division of labor did not necessarily mean that mom always washed the dishes and dad always mowed the lawn. While there has been some positive change and an increased flexibility in our thinking about the roles of mothers and fathers, there has also been some confusion about how to best apply these newly formulated definitions. I strongly support the lessening of sex-role stereotypes, but I also think that parents need to remember that their fundamental role as "parent" does not change whether they are drying dishes or mowing the lawn.

In my office, I have witnessed countless discussions between parents and children that were conducted as if between two adults, not a child and a parent. Negotiations worthy of our largest corporations have been carried out about everything from bedtime to allowance to household responsibilities. At times it has been hard to know who is the parent and who is the child.

We do our children a great disservice when we refuse to accept the authority of parenthood. If you don't like a program and think it is harmful or inappropriate for your child, then it is necessary for you, particularly if your child is young, to enforce your decisions. All of us are often tired and stressed and easily induced to take the path of least resistance. But when parents are uninvolved, children are frequently exposed to things they are ill-equipped to handle. *Ultimately, parental disengagement leads to a lessening of parental authority that invites our children into increasingly dangerous situations.*

The effects of media on children are not small and they are not incidental. We must approach decisions about our children's media viewing with the same deliberateness and seriousness we use when making decisions about other aspects of their well-being. We need to be as much a parent when we are deciding whether or not our four-year-old should be watching *X-Men* or our twelve-year-old should be watching Freddy Krueger as when we are deciding whether or not cookies are acceptable breakfast food or whether alcohol is a permissible beverage at our teenager's party.

While this last suggestion about reestablishing a parent-child gradient is not particular to children and media, it is a crucial element in making all of the previous suggestions truly viable. Parents need to maintain, and in many cases reestablish, their authority within the family. We are only fooling ourselves if we think that muttering about the violence on *Mighty Morphin Power Rangers* while allowing our children to parade around in Power Rangers T-shirts or eat Power Rangers–"endorsed" cereals has a dampening effect on our children's enthusiasm for the program. There is no point suggesting that the set be shut off if your teenagers' response is "To hell with you." Parents need to regain their authority by providing clear, appropriate, and forceful guidelines for their children.

14

Directions for Schools, Media, and Government

SCHOOLS AND MEDIA LITERACY

No form of mass media, whether commercials, newspapers, or movies, can present us with objective reality. Neither can television shows, regardless of whether they are National Geographic documentaries or *Star Trek* reruns. All media presentations have an agenda, and they construct a particular kind of reality, which is all too often consumed and accepted as real because it is so seamlessly authentic-looking. It is the job of media educators to teach our children that *what you see is not necessarily what you get* when it comes to the media.

Children are immersed in television, movies, computers, and video games. As astounding as the figures in this book have been—that the average American child watches three to four hours a day, that the average American household has the TV on some seven hours a day—these numbers are still a gross underestimation of how much involvement children have with the media. My teenage son can be reading the sports section of our local paper with the TV on in the background and his latest musical obsession blasting from his room. He is logging time on three different types of media, with his attention drifting between them. This is not an unusual use of media. How often do we read a book or magazine, picking our heads up for the opening stories of the evening news and maybe again for the weather so we know how to dress our kids the next day? It is hard to believe that television is such a large component of our lives and yet we remain so totally ignorant of its varied agendas and purposes.

Unfortunately, media studies have remained on the periphery of education in this country. This is a bizarre anomaly considering that for many people the media are their primary sources of information. For example, young adults say that the media are their main sources of information about political matters. Our children are growing up in a world that is dominated by images and yet they have absolutely no skills for understanding the meaning of those images in their lives. The power of the media rests on the fact that they can make things seem real, inevitable, and necessary. The media select their material, deliver a specific set of values, and are beholden to particular interests. (Often what they don't show us is just as important as what they do.)

Without understanding these basic facts about the media, children and adolescents (adults too) are susceptible to a subtle process of indoctrination. Aside from the most obvious issues of promoting consumerism and stereotypes, an uncritical reading of the media can have disastrous effects on our democratic processes. Already, political candidates are being merchandised much like breakfast cereals and laundry detergents. No longer are ideas or ideologies the basis on which political candidates are elected; rather, it is the "sound bite," the "negative campaign," the "political spot" that drives an election. Neil Postman points out that Abraham Lincoln could have walked down the street virtually unnoticed.[1] He was known and judged by his ideas. But our political images are far stronger and last longer than what little we know about our politicians' thinking: Gerald Ford tripping, Michael Dukakis looking ridiculous in a tank and hard hat, George Bush fainting at a state dinner in Japan. Repeated images such as these speak to our children with an immediacy and impact that print often lacks. More and more of our children's knowledge about the world will be derived from images rather than from print.

Why have schools been so reluctant to incorporate media literacy training into their curriculum? As a former teacher, I think that one of the things teachers like to believe is that they are the guardians of a "higher culture" than *Roseanne* or *Married . . . with Children*. I think there is an attitude that says that "important" pieces of programming are worthy of classroom time, such as a Bill

Moyers special or a BBC play. On the other hand, I think that many teachers would consider spending class time on *Cops* or Arnold Schwarzenegger's latest movie a trivial use of class time. But educators need to pay attention to the fact that, whether we like it or not, children spend hours on end with television and movies that are only partly understood. Schools are the institutions charged with educating our children, and they have the responsibility of preparing children to understand the world around them. A significant part of that world now includes various forms of electronic media.

Media literacy is not so much about content as it is about developing skills for decoding the messages that the media deliver. One could ask the same questions of *Married . . . with Children* as of *Sesame Street*, or the same questions of *Fatal Attraction* as of *Forrest Gump:* "Why is this pleasurable?" "What are the values implicit in the program or film?" "How is it marketed?" "Whose interests are being served?" "What information is being left out?" And so on. Media literacy is not simply about saying *Married . . . with Children* is bad and *Sesame Street* is good. It is about providing children with the tools they will need, in all subject areas and throughout their lives, to be able to understand different agendas of the media.

I do not mean to suggest that media, by definition, are evil and manipulative. Any medium must have a point of view. There is no way that we can reproduce "reality" because no two people see the world exactly alike. Even a photograph, the closest thing we can imagine to "capturing reality," is influenced by an untold number of decisions that the photographer makes—the lighting, camera angle, and distance all convey a particular vision of what is being photographed. The erotic lilies of Robert Mapplethorpe, the desolate tulips of André Kertész, and the monumental poppies of Georgia O'Keeffe hardly seem to exist in the same world. That they each photographed flowers is of course true, but that statement says nothing about the meanings they each saw and presented to their audience. Adults typically understand that they are being shown a particular version of reality; children, however, accept media at face value. Their experience with the world is limited and as a result they have very little to compare to television's or movies' portrayals.

My father was a police officer, one of the most commonly

depicted professions on television. He and I would watch police dramas, always looking out for mistakes and obvious distortions. My father would point out that much of police work is monotonous and routine, and he couldn't imagine anyone having the stamina to keep up with so many criminals. He was very proud of the fact that in twenty years on the police force, he had never once drawn his gun. So I suppose I learned early on that television police officers and real-life police officers have very little in common other than a predilection for coffee and donuts. With children spending more and more time with the media, and less time with competing sources of information, it becomes increasingly important that they understand to what extent the media are constructing rather than reflecting social reality.

There is another reason that I believe teaching media literacy in the schools is essential to maintaining a democracy. We are at a point of tremendous social unrest in our country. Increasingly, we find a third world country existing within the United States. Poverty continues to increase and to affect a disproportionate number of blacks, Hispanics, and Native Americans. Even those who enjoy relative affluence find that their family structures have been disrupted. Economic necessity has forced many people to move from their homes to find jobs in other parts of the country, and many families are far removed geographically from where they were born. Our society has become fragmented. The institutions that have traditionally held families together—marriage, religion, patriotism—are weak at best. This leads to diffusion of responsibility for the society, fragmentation for the family, and isolation for the individual.

Television has enormous power to shape our views about other groups of people. For a long time, African American people on television were either athletic superstars or thugs. A series of situation comedies expanded that repertoire, but it wasn't until 1995 that *Under One Roof*, the first dramatic series about African American families, was briefly aired. Many white children in America have very limited contact with black children, and so while most of their understanding derives from their families and from their community, a great deal is also learned through the media. The short-lived *All-American Girl*, about a Korean family, was the first glimpse for many children of the similarities and differences to be found in Asian culture. The potential of the media to explore rather than exploit the experience of other cultures is pathetically under-utilized. Programs such as *Sesame Street*, with its emphasis on multiculturalism, have taught several generations more than just their ABCs. More important, they have taught that children everywhere are pretty much the same.

Media literacy teaches children that television constructs a version of social reality. Watching American television, an uninformed observer could only conclude that the vast majority of people in this country are white men who rarely work but are always busy; that women never live past the age of about sixty-five; that almost everyone in this country enjoys a high level of affluence; and that children struggle with only the most trivial of problems. All of this is obviously false, but false with a purpose.

Television is not about raising social consciousness or even representing a more or less accurate view of reality. It is about selling people to an advertiser. So what we see on television reflects successful marketing techniques, but not reality. We see lots of men, since men hold more power and are seen as more authoritative; we see young, beautiful women, since erotic feelings make us euphoric; and we see people who are struggling with either outlandishly difficult or trivial problems, lest we be reminded of our own real life. Television encourages us not to think, but to want. Television creates desire, and is constructed to optimize our willingness to spend money.

Children and adolescents can understand these concepts, and it is imperative that they do. Media literacy teaches children that nothing the entertainment industry produces is an unproblematic reflection of external reality. The media need to be "read" and analyzed in order to be understood. Children who acquire the skills to do this are at a great advantage. Adolescent girls, for instance, can begin to understand that thinness or youth is an arbitrary ideal brought to them by a system that would like to see women spending lots of money on "improving" their appearance. Fully understanding this might help young women be more interested in improving their skills and their characters rather than eradicating their cellulite. At every level of development, children can be taught skills for interpreting and understanding the media.

WHAT THE MEDIA CAN DO

There are many things that the media can do to provide our children with a healthier and saner cultural environment. But I suspect that there will be few changes until those in positions of power in the media are able to confront the dilemma that they face. On the one hand, the networks are charged to "serve the public interest, convenience, and necessity"; on the other hand, they are in business only as long as they deliver a "demographically desirable" audience to their advertisers and profits to their stockholders. This dual mandate, serving the interests of the public and the interests of corporate America, sometimes works smoothly but often engenders a conflict of interest. When there is a conflict, the American public tends to lose. We are talking show *business*.

I think that the media have the potential to do many wonderful things. In the meantime, however, I think that they do a lot of bad things. They perpetuate stereotypes and racism. They present limited options for girls while glorifying unacceptably violent options for boys. They make children fearful, pessimistic, and aggressive. Do I think that the people who produce these programs are "bad" people? It's a difficult question because, at heart, I believe that we cannot separate our values from the ways in which we lead our lives. So the writers, directors, and producers have made choices about what to create and what not to create. I would say that they have made some very poor choices. And as a result of making poor choices, they find themselves in the position of having to justify what they do.

People in the entertainment industry know full well that what they produce is not "just entertainment" in the dismissive sense of having no enduring value. Children do not watch television once a week or even one hour a day. Aside from sleep, children spend more time watching television than participating in any other activity, *including school*. While I believe I have made it clear in this book that I consider it parents' responsibility to be their children's first line of defense, this does not suggest that the entertainment industry is without responsibility.

Recently Secretary of Education Richard Riley appealed to Hollywood to "stop glamorizing assassins and killers. I urge you to see this issue through the eyes of parents instead of script writers

. . . through the eyes of teachers instead of advertisers." Given the system of financing media in this country, it is not likely that those in the entertainment industry can afford to stop looking through the eyes of advertisers. Media are a business, and the sooner that fact is fully accepted, the sooner we can get to work on how to make entertainment that is both good for children and good for business. The two are not incompatible. *Forrest Gump* grossed $300 million, while Freddy Krueger's latest movie brought in $18 million. From 1984 to 1993, R-rated movies grossed, on average, $10 million less than PG-rated films.[2] The Nielsen ratings illustrate that violence is not "what the people want." According to Nielsen's 1994–95 rating report, of the top five television programs, not one is violent.[3] Situation comedies such as *Home Improvement* and *Seinfeld* consistently score higher than violence-laden fare.

The realization that responsible programming can also be commercially successful is vividly illustrated by Sheryl Leach, the creator of *Barney*. A mother and teacher, she found herself disappointed by what television offered her young son. "I thought I could build a better mousetrap," she said. And so she went about creating one of the most successful television programs for young children in broadcast history. "I knew about kids, about teaching, and about marketing," she explained. "The only thing I didn't know anything about was video and television, but I figured I could learn." Recognized with the Socially Responsible Entrepreneur of the Year Award in 1995, Barney's "mom" considers one of her greatest accomplishment proving that "it doesn't have to be violent to be successful in the marketplace."[4]

So how is it that bright, creative people keep insisting that "Violence is what sells" or "We're just giving them what they want." In psychology there is a well-documented concept called "cognitive dissonance." This very powerful phenomenon shows that when there is a gap between what people believe and the way they act, they fill this gap by rationalizing their behavior. We all know this from everyday life. We're on a diet and have just eaten half a box of cookies—it doesn't matter because they were "low-fat." We get home and find that the department store salesclerk has given us an extra ten dollars in change, but we don't go back to the store because "it's a huge company and it doesn't make any difference; besides, they charge too much anyway." People work very hard at coming up with rationalizations to legitimize their questionable behavior.

I believe that many people who work in the entertainment industry are exhibiting cognitive dissonance. It's pretty hard to justify making movies that are sensational and gratuitously violent. An "artist" can hardly feel that he has contributed something worthwhile to the world after spending thousands of dollars to make a child's murder appear realistic. Most of the people I spoke with in the entertainment industry have children of their own. How do you answer "Daddy, what did you do today?" by saying "I filmed a young girl being mutilated." On paper these look like absurd conversations, but in fact this is the dilemma faced by people who often find themselves working on projects that have little redeeming value.

It's probable that many people in the media live with their decisions by simply denying the negative impact of their work. On a 1995 PBS *Frontline* special on the effects of media violence on children, George Vradenberg, then vice president of the Fox network, said, "Well, I tend to think that the studies have received really too much attention."[5] Can you imagine this point of view coming from an equally powerful figure in another field affecting our children? "We know that children are safer when they use car seats, but let's not pay so much attention to the studies." Or perhaps the surgeon general saying, "We know teenage girls are running an increased risk of cancer by their rising cigarette consumption, but let's just forget about all that scientific stuff." Vradenberg, like everyone else in influential positions in the entertainment industry, is well aware that there is a large, consistent, and damning body of evidence that says that watching a lot of violence makes children aggressive and fearful. My intention is not to single Vradenberg out for condemnation but simply to suggest that one must go through astounding psychological contortions to justify things that are unjustifiable.

I would like to suggest that the media demand a higher level of honesty from themselves. To all media executives who disingenuously insist that the media do not create attitudes and behaviors, please consider that the magnitude of advertising budgets speaks volumes about the power of the media to influence viewers' choices. It is unlikely that America's largest corporations would be spending upwards of *$45 billion per year* on advertising if they did not have overwhelming evidence that media images can in fact alter attitudes and behaviors.

At a recent conference I attended, a question was asked about why the immensely popular *Mighty Morphin Power Rangers* chose to highlight racial and gender stereotypes by casting a black youth as the Black Power Ranger, an Asian youth as the Yellow Power Ranger, and a girl as the Pink Power Ranger.[6] Incredibly, the answer came back from Saban Entertainment that the original drawings from Japan had a pink skirted costume, and so the Pink Ranger had to be a girl. While original footage from Japan was used early in the series, Saban could undoubtedly have afforded to change the costumes. It is infuriating when media executives treat parents who are genuinely concerned with their children's welfare as if we had substandard IQs. A real dialogue is possible only when the participants, be they parents, politicians, academics, advertisers, studio heads, or writers, are honest and forthcoming about their motivations and the demands placed on them.

I think it is important to acknowledge that most of the people involved in the dialogue about children and the media have very different agendas. Parents are the group with the greatest interest in the welfare of their children, but they may have other pressures as well, such as fitting in with community standards or living up to their own image of what constitutes a "good person." Politicians need to be reelected, and academics need tenure. Studio heads need to keep advertisers happy, and advertisers need to sell their products. This doesn't mean that politicians or professors or those in the entertainment industry are unconcerned with children. Most of the people I met in the course of writing this book have a genuine interest in and concern for the welfare of children. But it is naive to assume that people aren't interested in keeping their jobs and paying their mortgages. The question for people in the media, and for our society as a whole, is how to encourage decisions that are moral as well as profitable.

We can take a lesson from the ways in which other countries have expanded the pool of educational media offerings available to children. France has a 3 percent tax on theater admission and a 2 percent tax on videotapes. These taxes go to a special fund that is made available to independent producers and helps provide breadth to the ideas and visions translated onto the screen. Such a system ensures that important, although not necessarily commercial ventures can become part of a nation's cultural offerings. This modest redistribution of capital helps lessen the tremendous amount of centralized power that a handful of top media executives hold.

Finally, we must support public broadcasting. While politicians have chosen to make PBS a political football, it is in fact one of our most valuable institutions. It assures us that some small corner of the media is safe from the demands of capitalism and is free to focus on the needs of the audiences it so richly serves. Ridiculous statements such as Newt Gingrich's "PBS is a playground for the rich" deserve comment only because his uninformed pronouncements carry weight. In fact, PBS is used by all kinds of children, but its benefits to lower socioeconomic children are particularly notable, since lower socioeconomic children have far fewer cultural opportunities than children from more comfortable homes.

I don't know how much of PBS's children's programming Gingrich has actually watched; I can only speculate. But after watching LeVar Burton's multicultural push for literacy on *Reading Rainbow* or Bill Nye's frenetic love affair with science on *Bill Nye the Science Guy*, I am hard pressed to figure out how Gingrich arrived at his conclusions. PBS is a national treasure, and it is nothing but classism that says that opera and theater and ballet are only the province of the rich. America's spending on public broadcasting is laughable compared with spending in other countries. In 1991, federal spending for public broadcasting in the United States was about $1 per person. For comparison, Japan spends $17, Canada spends $32, and Great Britain spends $38 per person. If we don't consider it worthwhile to foster a cultural environment that elevates our children, we may find ourselves with a cultural environment very much at odds with our values.

My invitation to the media is to work in collaboration with both parents and experts on child development to ensure a more balanced presentation to our children. Several studies conclude that children are even more affected by prosocial messages than by antisocial messages. With all of the interest in media and violence, this compelling finding is often overlooked. A particularly useful suggestion, utilizing the media's power to communicate positive messages, comes from Professor Bernard Friedlander. He proposes "a major, long-term, highly sophisticated professional media campaign to promote many themes and actions that have the single purpose of protecting and being decent to children."[7] Just as Smokey the Bear raised consciousness about protecting trees from forest fires, Friedlander urges that the media help raise our national consciousness about the value and vulnerability of our children.

It is unrealistic and unnecessary to suggest that all violence be dispensed with, although I cannot see any particular reason for gratuitous violence. Movies like *Crimson Tide* and television programs like *Law and Order* show that action and conflict and even violence can be produced effectively for a mass audience. The astronomical grosses of movies like *The Lion King* and *Forrest Gump* demonstrate that Americans are hungry for movies with a minimum of shoot-'em-ups, spectacular fires, deaths, explosions, and electrocutions. We want to know more about the human condition and how to deal with adversity. We are tired of being shell-shocked.

WHAT THE GOVERNMENT CAN DO

When I first began writing this book in August 1993, I went to visit Ephraim Margolin, a constitutional and criminal attorney in San Francisco. He is well known as a man of principle and intellect, and over the years he has handled many First Amendment cases. At that time I was feeling so disgusted with what my children were watching that I asked what kinds of government restrictions a parent might hope for. Mr. Margolin shook his head and knitted his eyebrows in that kind of bemused gesture parents often use when their children ask slightly off-center questions. "Why in the world would you want the government involved in this? Are you looking to attack the problem in the most ineffective way possible?" he asked. At the time, I was disappointed by not being given a blueprint for government regulation. Two years later, I understand the wisdom and reality of Mr. Margolin's advice.

Since the earliest days of television's popularity, some forty years ago, the government has threatened censorship, regulation, and interference. The result of reams of memos, hundreds of committee meetings, and thousands of political pronouncements has been minimal. Every ten years or so the government decides that "something must be done" about television and puts the networks on notice that if they don't clean up their act, they will have it cleaned up for them. This has the effect of briefly changing the

amount of violence in programming, which quick
former level or surpasses it.

We have recently witnessed a particularly vig
objections to the media on the part of politicians. I
Paul Simon of Illinois authored the Television Viol
allowed the major networks three years in which tc
self-regulating the amount of violence on televisio
line approached with little progress shown, Attorne
Reno said that without further steps, "government :
imperative." In January 1994, some two months afte
of the original Television Violence Act, Simon ann
had reached an agreement with cable and broadcast
independent monitoring plan.

However much politicians and parents demand changes in
programming, networks have found ways to sabotage intentions
and even legislation. The Children's Television Act of 1990, authored by Congressman Edward J. Markey of Massachusetts man-
dated that networks "serve the educational and informational needs
of children." Unfortunately, the legislation did not specify how
much programming was necessary to carry out this mandate. As a
result, the networks produce a minimum of children's programming. Currently, an FCC rule has been proposed that would require four hours a week of children's television programming to aid
in the implementation of this legislation. Lynn McReynolds, a
spokesperson for the National Association of Broadcasters, un-
abashedly said, "We don't like quotas period, which would make
the government a judge of what shows are educational."[8] The Children's Television Act of 1990 has failed to have much effect on the
networks because shows such as *The Flintstones*, *The Jetsons*, and *G.I.
Joe* have all been proffered as educational programs. If McReynolds
doesn't want government interference (a reasonable objection),
then I suggest that *G.I. Joe* not be offered as an example of educational programming.

An allotment of four hours per week of television programming directed at children seems rather anemic. Nonetheless, the
networks are proposing that they be allowed to "buy out" of their
obligation by paying other stations to produce three out of the
required four hours. The net effect of this would most likely be to
reduce rather than increase the total amount of children's programming available. Most networks would pay PBS, which already pro-

duces a great deal of children's programs, and thus the other networks would have to produce only one hour per week. This completely overturns the spirit of the Children's Television Act, which was to make good programming more readily available on a wide number of channels. The hypocrisy of allowing the major networks to pay someone else to discharge their responsibilities is outrageous. Like so much of what the networks produce, the message is that money buys anything—love, respect, even compliance with government regulation.

One of the most interesting ideas about how to protect children while not interfering with network decisions comes from Congressman Markey, who has suggested that a "V-chip" be programmed into all new televisions and be made available for older ones. This is the chip that allows parents to screen out programs they consider too violent for their youngsters. On the surface, it's hard to imagine much objection to this plan. It's voluntary and would simply give parents more information about and control over what their children are viewing. As this book goes to press, the V-chip, tacked onto the Telecommunications Bill of 1996, has become law. However, networks have been opposed to the V-chip. Like so many issues in this country, we can't seem to reconcile ourselves to a little intervention without fearing that we will be swamped with intervention. Those who oppose the V-chip argue that soon there will be S-chips for sexual material, R-chips for religious material, and so on. This is unlikely, but even if activist groups did begin to push their individual agendas, it would simply mean providing parents with additional information about other topics that they are concerned about.

We should be suspect of the motives of individuals who oppose parents obtaining more information and exerting greater control over their children's viewing habits. Fox executive Lucy Slahany is unaccountably frightened by the prospect of parental control. "Quite frankly, the very idea of a V-chip scares me," she said.[9] Jack Valenti, head of the Motion Picture Academy, has put forth the weak excuse that parents should be making decisions on violence on a case-by-case basis: "I'm opposed to indictment without appraisal. Parental discretion means it ought to be done individually."[10] In fact, networks who oppose the V-chip do so because they fear that parents may "indiscriminately" program out violent programs for their children. Since this represents a significant portion of what is on television, the potential of lost revenues to sponsors is staggering. Newton Minow, former FCC commissioner, recognizes that "the real fear is that the V-chip will chip into revenues."[11]

In the end, I don't believe that it is government or technology that will solve this problem for us. While this book has at times drawn a rather dark picture in broad strokes, the fact is that there are many bright spots on television. Television can teach tolerance and cooperation. It can reduce prejudice and increase helping behavior. It can introduce children to different peoples, cultures, and ideas. The media can be used to develop community, to reinforce the values of honesty and integrity, and to educate children to be citizens of the world.

Each one of us—parents, educators, child professionals, and media executives—makes decisions every day that affect our children's well-being. It is tempting for parents to point fingers at network executives and network executives to point fingers at advertisers and advertisers to point fingers back at parents. Bathing our children in violence and stereotypes to sell products harms us all, both in real and in spiritual terms. A country that is willing to sacrifice its children's welfare for the pursuit of money is bound to unravel. Ultimately, it is the responsibility of each and every one of us to insist that the well-being of our children comes before profits.

Resource Directory

e-mail: acahn@pbs.org
Web: www.pbs.org.

Turner Broadcasting System
1 CNN Center
Atlanta, GA 30303
(404) 885-4291

Government Agencies

The best way to make your views known is to contact your senators and representatives directly. If you don't know their names, you can call (202) 224-3121, the main Capitol switchboard, which can provide you with the names and phone numbers.

Consumer Product Safety Commission
Washington, DC 20207
24-hour hotline: 800-638-CPSC
This agency handles complaints about a wide range of products, including toys (such as toy guns looking like real guns).

Federal Communications Commission
Mass Media Bureau
2000 M St. NW, Room 539
Washington, DC 20554
(202) 739-0773
Independent government agency responsible for regulating telecommunications. Charged with implementing the Children's Television Act of 1990, which requires the FCC to review the educational programming efforts of the networks.

Federal Trade Commission
Attention: Marketing Practices
Room 238
6th St. and Pennsylvania Ave. NW
Washington, DC 20580
Fax: (202) 326-2050
Handles complaints related to advertising and marketing. Complaints have to be in writing or can be faxed.

United States House of Representatives
Subcommittee on Telecommunications and Finance
2125 Rayburn Bldg.
Washington, DC 20515
(202) 225-2927

UNITED STATES SENATE
Subcommittee on Communications
227 Hart Senate Office Bldg.
Washington, DC 20510
(202) 224-5184

MEDIA LITERACY

CENTER FOR MEDIA LITERACY
4727 Wilshire Blvd. Suite 403
Los Angeles, CA 90010
(800) 226-9494
Fax: (213) 931-4474
A nonprofit, community-based, membership organization dedicated to bringing media literacy education to children. The center produces and distributes media literacy resources: books, videos, and teaching materials for both parents and teachers.

CHILDREN'S TELEVISION RESOURCE AND EDUCATION CENTER
340 Townsend St. Suite 431
San Francisco, CA 94107
(415) 243-9943
A nonprofit educational corporation dedicated to creating services and products that promote children's social development and academic success. It focuses on helping parents, teachers, and other professionals deal with issues related to children and television.

CITIZENS FOR MEDIA LITERACY
34 Wall St., Suite 407
Asheville, NC 28801
(704) 255-0182
A nonprofit educational organization dedicated to linking critical thinking about media and advertising to citizenship and civic participation. This organization, through workshops, comic books, and other teaching materials, shines a light on the structure of media, emphasizing the fact that while we have many consumer choices, we have few citizen choices.

MEDIA WATCH
P.O. Box 618
Santa Cruz, CA 95061
(408) 423-6355
This nonprofit organization focuses on challenging sexism and violence in the media through education and action. Produces educational videos and

an international newsletter aimed at helping consumers to be more critical of the media.

NATIONAL ASSOCIATION FOR FAMILY AND COMMUNITY
EDUCATION/CHILDREN'S TELEVISION PROJECT
  P.O. Box 835
  Burlington, KY 41005
  (606) 586-8333
  Fax: (606) 586-8348
The goal of this grass roots organization is to strengthen individuals, families and communities through education, leadership and action. Provides media literacy materials.

NATIONAL TELEMEDIA COUNCIL
  120 E. Wilson St.
  Madison, WI 53703
  (608) 257-7712
  Fax: (608) 257-7714
A professional organization promoting media literacy education through partnership with educators, media producers, and consumers across the country. This nonprofit, membership organization publishes *Telemedium: The Journal of Media Literacy* and is the home of the Media Literacy Clearinghouse and Center.

STRATEGIES FOR MEDIA LITERACY, INC.
  1095 Market St., Suite 617
  San Francisco, CA 94103
  (415) 621-2911
A national nonprofit organization that promotes media literacy, beginning in early elementary education. The organization identifies, develops, and produces media education resources, conducts media education workshops, and serves as a center of support and contact for media teachers.

ADVOCACY GROUPS

CENTER FOR MEDIA EDUCATION
  1511 K St. NW, Suite 518
  Washington, DC 20005
  (202) 628-2620
  Fax: (202) 628-2554
A nonprofit organization dedicated to safeguarding the needs of children. Organizes and educates consumer groups and nonprofit organizations on issues of public policy and the media. The center's Campaign for Kids' TV is aimed at improving the quality of children's television.

CHILDREN NOW
1212 Broadway, Suite 530
Oakland, CA 94612
(510) 763-2444

A nonpartisan policy and advocacy organization for children. Children Now is spearheading a national commitment to improve the quality of media for children. The goal of its Children and Media Program is to help raise awareness among leaders in the news and entertainment industries about the needs of children and to encourage more effective portrayals of young people.

CHILDREN'S ADVERTISING REVIEW UNIT
Council of Better Business Bureau
845 Third Ave.
New York, NY 10022
(212) 705-0124

This agency deals only with advertising. Its mission is to promote responsible, truthful, and accurate advertising to children and to ensure that advertisers are sensitive to the particular nature of their audience. However, compliance with agency guidelines is voluntary. Prefers to receive complaints in writing.

CULTURAL ENVIRONMENT MOVEMENT
P.O. Box 31847
Philadelphia, PA 19104
(215) 387-5303
Fax: (215) 387-1560

CEM is a nonprofit educational corporation made up of a broad coalition of media, professional, labor, religious, environmental, health-related, and women's and minority groups working for a "freer and saner cultural environment." Focus is on reducing concentration of control by a small number of media conglomerates and expanding input of less affluent and more vulnerable groups.

FOUNDATION TO IMPROVE TELEVISION
50 Congress St. Suite 925
Boston, MA 02109
(617) 523-5520
Fax: (617) 523-4619

A nonprofit, public interest organization working to reduce the amount of violence shown on television. The foundation works to raise public awareness, contacts business leaders to enlist their support in reducing the attractiveness of advertising on shows that feature unnecessary violence, and initiates legal proceedings to ensure that regulators fulfill their mandate that television broadcasting is to serve the public interest.

MEDIASCOPE
12711 Ventura Blvd., Suite 280
Studio City, CA 91604
(818) 508-2080

Nonprofit, public policy organization founded to promote constructive depictions of health and social issues in media. Mediascope provides tools and information to help the entertainment community be more socially responsible without relinquishing creative freedom. Currently administering national television violence assessment study funded by National Cable Television Association.

PARENTS' CHOICE
P.O. Box 185
Waban, MA 02168
(617) 965-5913

Publishes a quarterly review of children's books, toys, videos, TV programming, computer programs, movies, and music. Parents' Choice Awards help parents identify the year's best in all fields of children's media.

Notes

Chapter 1 What We Know

(1) Eron, L. D., Testimony before the Senate Committee on Government Affairs, *Congressional Record*, June 18, 1992. (2) Hearing of the House Energy and Commerce Committee, Subcommittee on Health and the Environment, July 11, 1994. (3) *San Francisco Chronicle*, June 2, 1995. (4) *Newsday*, August 10, 1992, "Do Movies, Music Trigger Violent Acts?" p. 38. (5) Chen, M., *The Smart Parent's Guide to KIDS' TV*, KQED Books, San Francisco, 1994. (6) *Newsday*, August 10, 1992, "Do Movies, Music Trigger Violent Acts?" (7) Comstock, G., with Paik, H., *Television and the American Child*, Academic Press, 1991. (8) *TV Guide* poll, June 1992. (9) *TV Guide*, March 4–10, 1995. (10) Bogart, L., *Commercial Culture*, Oxford University Press, New York, 1995, p. 232. (11) *Scottish Daily Record*, October 20, 1994. (12) *TV Guide*, August 22, 1992. (13) Family Research Council, September 1993.

Chapter 2 Television in America

(1) Chen, M., *The Smart Parent's Guide to KIDS' TV*, KQED Books, San Francisco, 1994. (2) White, E. B. (1938), cited in Boyer, E. L., *Ready to Learn: A Mandate for the Nation*, Carnegie Foundation for the Advancement of Teaching, Princeton, 1991. (3) *Harper's*, Editorial, March 5, 1990. (4) Reuters Information Services, "Music Rocks into Political Arena," by Michael Miller, June 18, 1992. (5) Harris, R. J., *A Cognitive Psychology of Mass Communication*, Lawrence Erlbaum Associates, Hillsdale, NJ, 1994. (6) Gerbner, G., Morgan, M., and Signorielli, N., "Living with Television: The Dynamics of the Cultivation Process," in J. Bryant and D. Zillmann, eds., *Perspectives on Media Effects*, Lawrence Erlbaum, Hillsdale, NJ, 1986. (7) Harris, R., *Cognitive Psychology of Mass Communication*. (8) Minow, N. N., Address to the National Association of Broadcasters, Washington, DC, May 1961. (9) Minow, N. N., *How Vast Wasteland Now?* Gannett Foundation Media Center, Columbia University, New York, 1991. (10) Plato, *The Republic*, trans. by D. Lee, 2nd ed., Penguin, London, 1987. (11) Burns, S., "Tax Policy Works against Family Value," *Dallas Morning News*, July 11, 1993. (12) Williams, T. M., *The Impact of Television*, Academic Press, New York, 1986.

Chapter 3 Research and Theory

(1) *Cincinnati Post*, October 9, 1993. (2) *San Jose Mercury News*, October 2, 1993. (3) Harris, R., *A Cognitive Psychology of Mass Communication*, Lawrence Erlbaum Associates, Hillsdale, NJ, 1994. (4) Bandura, A., "Influence of Model's Reinforcement Contingencies on the Acquisition of Imitative Responses," *Journal of Personality and Social Psychology*, 1965, 1:589–95. (5) Singer, D. G., "Does Violent Television Produce Aggressive Children?" *Pediatric Annals*, 1985, 14:804–10; Bandura, A., Ross, D., and Ross, S., "Imitation of Film-Mediated Aggressive Models," *J. Abnormal Social Psychology*, 1963, 66:3–11. (6) *LA Times*, August 22, 1987. (7) Huesmann, L. R., Lagerspetz, K., and Eron, L. D., "Intervening Variables in the TV Violence-Aggression Relation: Evidence from Two Countries," *Developmental Psychology*, 1984, 20:746–75; Dorr, A., "Television and Affective Development and Functioning: Maybe This Decade," *Journal of Broadcasting*, 1981, 25:335–45. (8) Greenberg, B. S., and Atkin, C., "Learning about Minorities from Television: A Research Agenda," in G. Berry and C. Mitchell-Kernan, eds., *Television and the Socialization of the Minority Child* (pp. 215–43), Academic Press, New York, 1982. (9) Christenson, P. G., and Roberts, D. F., "The Role of Television in the Formation of Children's Social Attitudes," in M. J. A. Howe, ed., *Learning from Television: Psychological and Educational Research* (pp. 79–99), Academic Press, London, 1983. (10) Cook, T. D., Appleton, H., Conner, R. F., Shaffer, A., Tabkin, G., and Weber, J. S., *Sesame Street Revisited*, Sage, New York, 1975. (11) Bandura, A., "Influence of Model's Reinforcement Contingencies on the Acquisition of Imitative Responses," *Journal of Personality and Social Psychology*, 1965, 1:589–95. (12) Berkowitz, L., Corwin, R., and Heironimus, M., "Film Violence and Subsequent Aggressive Tendencies," *Public Opinion Quarterly*, 1963, 27:217–29; Berkowitz, L., and Geen, R., "Stimulus Qualities of the Target of Aggression: A Further Study," *Journal of Personality and Social Psychology*, 1967, 5:364–68. (13) Milgram, S., *Obedience to Authority*, Harper & Row, New York, 1974. (14) Donnerstein, E., Linz, D., Penrod, S., *The Question of Pornography: Research Findings and Policy Implications*, Free Press, New York, 1987. (15) Hearold, S., "A Synthesis of 1043 Effects of Television on Social Behavior," in G. Comstock, ed., *Public Communication and Behavior* (1:65–133), Academic Press, Orlando, FL, 1986. (16) Feshbach, S., "Reality and Fantasy in Filmed Violence," in J. Murray, E. Rubinstein, and G. Comstock, eds., *Television and Social Behavior* (2:318–45), Department of Health, Education, and Welfare, Washington, DC, 1972. (17) Cantor, J., "Fright Responses to Mass Media Productions," in J. Bryant and D. Zillmann, eds., *Responding to the Screen*, Lawrence Erlbaum, Hillsdale, NJ, 1991. (18) Cantor, J., and Reilly, S., "Adolescents' Fright Reactions to Television and Films," *Journal of Communication*, 1982, 32, 1:87–99. (19) Singer, J. L., Singer, D. G., and Rapaczynski, W., "Family Patterns and Television Viewing as Predictors of Children's Beliefs and Aggression," *Journal of Communication*, 1984, 34, 2. (20) FBI, *Crime in the United States*, 1993. (21) Gerbner, G., Gross, L., Morgan, M., and Signorielli, N., "The 'Mainstreaming' of America: Violence Profile No. 11," *Journal of Communication*, 1980, 30, 3:10–29. (22) Gerbner, G., Morgan, M., and Signorielli, N., "Television Violence Profile No. 16: The Turning Point," Cultural Environment Movement, Philadelphia, 1994. (23) Ibid. (24) Gerbner, G., "Television Violence: The Art of Asking the Wrong Question," *The World & I*, July 1994, p. 396. (25) Bandura, A., Blanchard, E. B., and Ritter, B., "The Relative Efficacy of Desensitization and Modeling Approaches for Inducing Behavioral, Affective, and Attitudinal Changes," *Journal of Personality and Social Psychology*, 1969, 13:173–99. (26) Kellerman, A. L., and Reay, D. T., "Protection or Peril? An Analysis of Firearm-Related Deaths in the Home," *New England Journal of Medicine*, June 12, 1986. (27) Lazarus, R., Speisman, J., Mordkoff, A., and Davison, L., "A Laboratory Study of Psychological Stress Produced by a Motion Picture Film," *Psychological Monographs*, 1962, 76. (28) Cline, V. B., Croft, R. G., and Courrier, S., "Desensitization of Children to Television Violence," *Journal of Personality and Social Psychol-*

ogy, 1973, 27, 3:360–65. **(29)** Ibid. **(30)** Drabman, R. S., and Thomas, M. H., "Does Media Violence Increase Children's Toleration of Real-Life Aggression?" *Developmental Psychology*, 1974, 10, 3:418–21. **(31)** Gaertner, S. L., and Dovidio, J. F., "The Subtlety of White Racism, Arousal, and Helping Behavior," *Journal of Personality and Social Psychology*, 1977, 35:691–707. **(32)** Hanratty, M., Thomas, M., Horton, R., Lippincott, E., and Drabman, R., "Desensitization to Portrayals of Real-Life Aggression as a Function of Exposure to Television Violence," *Journal of Personality and Social Psychology*, 1977, 35, 6.

Part Two Introduction

(1) Cantor, J., Wilson, B., and Hoffner, C., "Emotional Responses to a Televised Nuclear Holocaust Film," *Communication Research*, April 1986, 13:257–77.

Chapter 4   Attachment

(1) Burlingham, D., and Freud, A., *Young Children in War-time*, Allen & Unwin, London, 1942. **(2)** Rutter, M., "Functions and Consequences of Relationships: Some Psychopathological Considerations," in R. Hinde and J. Stevenson-Hinde, eds., *Towards Understanding Families.* Oxford University Press, Oxford, 1988. **(3)** Gilligan, C., *In a Different Voice*, Harvard University Press, Cambridge, 1993. **(4)** Park, K. S., and Waters, E., "Security of Attachment and Preschool Friendships," *Child Development*, 1989, 60:1076–81. **(5)** Sroufe, L. A., Fox, N., and Pancake, V., "Attachment and Dependency in Developmental Perspective," *Child Development*, 1983, 54:1615–27. **(6)** Troy, M., and Sroufe, L. A., "Victimization among Preschoolers: Role of Attachment Relationship History," *Journal of the American Academy of Child and Adolescent Psychiatry*, 1987, 26:166–72. **(7)** Magid, K., and McKelvey, C., *High Risk: Children without a Conscience*, Bantam Books, New York, 1987. **(8)** Chess, S., and Thomas, A., *Temperament in Clinical Practice*, Guilford Press, New York, 1986. **(9)** Singer, J. L., and Singer, D. G., "Family Experiences and Television Viewing as Predictors of Children's Imagination, Restlessness, and Aggression," *Journal of Social Issues*, 1986, 42, 3. **(10)** Korzenny, R., Greenberg, B. S., and Atkin, C. K., "Styles of Parental Disciplinary Practices as a Mediator of Children's Learning from Antisocial Television Portrayals," in D. Nimmo, ed., *Communication Yearbook 3* (pp. 283–94), Transaction Books, New Brunswick, NJ, 1979. **(11)** Comstock, G., with Paik, H., *Television and the American Child*, Academic Press, New York, 1991. **(12)** Desmond, R. J., Singer, J. L., and Singer, D. G., "Family Mediation: Parental Communication Patterns and the Influences of Television on Children," in J. Bryant, ed., *Television and the American Family* (p. 301), Erlbaum Associates, Hillsdale, NJ, 1990.

Chapter 5   Aggression

(1) Interpol, U.S. National Central Bureau, 1993. **(2)** *Bureau of Alcohol, Tobacco and Firearms Ready Reference Guide*, Washington, DC, 1994. **(3)** FBI Uniform Crime Report, 1993. **(4)** Desmond, R. J., Singer, J. L., and Singer, D. G., "Family Mediation: Parental Communication Patterns and the Influences of Television on Children," in J. Bryant, ed., *Television and the American Family*, Erlbaum Associates, Hillsdale, NJ, 1990. **(5)** Fingerhut, L. A., Centers for Disease Control and Prevention, "Firearm Mortality among Children, Youth, and Young Adults," No. 231, March 23, 1993. **(6)** *San Francisco Chronicle*, November 23, 1994. **(7)** Fingerhut, "Firearm Mortality." **(8)** Comstock, G., "Television and Film Violence," in S. J. Apter and A. P. Goldstein, eds., *Youth Violence: Programs and Prospects* (pp. 178–218), Pergamon Press, Elmsford, NY, 1986. **(9)** Belson, W. A., *Television Violence and the Adolescent Boy*, Saxon House, Teakfield, Limited, Westmead, England, 1978. **(10)** Centerwall, B. S.,

"Television and Violence," *Journal of the American Medical Association*, June 10, 1992. **(11)** Cloninger, C. R., and Gottesman, A., "Genetic and Environmental Factors in Antisocial Behavior Disorders," in S. A. Mednick, T. E. Moffitt, and S. A. Stack, eds., *The Causes of Crime: New Biological Approaches* (pp. 92–109), Cambridge University Press, New York, 1987. **(12)** Eron, L. D., Huesmann, L. R., Dubow, E., Romanoff, R., and Yarmel, P., "Aggression and Its Correlates over 22 Years," in D. Crowell, I. Evans, and C. O'Donnell, eds., *Childhood Aggression and Violence: Sources of Influence, Prevention, and Control*, Plenum Press, New York, 1987. **(13)** Huesmann, L. R., and Eron, L. D., *Television and the Aggressive Child: A Cross-National Comparison*, Lawrence Erlbaum, Hillsdale, NJ, 1986. **(14)** Buvinic, M., and Berkowitz, L., "Delayed Effects of Practiced versus Unpracticed Responses after Observation of Movie Violence," *Journal of Experimental Social Psychology*, 1976, 19:403–21. **(15)** Berkowitz, L., "Situational Influences of Reactions to Observed Violence," *Journal of Social Issues*, 1984, 42, 3:93–106. **(16)** Donnerstein, E., and Berkowitz, L., "Effects of Film Content and Victim Association on Aggressive Behavior and Attitudes," unpublished manuscript, University of Wisconsin—Madison, 1983.

Chapter 6   Cognitive Development (Thinking)

(1) Saint-Exupéry, A. de, *The Little Prince*, Harcourt Brace Jovanovich, New York, 1943. **(2)** Huesmann, L. R., and Miller, L. S., "Long-term Effects of Repeated Exposure to Media Violence in Childhood," in L. R. Huesmann, ed., *Aggressive Behavior: Current Perspectives*, Plenum, New York, 1994. **(3)** Huesmann, L. R., and Malamuth, N. M., "Media Violence and Antisocial Behavior: An Overview," *Journal of Social Issues*, 1986, 42, 3:1–6. **(4)** Ted Turner, speaking before the Subcommittee on Telecommunications and Finance, May 12, 1993, p. 111, Serial No. 103-79. **(5)** Postman, N., *The Disappearance of Childhood*, Vintage Books, New York, 1982, p. 97.

Chapter 7   Moral Development (Conscience)

(1) Sergeant David Thompson, Manteca, California, Police Department, personal communication, February 1996. **(2)** Kohlberg, L., *Collected Papers on Moral Development and Moral Education*, 1973, Harvard University Center for Moral Education, Cambridge; *The Stages of Ethical Development*, Harper, New York, 1986. **(3)** Kohlberg, L., "Stage and Sequence: The Cognitive-Developmental Approach to Socialization," in D. A. Goslin, ed., *Handbook of Socialization Theory and Research*, Rand McNally, Chicago, 1969. **(4)** Bandura, A., "Social Cognitive Theory of Moral Thought and Action," in W. Kurtines, J. Gewirtz, ed., *Handbook of Moral Behavior and Development*, vol. 1, *Theory*, Lawrence Erlbaum, Hillsdale, NJ, 1991. **(5)** Gilligan, C., *In a Different Voice*, Harvard University Press, Cambridge, 1993. **(6)** Freud, S., *Some Psychical Consequences of the Anatomical Distinctions between the Sexes*, 1925, vol. 19. **(7)** Bandura, A., *Social Foundations of Thought and Action*, Prentice-Hall, Englewood Cliffs, NJ, 1986.

Chapter 8   The Cartoon Dilemma: Ages 3, 4, and 5

(1) Berlyne, D., "Curiosity and Exploration," *Science*, 1966, 153:25–33. **(2)** Gerbner, G., Morgan, M., and Signorielli, N., "Television Violence Profile No. 16: The Turning Point," Cultural Environment Movement, Philadelphia, 1994. **(3)** Associated Press, August 3, 1993. **(4)** DeVries, R., "Constancy of Generic Identity in the Years Three to Six," *Monographs of the Society for Research in Child Development*, 34, ser. no. 127. **(5)** Singer, J. L., and Singer, D. G., "Family Experiences and Television Viewing as Predictors of Children's Imagination, Restlessness, and Aggression," *Journal of Social Issues*, 1986, 42, 3:113. **(6)** Fowler, quoted in Gitlin, T., ed., *Watching Television*, Pantheon Books, New York, 1986, p. 76. **(7)** " 'Wuzzles' to 'Insectoids' Come Alive at Toy Fair," *New York Times*, February 11, 1985. **(8)** Nossiter, B. C., "The FCC's Big Giveaway Show," *The Nation*, October 26, 1985, p. 402. **(9)** Robertson, G., "Law for the Press," in J. Curran, ed., *The British Press: A Manifesto* (p. 205), Macmillan, New York, 1978. **(10)** Engelhardt, T., in T. Gitlin, ed., *Watching Television*, Pantheon, New York, 1986. **(11)** Elicker, J., Englund, M., and Sroufe, L., "Predicting Peer Competence and Peer Relationships in Childhood from Early Parent-Child Relationships," in R. Parke and G. Ladd, eds., *Family Peer Relationships: Modes of Linkage*, Lawrence Erlbaum, Hillsdale, NJ, 1992. **(12)** Meltzoff, A. N., and Moore, M. K., "Imitation of Facial and Manual Gestures by Human Neonates," *Science*, 1977, 198:75–78. **(13)** Meltzoff, A., "Imitation of Televised Models by Infants," *Child Development*, 1988, 59:1221–29. **(14)** Bandura, A., Ross, D., and Ross, S., "Vicarious Reinforcement and Imitative Learning," *Journal of Abnormal Social Psychology*, 1963, 67:601–7. **(15)** Friedrich, L., and Stein, A., "Aggressive and Prosocial Television Programs: The Natural Behavior of Preschool Children," *Monographs of the Society for Research in Child Development*, ser. no. 151, August 1973. **(16)** Singer, J., Singer, D., and Rapaczynski, W., "Family Patterns and Television Viewing as Predictors of Children's Beliefs and Aggression," *Journal of Communication*, Spring 1984. **(17)** Ibid. **(18)** Bandura, A., Ross, D., and Ross, S., "Vicarious Reinforcement and Imitative Learning," *Journal of Abnormal Social Psychology*, 1963, 67:601–7. **(19)** Chess, S., and Thomas, A., *Temperament in Clinical Practice*, Guilford Press, New York, 1986. **(20)** Flavell, J., "The Development of Children's Knowledge about the Appearance-Reality Distinction," *American Psychologist*, April 1986, 419. **(21)** Singer, J., and Singer, D., "Imaginative Play in Early Childhood: Some Experimental Approaches, in A. Davids, ed., *Child Personality and Psychopathology* (pp. 69–112), Wiley, New York. **(22)** Singer, D. G., and Singer, J. L., *House of Make Believe*, Harvard University Press, Cambridge, 1990. **(23)** Salomon, G., "Effects of Encouraging Israeli Mothers to Co-observe *Sesame Street* with Their Five-Year-Olds," *Child Development*, 1977, 48:1146–51. **(24)** Johnston, J., and Ettema, J., 1986, "Using Television to Best Advantage: Research for Prosocial Television," in J. Bryant and D. Zillmann, eds., *Perspectives on Media Effects* (pp. 143–64), Lawrence Erlbaum, Hillsdale, NJ, 1986. **(25)** Bryan, J. H., "Model Affect and Children's Imitative Behavior," *Child Development*, 1971, 42:2061–65. **(26)** Singer, J. L., and Singer, D. G., "Executive Summary on *Barney and Friends*," Family Television Research and Consultation Center, Yale University, 1995. **(27)** Singer, J. L., and Singer, D. G., "Family Experiences and Television Viewing as Predictors of Children's Imagination, Restlessness, and Aggression," *Journal of Social Issues*, 1986, 42, 3:107–24.

Chapter 9   Middle Childhood: Ages 6, 7, and 8

(1) Elicker, J., Englund, M., and Sroufe, L. A., "Predicting Peer Competence and Peer Relationships in Childhood from Early Parent-Child Relationships," in R. Parke and G. Ladd, eds., *Family-Peer Relationships: Modes of Linkage*, Lawrence Erlbaum, Hillsdale, NJ, 1992. **(2)** Huston, A. C., Carpenter, C. J., and Atwater, J. B., "Gender, Adult Structuring of Activities, and Social Behavior in Middle Childhood," *Child Development*, 1986, 57:1200–1209; Hoffman, L., "Changes in Family Roles, Socialization, and Sex Differences," *American Psychologist*, 1977, 84:712–22. **(3)** Block, J. H., "Personality Development in Males and Females: The Influence of Different Socialization," *Master Lecture Series of the American Psychological Association*, New York, 1979; Sadker, M., and Sadker, D., *Failing at Fairness*, Simon & Schuster, New York, 1994. **(4)** Reynolds, C., *Hollywood Power Stats*, Cineview Publishing, 1995. **(5)** Daven, J., O'Conner, J. F., and Briggs, R., "The Consequences of Imitative Behavior in Children: The 'Evel Knievel Syndrome,'" *Pediatrics*, March 1976. **(6)** Cantor, J., and Omdahl, B. L., "Effects of Fictional Media Depictions of Realistic Threats on Children's Emotional Responses, Expectations, Worries, and the Liking for Related Activities," *Communication Monographs*, 1991, 58:384–401. **(7)** Cantor, J., "Confronting Children's Fright Response to Mass Media," in D. Zillmann, J. Bryant, and

J. Huston, *Media, Children, and the Family*, Lawrence Erlbaum, Hillsdale, NJ, 1994. **(8)** Greenberg, B. S., and Brand, J. E., "Cultural Diversity on Saturday Morning Television," in G. Berry and J. Asamen, eds., *Children and Television*, Sage Publications, Newbury Park, CA, 1993. **(9)** Maccoby, E., *Social Development*, Harcourt Brace Jovanovich, New York, 1980. **(10)** Baumrind, D., "Rearing Competent Children," in W. Damon, ed., *Child Development Today and Tomorrow*, Jossey-Bass, San Francisco, 1989. **(11)** Baldwin, A., Cole, R., and Baldwin, C., "Parental Pathology, Family Interaction, and the Competence of the Child in School," *Monographs of the Society for Research in Child Development*, 1982, 47, 5. **(12)** Emmerich, W., "Structure and Development of Personal-Social Behaviors in Economically Disadvantaged Preschool Children," *Genetic Psychology Monographs*, 95:191–245. **(13)** Becker, W., "Consequences of Different Kinds of Parental Discipline," in M. Hoffman and L. Hoffman, eds., *Review of Child Development Research*, Russell Sage, New York, 1964. **(14)** Reynolds, C., *Hollywood Power Stats*, Cineview Publishing, 1995. **(15)** Huesmann, R., "Psychological Processes Promoting the Relation between Exposure to Media Violence and Aggressive Behavior by the Viewer," *Journal of Social Issues*, 1986, 42:125–39. **(16)** Huesmann, L. R., Eron, L. D., Lefkowitz, M. M., and Walder, L. O., "The Stability of Aggression over Time and Generations," *Developmental Psychology*, 1984, 20, 6:1120–34. **(17)** Huesmann, L. R., Eron, L. D., *Television and the Aggressive Child*, Lawrence Erlbaum, Hillsdale, NJ, 1986. **(18)** Ibid., 9. **(19)** Stein, S., Kraemer, H., and Spiegel, D., "The Impact of Media Coverage of a Violent Crime on Children in Three States," in press. **(20)** McGhee, E. E., "Children's Appreciation of Humor: A Test of the Cognitive Congruency Principle," *Child Development*, 1976, 47. **(21)** Dorr, A., "No Shortcuts to Judging Reality," in J. Bryant and D. Anderson, eds., *Children's Understanding of Television*, Academic Press, New York, 1983. **(22)** Hawkins, R., "The Dimensional Structure of Children's Perceptions of Television Reality," *Communication Research*, 1977, 4, 3:299–320. **(23)** Lickona, T., *Raising Good Children*, Bantam Books, New York, 1983, p. 140.

Chapter 10 Older Childhood: Ages 9, 10, and 11

(1) Ruble, D., "The Development of Social Comparison Processes and Their Role in Achievement-Related Self-Socialization," in T. Higgins, D. Ruble, and W. Hartup, eds., *Social Cognitive Development*, Cambridge University Press, Cambridge, 1983. **(2)** Rosenberg, *Conceiving the Self*, Basic Books, New York, 1979. **(3)** Erikson, E., *Childhood and Society*, Norton, New York, 1993. **(4)** Hoffman, M. L., "Altruistic Behavior and the Parent-Child Relationship," *Journal of Personality and Social Psychology*, 1975, 31:937–43. **(5)** Radke-Yarrow, Zahn-Waxler, C., and Chapman, M., "Prosocial Dispositions and Behavior," in P. Mussen, ed. *Handbook of Child Psychology*, Wiley, New York, 1983. **(6)** Spivack, G., Marcus, J., and Swift, M., "Early Classroom Behaviors and Later Misconduct," *Developmental Psychology*, 1986, 22:123–31. **(7)** Dweck, C. S., Davidson, W., Nelson, S., and Erra, B., "Sex Differences in Learned Helplessness," 2: "The Contingencies of Evaluation Feedback in the Classroom"; 3: "An Experimental Analysis," *Developmental Psychology*, 1978, 14:268–76. **(8)** Ibid. **(9)** Gilligan, C., *In a Different Voice*, Harvard University Press, Cambridge, 1982. **(10)** Huesmann, R. L., "Learning of Aggression from Television Violence," paper delivered to Third International Conference on Standards in Screen Entertainment, London, March 1992. **(11)** Williams, P. A., Haertel, E. H., Haertel, G. D., and Walberg, H. J., "The Impact of Leisure-Time Television on School Learning: A Research Synthesis," *American Educational Research Journal*, Spring 1982, pp. 19–50. **(12)** Ibid. **(13)** Hearold, S., "A Synthesis of 1043 Effects of Television on Social Behavior," in G. Comstock, ed., *Public Communication and Behavior* (1:65–133), Academic Press, Orlando, FL, 1986. **(14)** Berkowitz, L., and Rawlings, E., "Effects of Film Violence on Inhibitions against Subsequent Aggression," *Journal of Abnormal and Social Psychology*, 1963, 66:405–12. **(15)** Donnerstein, E., and Berkowitz, L., "Victim Reactions in Aggressive-Erotic Films as a Factor in Violence against Women,"

Journal of Personality and Social Psychology, 1981, 41:710–24. **(16)** Rosekrans, M. A., "Imitation in Children as a Function of Perceived Similarities to a Social Model of Vicarious Reinforcement," *Journal of Personality and Social Psychology*, 1967, 7:305–17. **(17)** Berkowitz, L., and Rawlings, E., "Effects of Film Violence on Inhibitions against Subsequent Aggression," *Journal of Abnormal and Social Psychology*, 1963, 66:405–12. **(18)** Feshbach, S., "Reality and Fantasy in Filmed Violence," in J. Murray, E. Rubinstein, and G. Comstock, eds., *Television and Social Behavior*, vol. 2, Department of Health, Education, and Welfare, Washington, DC. **(19)** Gerbner, G., Gross, L., Morgan, M., Signorielli, N., "The 'Mainstreaming' of America: Violence, Profile No. 11," *Journal of Communication*, 1980, 30:10–29. **(20)** Singer, J. L., Singer, D. G., and Rapaczynski, W. S., "Family Patterns and Television Viewing as Predictors of Children's Beliefs and Aggression," *Journal of Communication*, 1984, 34, 2. **(21)** Gerbner, G., "Television Violence: The Art of Asking the Wrong Question," *The World & I*, July 1994. **(22)** Gerbner, G., *The Amplifier*, American Psychological Association, Summer 1994. **(23)** Eron, L. D., "Prescription for Reduction of Aggression," *American Psychologist*, 1980, 35, 3:244–52. **(24)** Mander, J., *Four Arguments for the Elimination of Television*, Quill, New York, 1978. **(25)** Gerbner, G., Gross, L., Morgan, M., and Signorielli, N., "The 'Mainstreaming' of America: Violence," Profile No. 11, *Journal of Communication*, 1980, 30, 3:10–29. **(26)** Clemente, J., unpublished manuscript, International Conference of Child and Adolescent Psychiatry, San Francisco, August 1994. **(27)** Drabman, R. S., and Thomas, M. H., "Does Media Violence Increase Children's Toleration of Real-Life Aggression?" *Developmental Psychology*, 1974, 10, 3:419. **(28)** Reynolds, C., *Hollywood Power Stats*, Cineview Publishing, 1995.

Chapter 11   Early Adolescence: Ages 12, 13, and 14

(1) Douvan, E., and Adelson, J., *The Adolescent Experience*, Wiley, New York, 1966; Montemayor, R., "Parents and Adolescents in Conflict," *Journal of Early Adolescence*, 1983, 3:83–103. **(2)** Rutter, M., Graham, P., Chadwick, O., and Yule, W., "Adolescent Turmoil: Fact or Fiction?" *Journal of Child Psychology and Psychiatry*, 1976, 17:35–56. **(3)** Uhlenhuth, E. H., Balter, M. B., et al., "Symptom Checklist Syndromes in the General Population: Correlations with Psychotherapeutic Drug Use," *Archives of General Psychiatry*, 1983, 40:1167–73. **(4)** Helfer, R., and Kempe, C. H., *Child Abuse and Neglect: The Family and the Community*, Ballinger, Cambridge, MA, 1976. **(5)** *Business Week*, April 11, 1994, pp. 76–86. **(6)** Moog, C., "The Selling of Addiction to Women," *Media & Values*, Spring/Summer 1991, 20–22. **(7)** Montgomery, K., "Alcohol and Television," *Media & Values*, Spring/Summer 1991, 18–19. **(8)** Hechinger, F., *Fateful Choices: Healthy Choices for the 21st Century*, Hill and Wang, New York, 1992, p. 110. **(9)** Cooper, C., Grotevant, H., and Condon, S., "Individuality and Connectedness in the Family as a Context for Adolescent Identity Formation and Role-taking Skill," in G. D. Grotevant and Cooper, eds., *Adolescent Development in the Family*, Jossey-Bass, San Francisco, 1983. **(10)** Fingerhut, L. A., Centers for Disease Control and Prevention, "Firearm Mortality among Children, Youth, and Young Adults 1–34 Years of Age," *Trends and Current Status: United States*, March 23, 1993. **(11)** AIDS Information Clearing House, 1994. **(12)** Jhally, S., *Dreamworlds: Desire/Sex/Power in Rock Video*, Media Education Foundation, Northampton, MA, 1995. **(13)** Donnerstein, E., "Aggressive Erotica and Violence against Women," *Journal of Personality and Social Psychology*, 1980, 39; Malamuth, N., Haber, S., and Feshbach, S., "Testing Hypothesis Regarding Rape: Exposure to Sexual Violence, Sex Differences, and the 'Normality' of Rapists," *Journal of Research in Personality*, 1980, 14:121–37. **(14)** Josephson Institute, *Ethics in Action*, Character Counts Week, 1994. **(15)** Eron, L. D., Gentry, J., and Schlegel, P., *Reason to Hope*, American Psychological Association, Washington, DC, 1994. **(16)** "Mr. MTV," *W*, May 1995.

Chapter 12   Adolescence: Ages 15, 16, 17, and 18

(1) Erikson, E., "Autobiographic Notes on the Identity Crisis," *Daedalus,* Fall 1970. **(2)** Mc-Cord, J., "Problem Behaviors," in S. Feldman and G. Elliot, eds., *At the Threshold: The Developing Adolescent* (pp. 414–30), Harvard University Press, Cambridge, 1990. **(3)** Miller, B. C., and Dyk, P., *Sexuality in Clinical Research and Practice with Adolescents,* P. Tolan and B. Cohler, eds., Wiley, New York, 1993. **(4)** Roberts, D. F., "Adolescents and the Mass Media: from 'Leave It to Beaver' to 'Beverly Hills 90210,' " *Teachers College Record,* Spring 1993. **(5)** Erikson, E., *Childhood and Society,* Norton, New York, 1993, p. 262. **(6)** Snoop Doggy Dog, *Doggy Style,* Death Row Records, distributed by Atlantic Recording, 1993. **(7)** Greenberg, B. S., et al., "Sex Content on Soaps and Prime Time Television Series Most Viewed by Adolescents," in B. S. Greeenberg, J. D. Brown, and N. L. Buerkel-Rothfuss, eds., *Media, Sex and the Adolescent,* Hampton Press, Cresskill, NJ, 1993. **(8)** Miedzian, M., *Boys Will Be Boys,* Anchor, Doubleday, New York, 1991, p. xxiii. **(9)** Donnerstein, E., Linz, D., and Penrod, S., *The Question of Pornography: Research Findings and Policy Implications,* Free Press, New York, 1987. **(10)** Donnerstein, E., Berkowitz, L., and Linz, D., "Role of Aggressive and Sexual Images in Violent Pornography," unpublished manuscript, University of Wisconsin—Madison, 1986. **(11)** Donnerstein, Linz, and Penrod, *Question of Pornography,* p. 136. **(12)** Postman, Neil, *The Disappearance of Childhood,* Vintage Books, House, New York, 1982, 1994. **(13)** Ibid., pp. 104–5.

Chapter 13   Suggestions, Solutions, and Directions for Parents

(1) Hechinger, F. M., *Fateful Choices: Healthy Youth for the 21st Century,* Hill and Wang, New York, 1992. **(2)** Walsh, D., *Selling Out America's Children,* Fairview Press, Minneapolis, 1994. **(3)** Heintz-Knowles, K., "Television's Image of Children," study commissioned for Children Now, 1995. **(4)** Children Now Conference, Stanford University, March 1995. **(5)** Josephson Institute of Ethics, Aspen Declaration, 1992. **(6)** Desmond, R. J., Singer, J. L., and Singer, D. G., "Family Mediation: Parental Communication Patterns and the Influences of Television on Children," in J. Bryant, ed., *Television and the American Family* (pp. 293–310), Lawrence Erlbaum, Hillsdale, NJ, 1990. **(7)** Hearold, S., "A Synthesis of 1043 Effects of Television on Social Behavior," in G. Comstock, ed., *Public Communication and Behavior* (1:65–133), Academic Press, Orlando, FL, 1986. **(8)** Friedrich, L. K., and Stein, A. H., "Aggressive and Prosocial Television Programs and the Natural Behavior of Preschool Children," *Monographs of the Society for Research in Child Development,* 1973, 38:1–64. **(9)** Singer, J. L., and Singer, D. G., "Executive Summary on *Barney and Friends,*" Family Television Research and Consultation Center, Yale University, 1995. **(10)** Collins, W. A., and Getz, S. K., "Children's Social Responses Following Modeled Reactions to Provocation: Prosocial Effects of a Television Drama," *Journal of Personality,* 1976, 44:488–500. **(11)** Friedrich, L. K., and Stein, A. H., "Prosocial Television and Young Children: The Effects of Verbal Labeling and Role-Playing on Learning and Behavior," *Child Development,* 1975, 46:27–38. **(12)** Hearold, S., "A Synthesis." **(13)** Dietz, W. H., "You Are What You Eat—What You Eat Is What You Are," *Journal of Adolescent Health Care,* 1990, 11, 1:76–81. **(14)** Comstock, G., with Paik, H., *Television and the American Child,* Academic Press, New York, 1991. **(15)** Postman, N., *Amusing Ourselves to Death,* Penguin, New York, 1985. **(16)** *Oregonian,* April 7, 1989. **(17)** "How One Woman Pushed Big Firms to Kill Ads," *San Jose Mercury News,* March 3, 1989. **(18)** Boyer, E., from National Telemedia Council, Madison, WI.

Chapter 14   Directions for Schools, Media, and Government

(1) Postman, N., *Amusing Ourselves to Death*, Penguin Books, New York, 1985, p. 63. (2) Paul Kagan and Associates, quoted in *Washington Post*, February 27, 1994. (3) A. C. Nielsen Co., April 1994. (4) Personal communication, June 1995. (5) "Does TV Kill?" *Frontline*, PBS, January 1995. (6) Children Now Conference, Stanford University, March 2–4, 1995. (7) Friedlander, B., "Community Violence, Children's Development, and Mass Media," in D. Reiss, J. Richter, M. Radke-Yarrow, and D. Scharff, *Children and Violence* Guilford Press, New York, 1993. (8) *Washington Times*, April 6, 1995. (9) Frank Swertlow, "Fox Executive Fears High-Tech Devices May Lead to Censorship," *Daily News of Los Angeles*, July 12, 1993. (10) House Energy and Commerce Telecommunications Subcommittee hearing, July 1, 1993. (11) Minow, N., "How to Zap TV Violence," *Wall Street Journal*, August 3, 1993.

Index